GERMAN FIGHTER AIRCRAFT IN WORLD WAR I
DESIGN, CONSTRUCTION, AND INNOVATION

CASEMATE | ILLUSTRATED

CASEMATE | ILLUSTRATED

GERMAN FIGHTER AIRCRAFT IN WORLD WAR I

DESIGN, CONSTRUCTION, AND INNOVATION

MARK C. WILKINS

CASEMATE | ILLUSTRATED

| Acknowledgements

I would like to express my sincerest thanks to Fokker Team Schorndorf, and Achim Engels, for all his help regarding the design, construction, and development of the Fokker aircraft. In addition, I would also like to thank Kolomon Mayrhofer of Craftlab for all of his fine help regarding design and construction of the Albatros aircraft. Greg VanWyngarden was a tireless source of images and information for several different types of aircraft—many thanks Greg. Michael O'Neal, president of the League of WWI Aviation Historians, was also helpful in his insights into various manufacturers and historical information concerning some of the individuals described herein. Many thanks too to the staff of the National Archives and Records Administration at College Park, MD, for all their help locating images. Finally, I would like to dedicate this book to Mozart.

Published in the United States of America and Great Britain in 2019 by
CASEMATE PUBLISHERS
1950 Lawrence Road, Havertown, PA 19083, USA
and
The Old Music Hall, 106–108 Cowley Road, Oxford OX4 1JE, UK
Copyright © 2019 Mark C. Wilkins

Hardback Edition: ISBN 978-1-61200-6192
Digital Edition: ISBN 978-1-61200-6208

A CIP record for this book is available from the British Library

Design by Battlefield Design
Color profiles by Ronny Bar
Printed and bound in the Czech Republic by FINIDR, s.r.o.

For a complete list of Casemate titles, please contact:
CASEMATE PUBLISHERS (US)
Telephone (610) 853-9131
Fax (610) 853-9146
Email: casemate@casematepublishers.com
www.casematepublishers.com

CASEMATE PUBLISHERS (UK)
Telephone (01865) 241249
Email: casemate-uk@casematepublishers.co.uk
www.casematepublishers.co.uk

All black and white drawings are from *Flight* magazine unless otherwise noted.
Facing Title Page: Fantastic flying shot of the Craftlab Oeffag Albatros D.III. (Craftlab)
Title Page: The SS D.III had an impressive rate of climb due to its powerful Sh.III engine, had a semi-monocoque fuselage, thin airfoil wings with interplane struts that supported two spars in the lower wings (like Pfalz), balanced control surfaces including ailerons on bottom and top wings, a nicely cowled engine, spinner, and a four-bladed propeller.
Contents Page: An Albatros factory worker working on smoothing the lightening holes of a D.V or D.Va former using a sanding board. It is clamped in a bench vise; there are other sanding boards lying on the bench.

Contents

| Glossary

Adlershof—a town located in the borough Treptow-Köpenick of Berlin, Germany. Aircraft, engines, and armaments were tested here for potential contract awards, and to decide on efficacy of a given type.

Aerodrome—military airfield comprised of hangars, maintenance facilities, mess, and billets.

Ailerons—control surfaces on wings used to induce roll in an aircraft.

Angle of Incidence –usually expressed in positive and negative degrees relative to 0 degrees which indicates a horizontal line running through the LE and TE parallel to the thrust line of the fuselage.

Cabane struts—Struts that attach the upper wing to the fuselage forward of the cockpit.

Cam lock—a lozenge-shaped metal fitting that has a pin set off-center, such that when rotated it will apply pressure to whatever it abuts.

Cantilever—a structure that can project from a given attachment point and requires no external bracing such is its strength.

Cellule—a wing structure comprised of an upper and lower wing i.e. a biplane.

Clausewitz, von, Carl—Prussian military theorist whose tract *On War* was read, endorsed, and practiced by all leadership during World War I.

Clinker—a method of planking boats where the planks overlapped each other like clapboards on a house.

Doppeldecker—biplane.

Dreidecker—three-winged aircraft or "triplane."

Elevator—control surface used to control pitch on an aircraft. Elevators join the aft edge of the horizontal stabilizer.

Empennage—refers to the entire tail assembly; horizontal stabilizer, elevators, rudder and fin. Also referred to as "tail feathers" much like a bird.

Eindecker—monoplane or "one wing."

Fairness—in referencing a curve it should have no humps or hollows but be a continuous and "fair" curve.

Flugzeugwerke—Aircraft plant or factory.

Full flying rudder—a rudder that has no fin and is hinged such that the entire structure moves. Nieuports, Fokker D series and Dr.1, and Halberstadt D.IIs all had full flying rudders.

Fuselage—body of the airplane.

Gores—tapered shapes that allow a compound curve to be rendered from material that will not easily conform to curves.

Gyroscopic effect—this is produced by the aggregate weight and mass of a spinning rotary engine. It would cause the airplane to move quickly in one direction while making it difficult to turn in the other direction; this could be used to advantage in combat.

IdFlieg—Inspektion der Fliegertruppen, or Inspectorate of Flying Troops, was the German Empire bureau that oversaw the development of the military aviation industry prior to and including World War I.

Interplane Struts—struts that connect the upper and lower wings near the tips.

Jasta—short for *Jagdstaffel*; was a fighter *Staffel* (squadron) of the German Imperial Luftstreitkräfte during World War I.

Lightening holes—these were holes of irregular shape that were cut out of bulkheads, formers, ribs, etc. to "lighten" the weight of said object without sacrificing strength. Obviously placement and size of these apertures was crucial.

Longerons—usually made from spruce or ash, these were long and resilient stringers that ran fore and aft in the fuselage and usually defined the bottom, sides, and turtle deck portions of a given fuselage.

Parseval—An airship built between 1909 and 1919 by the Luft-Fahrzeug-Gesellschaft (LFG) following the design of August von Parseval. There were 22 of these built in this time period.

RFC—Royal Flying Corps; at the war's conclusion this had been replaced by the Royal Air Force.

Stabilator—similar to the full flying rudder, this is a combination of horizontal stabilizer and elevator in one; the entire plane moves and was typically fairly sensitive. These were used in Eindeckers, and Halberstadt D.IIs.

Symmetrical airfoil—an airfoil that has the same curve on the top and bottom of the wing rib from profile view.

Teves & Braun—a type of in-wing, airfoil-shaped radiator that could be dropped into an aperture of an upper wing.

Turtle Deck—the compound curved area on the top of the fuselage. It was usually made up of formers and stringers and was either covered with linen or paneled with plywood or aluminum.

Typenprufung—"type testing" of aircraft which was usually conducted at facilities such as Adlershof. The results of this testing would determine whether a given aircraft was suitable for military service.

Washout—a slight upward warping of the trailing edge of a wing at the tip. The purpose of washout is to prevent a "hard stall" when an aircraft has reached stalling moment and drops a wing.

Wing-warping—a method of roll control devised by the Wright Brothers. Using a series of cables and pulleys the wings of an aircraft were literally warped to induce roll. Ailerons were devised by Glenn Curtiss as a method of roll control that did not infringe on the Wright patent.

START mit GARUDA Propeller

A bold graphic promoting Garuda Propellers. Seen in this image is the silhouette of a either a *Taube* or Eindecker. Garuda propellers were used on Fokker E, D.I–IV, D. VII types; Albatros D.V; and various C types.

| Introduction

Aircraft reconnaissance was born out of the stasis of trench warfare and the impossible topography of "no man's land." Traditional means such as cavalry or even scouting parties found navigating the devastated landscape difficult, which included massive artillery craters, barbed wire, and a host of obstacles. However, this terrain posed no difficulty for aircraft thus galvanizing its efficacy in military operations. With the ever-increasing numbers of reconnaissance aircraft came the desire to shoot the opposing side's down, thereby creating the need for the armed reconnaissance aircraft and the fighter.

Both the Allies and Central Powers developed aircraft during World War I at an unprecedented rate. Each sought to achieve and maintain air supremacy and, importantly, each side was influenced by the other—a fact often overlooked or marginalized in many historical tracts on the subject. Innovation occurred on a compressed timeline with one power scrutinizing the other, improving upon, and attaining the (albeit fleeting) upper hand. Even within a given country competition was fierce and sometimes perfidious. Occurring simultaneously was the notion of mass production: could a given design be built cost-effectively to uniform timelines given the exigencies of wartime shortages of materials and equipment? And, as importantly: what materials were available in one country in large quantities? Moreover, given the exceptional rate of innovation, production techniques to produce a given aircraft had to be invented—fast. Another important aspect was whether a particular design could be assembled/disassembled quickly and efficiently at the Front. Aircraft had to be transported via rail or truck to access the fighting so this aspect became very important to the design. Thus German aircraft tended to incorporate better modular engineering than most French (e.g. Spads) or British aircraft (profusion of rigging and somewhat difficult to disassemble/assemble). Additionally, British planes had to be flown to bases in France. Why Germany did not follow suit could be due to early aspirations of a more mobile war, or uncertainty as to the role of aircraft once at the front; that they could be towed to the combat zone tends to support the mindset that aircraft, like artillery pieces, were simply another tool at the army's disposal. Fokker, Albatros, and Pfalz all capitalized on this aspect as all their aircraft were built in a similar fashion—wooden wings with welded steel fuselages, in the case of Fokker, and semi-moncoque for Pfalz, Albatros, and Roland. Thus many German aircraft could be quickly assembled in the field—something that could not be said of many Allied aircraft.

Pfalz and Albatros were the first to realize the importance of a streamlined fuselage—the precursor of all that would follow. Both of these companies built semi-monocoque fuselages using plywood to develop semi-stressed skin; the Allies had nothing similar. Moreover, the Germans were quick to realize the importance of powerful inline engines as exemplified by the Halberstadt and Albatros fighters. These engines did not have the gyroscopic effect of the rotary engines and as such were easier and more stable to fly. Fokker was slow to give up his rotary engines but once he did, the result was the iconic and deadly Fokker D.VII. However, many design decisions were made due to the availability of materials or engines; Germany, for example, eventually faced shortages of high-quality castor oil, thus rendering rotaries undesirable. Although Fokker had a controlling share in Oberursel, and profits dictated that he use rotaries, combat performance, fast-tracked training for new pilots, and a mandate from Idlfieg compelled him to turn to inline engines.

The companies profiled in this book demonstrate most of the major fighter-producing operations that materially contributed to the war effort. There are some companies that produced a few fighters—DFW, AEG, Gotha, Phonix—that are mentioned where appropriate but they are referenced insofar as their contributions warrant.

Unification, Industrialization, Aeronautical Research

In 1914 Germany had been a "unified state" for less than half a century. In 1848—the year of European revolution—a series of movements and upheavals in Prussia, Bavaria, Baden, and Saxony all demanded change and political restructuring, the dominant theme being German unification. Germany at this time was an uneasy aggregation of 25 states, city states, and duchies that in times of war all fell under the leadership of the Kaiser. German nationalism gathered steam through the mid-1800s, spearheaded by Prussia, which was the largest, richest, and most influential of the states. The nationalistic flashpoint for Germany was the brief but victorious Franco-Prussian War of 1870–71. At the conclusion of this conflict, and guided by the skillful diplomacy of Prussian statesman Otto von Bismarck, the long-awaited unification of Germany was formalized. The new German empire or "Second Reich" was led by its new Kaiser, Wilhelm I. The fledgling constitution was a strange mix of authoritarian monarchical power and liberal individual rights. The Kaiser retained absolute power over government: he could hire and fire the chancellor (prime minister), determine foreign policy and was commander-in-chief of the armed forces of the entire German nation.

Although in reality largely aspirational, the notion of a unified Germany—featuring a proud cultural heritage, decisive government, robust economy, and a strong army and navy—was a dream that was held by many. Prussia was in the vanguard with many of these aspirations, and, as a result, Prussian influence remained pervasive after unification, creating "Prussianism" which was characterized by fierce nationalism and militarism. Also at this time the writings of Carl von Clausewitz, a military theorist and strategist who attained widespread acceptance, became enduringly influential; the Clausewitzian notion of the "decisive victory" would attain near gospel status during World War I, although of equal, if not more, importance, his "fog of war" seems to have been disregarded by German and Allied military leadership, something that would cost them millions of lives.

Regardless of unification, some states like Bavaria remained fiercely independent. Bavaria had been an autonomous dukedom and later kingdom until 1871, when it was (grudgingly) incorporated into the German nation-state. For Bavarians, anything beyond the state's borders might as well be Russia or France. The state had its own anthem and its own flag, part of which—the blue-and-white checkers—symbolized quality and tradition. Bavarian political rhetoric exuded the notion of Bavaria as a separate nation-state—its official name "der Freistaat" meaning "the Free State." The Bavarian republic is mentioned in the first line of the separate Bavarian constitution (its fourth constitution since 1808) that was signed under the aegis of the American forces of occupation in 1946.

From the perspective of political representation in post-unification Germany, this translated to a nation being represented by the interests of a small percentage of its people (the Kaiser, Junkers) whose view was skewed: none of the ruling class had ever worked in a factory, or known hunger or privation. Catholics, Jews, and factory workers were treated with suspicion and exerted little influence on Germany's governance, at a time when Germany was rapidly industrializing; this would come to a head during the latter part of the war. Manufacturing of electrical products (Siemens and AEG), chemicals (BASF) and internal combustion engines (Karl Benz and Gottlieb Daimler) replaced agrarian enterprises as the most important growth sectors of the German economy, and by 1900 Germany boasted the largest industrial economy in Europe.

The burgeoning aircraft industry was an extension of this industrial surge as it capitalized on preexisting engine industry. Industrialization influenced the demography of Germany, and, by 1910, 60 percent of Germans lived in urban areas: the population of Berlin doubled between 1875 and 1910 and other cities like Munich, Essen, and Kiel grew exponentially. Industrialization and the resultant demographic changes thus produced social changes in the growing towns and cities. However, the basic hierarchy of German society and government remained, regardless of the now drastically disproportionate numbers.

By 1910 there were over 10 million factory workers in Germany—the largest single faction in German society—who faced generally poor living and working conditions. On a positive note, all adult males could vote, and most of them supported the Social Democratic Party (SDP), which grew rapidly during this period to become the largest party in the Reichstag by 1912. The popularity of and support for the SDP worried the Kaiser and the ruling class. During the 1880s Chancellor Bismarck shrewdly introduced a liberal reform package such as insurance against accidents, health care, disability, and old age pensions to reduce support for the SDP. He also worked to enact laws to weaken the influence of the SDP. However, the socialist party made labor reform their top party plank and worked to pass laws that benefited the average factory worker: the 1891 Social Law banned work on Sundays and child labor for children under 13; in 1900 accident insurance coverage was expanded; in 1901 special "industrial arbitration courts" were established to mediate worker/employer disputes; and in 1903 health insurance was expanded and further restrictions were placed on child labor. The Junkers responded by supporting their own modest labor reforms to try to maintain loyalty to the German state, but the tension between the two did not subside.

The burgeoning aircraft manufacturing industry was thus created and fostered in this context. A world war would bring the plight of the worker to a head with wartime restrictions on food, wages, and expanded hours to meet the demands of winning the war. In addition, the influx of a completely new demographic—women—would transform further the context of wartime production, as most of the men were needed to fight the war. This was not only true for Germany but all warring nations, which would empower women in this period with a purpose heretofore unheard of, giving rise to nascent notions of equality in the workplace, and women's suffrage and rights.

Moreover, given the state of rationing during the war in Germany, working in a military factory could mean increased rations as well as job security. While most food reserves went to feed the army, munitions and military contractors could make a case for additional food for their workers who were materially supporting the war effort. This made these jobs attractive, as the chief worry on home-front was finding the next meal. However, by the end of the war rioting, picketing, and walkouts became more common as dissatisfaction with the war grew, and the upheavals in Russia caused ordinary Germans to wonder if they too should adopt pro-worker ideologies and governments.

In addition, the development of the aircraft industry just before and during World War I must take into account the availability of raw materials and supplies within Germany. This is important, as the British blockade prevented other types of materials from reaching Germany—for example, castor oil, crucial in rotary engines. The two principal materials that account for the trajectory of German aircraft design and production were steel and plywood. Without either of these the developmental path of German aircraft design and production would have been very different. On the eve of World War I Germany was the second largest producer of steel in the world (the United States was number one). It was also the first to build factories for the manufacture of veneer (used in plywood) in the middle of the 19th century. The rotary peeling lathes (called "peelers") were mostly of French origin, but American-made peelers were also imported by Germany. After 1870, the firm A. Roller in Berlin delivered simple peelers. The rapid development and improvement of the rotary peelers fostered and accelerated the German plywood industry prior to World War I.

Finally, in the decade leading up to the outbreak of World War I, there was a growing community of scholars in Germany intent on investigating the rapidly growing field of aerodynamics. There were a few epicenters of study in Germany, namely the Technical Institute at Charlottenburg and Gottingen University, as well as Aachen. At Gottingen, Dr Prandtl and his disciples were intent on studying the performance of the airfoil via wind-tunnel experiments. Airfoils of various aircraft manufacturers were tested there; for example, Fokker's Dr.1 airfoil was tested and numbered. Scientists at Gottingen kept the German aircraft industry informed as to significant breakthroughs—such as Prandtl's news that thick airfoils did not produce more drag than thin ones, validating Junkers's work and infusing Fokker with ideas as to his best designs and most famous direction.

After war broke out, the study did not cease; in fact it was accelerated based on the need to win the war. Innovations were quickly put into practice and if successful would be fast-tracked into production for frontline service. The testing facility at Adlershof was one such example of a real-time method to test aircraft, with associated devices being tested before being put into production. When problems arose, such as early Dr.1 wing failures, Adlershof testing was reactivated on an already approved aircraft. Some of the academic community's best, like Hugo Junkers, were not interested in winning the war per se but rather using it as a vehicle for research.

Graphic poster image promoting Fokker's affiliation with the Imperial German air force, as well as alluding to his synchronizing gear that permitted the machine gun to fire through the propeller without hitting it.

1

The *Taube*

A replica *Taube* flying—the *Taube* resembled a large mechanical bird and featured wing and elevator warping with a hinged rudder.

Germany would make a direct connection with nature—specifically biology—in her aircraft, be they Zanonia seeds or birds, while the Allies would employ only the principles contained therein. Both the Wright brothers and German aviation pioneers studied the mechanics of how birds flew to inform their flying machines. The Wrights had a very different solution to the challenge of flight from that of the European aviation pioneers who adopted in its entirety the shape of the bird for their early flying machines, examples being the French Antoinette and Deperdussin aircraft. The *Taube* (Dove) resembled a giant bird and this would make a lasting impression on the Albatros company designers.

The ubiquitous *Taube* monoplane was the first aircraft that appeared on the German aviation scene in quantity before the war. The *Taube* was the brainchild of Austro-Hungarian Igo Etrich who designed this bird-like monoplane in 1909, and flew it in 1910. Igo Etrich was schooled in Leipzig where he learned of the work of Otto Lilienthal. He became fascinated with solving the problem of flight. With his father's help, he built a laboratory for his aviation experiments. After Lilienthal was killed, Etrich's father acquired some of his advanced gliders.

Franz Wels graduated as an industrial engineer in 1891. After serving in the army between 1893 and 1897, he spent some time in England. His interest in flying machines led to a meeting with the Austrian aviation pioneer Wilhelm Kress in 1901. Following Kress's recommendation, Wels was employed by Igo Etrich in Trutnov (Czech Republic) who tasked him with researching relevant aviation literature. Wels found "The Stability of the Flying Apparatus" by Professor Friederich Ahlborn, who taught at the Real Gymnasium des Johanneums in Hamburg, and who was also co-founder of the Hamburg Association of Airship Aviation. His background in zoology led to the study of various things occurring in nature that might have favorable hydro- and aerodynamic properties. The article analyzed the flying seed of *Zanonia Macrocarpa* as possessing particularly stable flight characteristics. Ahlborn, a graduate of Gottingen University, was interested in the science and development of flow dynamics as they related to water and air (he would become head of the Hydrodynamic Research Institute of the (military) Aviation Department at Adlershof in 1916).

Franz Wels.

Igo Etrich.

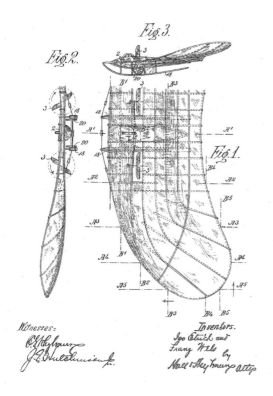

Flying seed of *Zanonia Macrocarpa*. Note how closely this shape resembles the wing plan of the *Taubes*.

The patent illustration for the flying machine created by Wels and Etrich. Note the pronounced similarity to the Zanonia flying seed.

In 1903, Etrich used the principles outlined in Ahlborn's article to construct his first glider that was based on the Zanonia seed, which produced the effect of keeping the wing parallel to the freestream of air induced by air flowing off the tips. On March 3, 1905, Etrich filed an Austrian patent on the Zanonia wing shape (patent no. 23465). It was described in the document as "Igo Etrich and Franz Wels in Oberaltstadt Trautenau (Slovakia)—a flying machine." It was filed in the U.S. on February 28, 1906 as patent no. 952,316. According to the patent drawing, this flying machine had just wings, two inset propellers and one engine. First, the airplane was tested without the engine, but as a glider, it proved unstable over 15 meters.

At the beginning of 1907 Etrich and Wels tested a smaller motor airplane, the *Etrich I*, or *Praterspatz* aka "Prater park sparrow." Karl Illner flew the *Etrich I* but due to its weak (24-hp) engine and the limited space in which to fly it, the aircraft flew only 40 metres at 4 meters off the ground. After the glider was remodeled, Wels succeeded in flying it for the first time on October 2, 1907. Etrich rented two hangars and continued to develop his *Taube* design. Wels traveled to Paris in 1908, to witness the successful flight of the Wright Brothers' model B and suggested to Etrich to change from monoplane to biplane design. This caused an irreconcilable rift between Wels and Etrich and they parted company.

In 1909, the first airfield in the Austro-Hungarian Empire was founded at Wiener-Neustadt. At this time Karl Illner and Pavel Podgornik became associates of Etrich's, and while Wels was in France, the three successfully built a monoplane called *Taube II*.

On May 17, 1910 Karl Illner flew an advanced version of the *Taube* cross-country from Wiener-Neustadt to Vienna, a distance of 25 miles, at an altitude of 948 feet. Wels subsequently worked as an independent inventor. Etrich filed for another patent in the U.S. on August 12, 1910: serial no. 576,853. In 1912, Etrich founded the Etrich Flieger Werke in Liebau, Silesia (now Poland), whose chief designer starting in the spring of 1914 was Ernst Heinkel.

The design of the *Taube* was and is interesting to say the least. Etrich coopted Blériot's undercarriage structure to improve ground handling and make bumpy landings easier on the airframe, as the German military stipulated that these aircraft should be able to land on a ploughed field. The wing was comprised of three spars around which the rib webs were installed, supported by a steel tube truss—a "bridge" or *brücke*—underwing,

The only surviving Etrich Taube is located at the Vienna Technical Museum. Note the simple fuselage, complex undercarriage, and open cockpit. (Image courtesy of ldflieg.com)

The Etrich Taube looking forward. Note the steering wheel–type roll control; this was common during this period and was a direct coopting from early automobiles. Note also the profusion of rigging cables that were led from an armature just in front of the pilot to the wings.

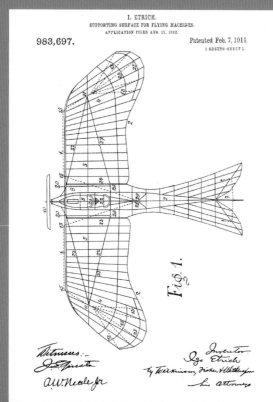

Etrich's patent for his Taube which was filed in 1910 and granted in 1911. In planform the Taube borrows heavily from nature.

The tail of the Taube is very similar to a bird and features no separate elevators; instead the aft portion of the tail wass made from flexible wood that was then simply bent upward or downward using a web of rigging that was led forward.

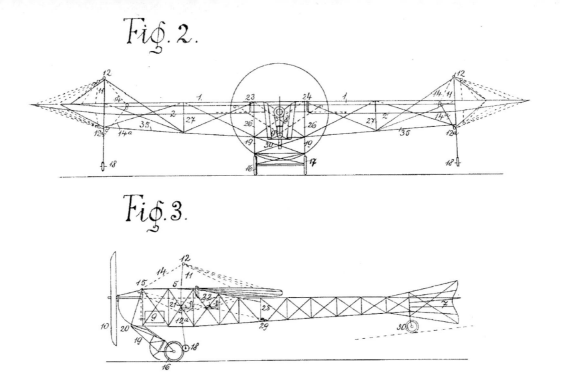

Fig. 2.

Fig. 3.

The second drawing of the 1910 patent, which looks decidedly manmade with its spiderweb of cables, and awkward system of girders and struts.

which in turn was braced by cable and hardened by turnbuckles. At the outboard end of each truss, a kingpost ran perpendicular to the truss and plane—which it pierced and projected above to support rigging for wing-warping and the support of the wing itself. Like many contemporary aircraft, especially monoplanes, the original *Taube* used wing-warping for lateral (roll) control, and also warped the rear half of the stabilizer to function as the elevator. Only the vertical, twin triangular rudder surfaces were initially hinged. However, *Taubes* would eventually employ hinged ailerons and elevators.

The Etrich *Taube II* was originally licensed for production by Lohner-Werke in Austria. It should be noted how trades such as coachbuilding and boat building—specialized woodworking— were coopted or leveraged by the growing aircraft industry. Since "aircraft builders" per se had not existed as a long-established trade, the trade had to be "invented" using those with woodworking, metalworking, engine, and rigging experience to develop the new craft.

Rumpler also licensed the Etrich *Taube II* in Germany and soon changed the name to Rumpler *Taube*, and stopped paying royalties to Etrich, who subsequently abandoned his patent. This was due to the fact that since Ahlborn had already published on the Zanonia wing form, it could not be patented by another party. This led to a glut of *Taube* designs by just about everyone producing aircraft in Germany during the ramp-up to World War I.

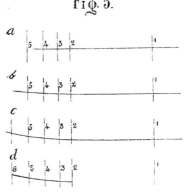

Fig. 4.

Fig. 5.

This drawing from the patent describes the "washout" at the wingtips of the Etrich *Taube*. In the event of a stall, this feature insured a smoother recovery of the aircraft, than if the tips were not warped upward.

A coach made by Lohner-Werke coachworks; the same curves used to make this beautiful coach were re-purposed to build the curved shapes of aircraft.

A Rumpler *Taube* built under license from Etrich.

Later *Taube*-type aircraft from other manufacturers replaced the Blériot-type main gear with a simpler V-strut main gear design, and also replaced the underwing "bridge" structure with wire cables to reduce drag. These gradual and systematic improvements paved the way for the transition from the *Taube* form to the biplane reconnaissance planes, which were subsequently produced by every manufacturer who had originally produced *Taubes*. The following are brief descriptions taken from *Flight* magazine regarding the different manufacturers who produced *Taubes*, and the design traits specific to same.

The first Albatros *Taube* was similar to the Etrich and Rumpler *Taubes*. Even during this early period, German authorities and aircraft industries were thinking about ease of transport and assembly/disassembly of aircraft:

> The Albatros *Taube* was characterized by a fuselage similar to that of the biplane. The wings are of the Taube type having back-swept upturned tips, and there is the usual girder structure forming the lower wing bracing as in nearly all Taube monoplanes. It consists of a steel tube running parallel to the wing spars and placed some distance below the wing to which it is connected by a number of steel tube struts and diagonal cross bracing. Although offering a considerable amount of head resistance [drag]

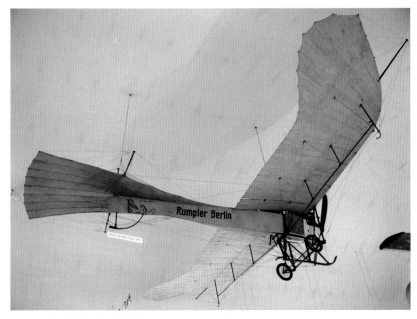

A surviving Rumpler *Taube* in the permanent collection of the Deutsches Museum in Munich.

this type of construction is employed as it provides a structure of almost equal strength to that of a biplane. The stabilizer and elevator [stabilator] are formed by a single plane the front portion of which is rigidly attached to the fuselage whilst the rear part acts as an elevator by being flexed up and down. Steering is effected by means of two rudders, one above and one below the tail plane. Lateral control is maintained by flexing the upturned wingtips. Provision has been made for rapidly folding the wings for purposes of storage or transport [consistent with the military's desire to have such characteristics]. The chassis is similar to that of the biplane, the different parts have been standardized in order to facilitate interchange.

The Albatros *Taube* of the type used in the Constance Race in 1913 was a significant breakthrough for Albatros, as this racer featured an almost completely streamlined fuselage of plywood on ply formers (just as later Albatros would be built), It had a rudder and vertical fin, stabilizer and elevators, and the wings were braced with wire; not the cumbersome steel truss system. It is difficult to tell, but wing-warping still is being used: note the Zanonia form in the floatplane version Also the aircraft was able to be completely broken down for transport. The description in *Flight* appears to contain inaccuracies as the main planes are not the usual *Taube* type:

> Its main planes are of the usual *Taube* type, being of Zanonia form. The body is of particularly good stream line form, having no sharp angles in its outline. Pilot's and passenger's seats are arranged in tandem as in the land machines, and just in front of the passenger is mounted a 100 hp Mercedes engine. The tail planes are similar to those fitted on the Albatros biplanes, and consist of a horizontal stabilizer, to which is hinged the divided elevator, and of vertical fins above and below the body, to which is hinged the rudder.

The [Karl] **Jatho** and **Jeannin Steel *Taubes*** were unusual for the time in that they utilized welded steel fuselages. The Jatho had wings comprised of steel tube spars and steel ribs, whereas the Jeannin had traditional wooden wing framing; perhaps steel was not as good a system for wing-warping as wood. *Flight* described the Jatho as having:

> Very roomy cockpits, where the occupants are protected against the wind. In front of the pilot is a dashboard with a very complete set of instruments, including barograph, tachometer, map case, watch, inclinometer, compass, &c. The petrol and oil tanks, which are placed low down in the fuselage, contain a supply sufficient for a flight of 7 hours' duration it has a radius of action of something like 273 miles … on each side of the fuselage part of the wings have been left uncovered in order to provide a better view in a downward direction … the constructors of the Jatho steel *Taube* also build a racing type monoplane with a 150 hp engine, and a light sporting monoplane fitted with a Gnome motor.

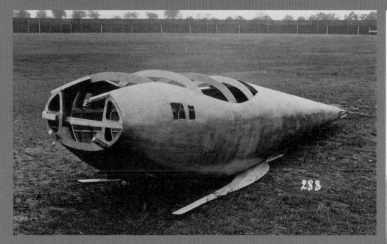

Fuselage of a *Taube* made by Albatros—a double-seat single-cockpit model. Note the company's early facility with curved plywood panels over plywood formers. (Craftlab)

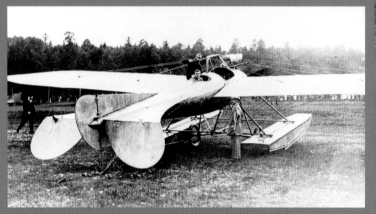

A front view of the Albatros *Taube*. Note the modular nature of this aircraft and the purpose-made troughs that hold the leading edge of the wings. This was a mandate from the German military: these early planes had to be portable. (Craftlab)

The clean lines of the Albatros floatplane *Taube* that performed so well at Lake Constance in 1913.

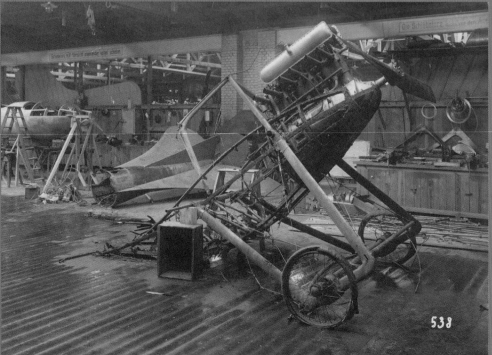

In this very unusual and vexing image, an Albatros *Taube* has apparently either been set on fire, or has accidentally caught fire. The semi-intact aft fuselage section is just behind the charred forward fuselage section. Another one is under construction farther in the background; in the distance a *Taube* Zanonia-shaped wing is just visible. (Craftlab)

The Jeannin Steel *Taube* is described as having eliminated the awkward steel girder under its wood-framed wings and instead having cable bracing consistent with "the latest models." Like the Jatho, it too has a 100-hp Mercedes engine and also has "a radiator similar to that on the Albatros biplane … the chassis is of a very simple type, and consists of a short skid, carried on four streamline steel tube struts, and to it is hinged the divided axle, which is sprung by means of telescopic tubes running to the fuselage at the attachment to which are incorporated rubber shock absorbers." Seeing the evolution of the early *Taubes*, it is easier to make the technological transition to the next series of monoplanes: the Eindeckers.

The DFW *Taube* presented no significant improvements over the other *Taubes*, except for the notation that "The wheels are carried on stub axles pivoted on the center skid, and springing is effected by coil springs on telescopic steel tubes running to the upper longerons of the fuselage. The radiators are mounted on each side of the body." Again, looking at the landing gear structure of the Eindecker monoplanes such as those built by Pfalz and Fokker, it is easy to trace their structural developments by comparing them to the *Taubes,* and the positioning of "ear-type" radiators on either side of the fuselage also began here.

The Jeannin Steel *Taube* ("*Stahltaube*") had an-all steel framework for the fuselage and wings. The awkward girder running under the main planes has disappeared and has been replaced with all-cable bracing.

The Goedecker *Taube* reflected the German army's desire for mobility and flexibility and also incorporated steel tube spars into the wings "and provision has been made for quick erecting and dismantling. By substituting a pair of floats for the wheels, this machine can be very quickly converted into a hydro." Goedecker and Fokker collaborated on his *Spin*, and doubtless Fokker learned from Goedecker—perhaps regarding the potential of steel in aircraft, and how to engineer an aircraft to dis/assemble efficiently.

This Jeannin "*Stahltaube*" is in the permanent collection of the Deutsches Technikmuseum in Berlin. (Public domain)

The Gotha *Taube* was noteworthy in its cowling and streamlining of its engine, use of streamlined steel tubes for landing gear struts, and shock absorbing set-up; as with all the *Taubes* the German army required that they be able to land on a ploughed field.

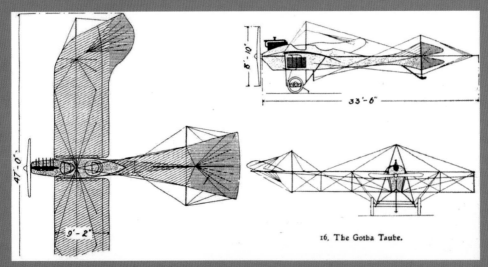

16. The Gotha Taube.

The Gotha *Taube* was similar to the other *Taube* copies and reverted to the girder, strut, and cable system of wing bracing.

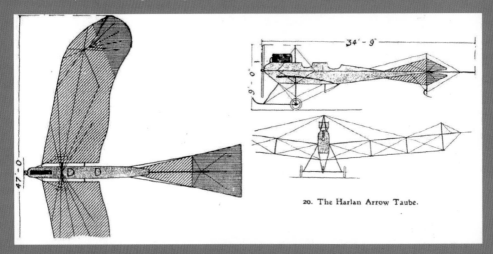

20. The Harlan Arrow Taube.

The Harlan Arrow *Taube* had tandem cockpits, a preventer ski to prevent nose-overs and a space between the fuselage and wings to allow better downward visibility.

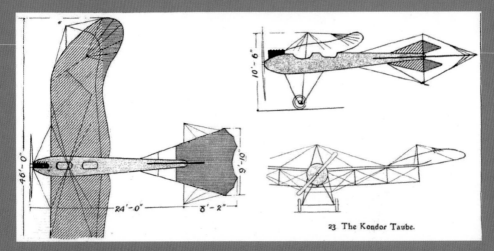

23 The Kondor Taube.

The Kondor *Taube* featured a very streamlined fuselage, and extreme washout at the wingtips.

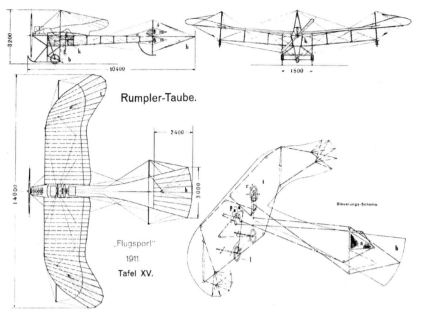

Rumpler-Taube.

„Flugsport"
1911
Tafel XV.

A diagram showing the control arrangement of the Rumpler *Taube* that was published in *Flugsport* in 1911. Note the continued use of the car wheel to control roll.

The Halberstadt *Taube*, like Albatros, was characterized by a semi-monocoque fuselage, a technique Halberstadt would return to with its famed CI. II two-seater. *Flight* mentions that it was "covered with fabric inside and out," again, lending precedent to the fabric-taped interiors of Pfalz, Roland, and Albatros. The Halberstadt *Taube* followed suit with steel cables to support the wings, and featured an impressive speed due to the streamlining efforts. *Flight* had the following to say:

> For purposes of observation, and in order to facilitate photography, openings have been provided in the wings on each side of the observer's seat, and these openings are fitted with glass covers." The landing gear has become standard for World War I aircraft, which chassis consisted of "two pairs of V" tubes, from which the tubular axle is slung by means of rubber shock absorbers … the peculiar flexing tail plane found on most Tauben has been replaced in this machine by an ordinary flat non-lifting stabilizing plane, to the trailing edge of which is hinged the divided elevator. Mounted on top of the fuselage is a vertical fin of comparatively large area, to the trailing edge of which is hinged the rudder. Evidently the monocoque type fuselage, and the absence of the usual girder structure below the wing, has reduced the head resistance enormously, for with a 100 hp Mercedes engine this machine is said to be capable of a speed of 92 miles per hour.

The Halberstadt *Taube* featured many innovations that would become standard on all subsequent aircraft: the hinged rudder and elevators, twin V strut gear, and a novel feature—glass panels inset into the wing to allow downward visibility for photography.

The Hansa *Taube* (72 mph), **Harlan Arrow *Taube*,** and **Kondor *Taube*** (60 mph) showed no great improvement over any of the other *Taubes*, differing in no way from the usual form. Although, it was noted that the Harlan Arrow, using either an Argus or Mercedes 100-hp engine, fully loaded, could climb 1,000 meters (3,281 feet) in 15 minutes. Also, the Kondor *Taube* showed a nicely streamlined fuselage, but apparently it was too heavy judging from its overall speed.

Rumpler made a variety of *Taubes* beginning with the licensed Etrich model all the way up to what could be rightly called an Eindecker. The Rumpler *Taubes* built between 1911 and 1912 closely resemble the Etrich *Taube*. However, Rumpler did build a floatplane version, the Rumpler Wasser Eindecker Type 3F, in 1913 to satisfy the navy's desire for reconnaissance aircraft. Moreover, he experimented within the *Taube* class: a three-view drawing dated 1912 shows a very streamlined Rumpler *Taube* with none of the steel girderwork under the wings, suggesting that he had abandoned this system by this date, or was building both types. Moreover, the fuselage is very streamlined and the engine is well cowled. However, it still featured wing- and potential elevator-warping which continued through 1913 although the landing gear is moving in the V-strut direction.

A detail of a Rumpler *Taube* in the Luftwaffenmuseum (Air Force Museum) at Berlin-Gatow. Note the finely formed aluminum cowling of this replica, and the thin radiator that was installed under the starboard wing against the fuselage.

A replica of the Rumpler *Taube* in the Museum of Flight in Seattle, Washington. Note the small skid located just aft of the main wheels; this could be pulled from the cockpit to act as a brake. Also visible is the slightly flaring framing of the wingtips, and the rigging for actuating the wingtip warping.

Another image of the *Taube* in the Luftwaffenmuseum. Note the rigging at the tips of the wings that served as ailerons.

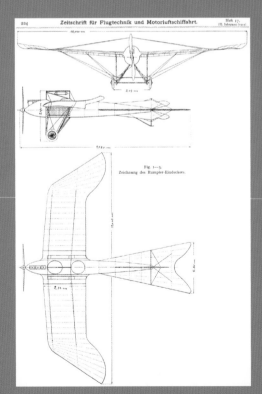

This Rumpler Eindecker drawing shows a finely streamlined fuselage, and apparently a hinged elevator, which was a break from the typical elevator-warping system.

A rare image of the wing framing for an Etrich Rumpler *Taube*. The ribs are made from thin strips with spacers glued at set distances to form the lightening spaces. The bottom flange extends far aft, making a very flexible trailing edge once covered. Also note the aft spar curves forward sharply to allow the wingtip framing to be very flexible and facilitate warping. (Public domain)

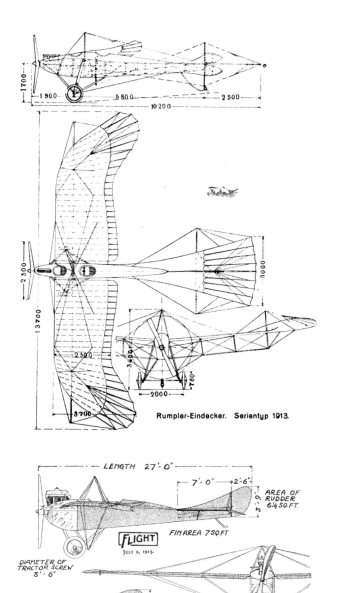

Rumpler-Eindecker. Serientyp 1913.

LENGTH 27'-0"

7'-0"   2'-6"

AREA OF RUDDER 6¼ SQ.FT.

FIN AREA 7 SQ.FT

FLIGHT
JULY 9, 1915.

DIAMETER OF TRACTOR SCREW 8'-6"

AREA OF MAIN PLANES 300 SQ.FT.

AREA OF AILERONS 30.SQ.FT.

7'-0"

SPAN 96'-0"

RUMPLER TAUBE
MONOPLANE
100 HP MERCEDES

SCALE OF FEET
0 1 2 3 4 5 6 7 8 9 10 11 12 13 14 15

2'-0"   9'-6"   5'-6"   7'-0"

1'-6"

AREA OF ELEVATORS 13 SQ.FT.

AREA OF TAIL PLANES 32 SQ.FT.

2'-9"

A large Rumpler *Taube* circa 1913, a two-seater that featured older-style construction methods.

By late 1913/early 1914, Rumpler *Taube* was described by *Flight* as a:

> Very compact business-looking machine. The upper wing bracing, it will be seen, is now effected by cables running to a pyramidal pylon of steel tubes, and the Zanonia form of wing has been retained. Instead of the usual flexing wingtips, ailerons are fitted. These, it should be noted, are hinged along an axis forming an angle with the transverse axis of the main planes. The bracing cables are taken to pyramidal cabanes or pylons above and below the fuselage, and instead of the flexing wingtips usually found on monoplanes of the Taube type, upturned ailerons are fitted These, it should be noted, are hinged along an axis forming an angle with the transverse axis of the main planes. The only feature constituting this machine one of the Taube class is its Zanonia-form wings, it otherwise following standard practice as regards its fuselage, tail planes and chassis. The flexing elevator has been replaced by one of the hinged, divided type, whilst the rudder is hinged to the stern post, and not half above and half below the fuselage. The chassis is built up of four steel tubes forming two pairs of Vs, in the angle of which rests the axle, which is sprung by rubber shock-absorbers. Evidently the reduction of head resistance effected by substituting cable bracing for the girder structure under the wings has considerably increased the speed, for with a 100-hp Mercedes engine this machine is capable of doing about 74 mph.

The use of *Taubes* began to wane shortly after the outbreak of war in 1914, being replaced by biplane two-seaters as these proved a bit sturdier and more maneuverable. However, Rumpler continued to build *Taubes* as late as 1915. The Rumpler *Taube* of 1915 more closely resembles something out of the E series

This Rumpler *Taube* could be considered a true antecedent to the *Eindeckers* that would follow—actually it had some more advanced features than these in that it had hinged ailerons, a semi-streamlined fuselage, hinged elevators and rudder. It had only cable bracing on the wings.

except more streamline, like the Bristol Bullet. The late model Rumpler *Taube* was described by *Flight* as such:

> [it has an] absence of the girder understructure bracing the wings—a distinctive characteristic of nearly all Taubes—the hinged balancing flaps [ailerons], and the orthodox type of tail planes in place of the original flexing plane. Though somewhat modified, the main planes still have the Zanonia form … the angle of incidence decreases toward the tips, where the … [ailerons] present a slight negative angle of incidence [washout]. [The ailerons] have an area of 15 sq. ft. each … they also operate in an upward direction only … Cable bracing is employed top and bottom … anchored to pyramids of tubular steel struts mounted above and below the body respectively; the underbracing is thus quite independent of the undercarriage … Ash and American white pine are employed in the construction of the main planes, which are built up on two main spars situated fairly close together. Portions of the planes adjacent to the pilot's cockpit are cut away in order to provide a view below. The tail consists of a triangular stabilizing surface, in two portions mounted one on either side of the body, and two elevator flaps hinged similarly to the balancing flaps, *i.e.*, at an angle. The vertical rudder is mounted between the elevators with a triangular vertical fin in front. The body is rectangular in section, tapering to a vertical knife-edge at the rear. Ash is the material employed in its construction, and the portion forward of the cockpits is covered with sheet metal, and that aft with fabric. The engine, a 100 hp 6-cylinder water cooled Mercedes, is mounted in the nose, with the Windhoff radiator directly above it … The engine drives direct a Reschke tractor screw 8 ft. 6 ins. diameter and 4 ft. 9 ins. pitch. Immediately behind the engine are the fuel tanks, and then [the passenger's and pilot's cockpits in that order]. The control consists of a vertical wheel mounted on a rocking column, the former operating the [ailerons] and the latter the elevator, whilst the rudder is actuated by pedals. A simple but strong under carriage is fitted consisting of two pairs of steel V struts of streamline section, with a tubular axle carrying a pair of disc wheels, attached, by means of rubber bands, to the apex of each V. A short skid attached to the body at the rear protects the tail. The following are the main characteristics of the Rumpler-Taube: Span, 46 ft.; maximum chord, 9 ft. 6 ins.; overall length, 27 ft.; supporting area, 300 sq. ft.; weight fully loaded, 1,840 lbs.; speed, 74 mph.; climbing speed, 2,600 ft. in 6 mins. (full load, 4 hours fuel and 400 lbs. useful load).

It is obvious this is where Rumpler, Albatros, etc. derived inspiration for the fuselage for their two-seater C series of observation biplanes, or vice versa: if you were to replace the Zanonia single plane with a biplane cellule structure the result would resemble very closely the Albatros, Rumpler, and Aviatik B and C series.

This Rumpler *Taube* was brought down in September 1917, proof that this type of aircraft was still in use at this relatively late date. Also visible is the V-strut landing gear that featured streamlined fairings, and rebound slot for the axle which was set up with bungees—common practice for all aircraft during World War I. (NARA)

An Aviatik two-seater—note the radiator mounted to the forward faces of the cabane struts. Working out the cooling system for WWI aircraft was problematic. (NARA)

2
Aviatik

Automobil und Aviatik AG was founded in December 1909 by Alsatian Georges Chatel, and Emil Jeannin, a successful German pilot and builder who, as mentioned, was the creator of the Stahltaube. Their original intent was to sell Peugeot cars and aircraft under license. The factory was originally established at Mühlhausen, Alsace, in 1910. Aviatic soon became a leading aircraft producer, building French Hanriot monoplanes and Farman biplanes under license, just as others had done. Under the design direction of Robert Wild, Aviatik began building its own biplanes in 1912, but was nearly closed due to a letter sent by Otto Weiner at Albatros to IdFlieg—Albatros claimed it originated from DFW and Rumpler—stating that Aviatik was in fact a French

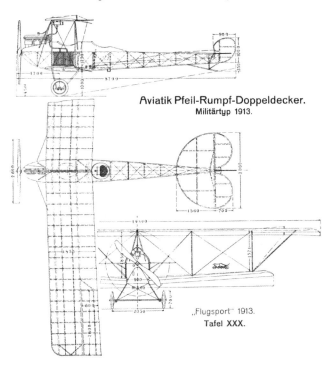

Aviatik Pfeil-Rumpf-Doppeldecker.
Militärtyp 1913.

„Flugsport" 1913.
Tafel XXX.

An early Aviatik two-seater biplane. Note the box-girder construction of the fuselage, and the relatively minimal use of compound curved panels: e.g. turtle deck area.. This appeared in *Flugsport* in 1913.

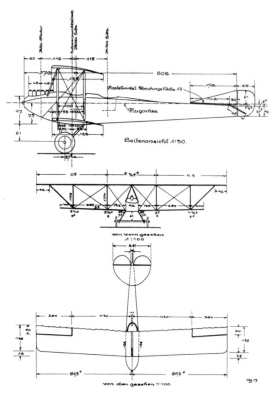

The Aviatik B.I reconnaissance biplane of 1915. The interplane structure is reminiscent of Farman- or Caudron-style bracing, and also note the high angle of incidence of the wings.

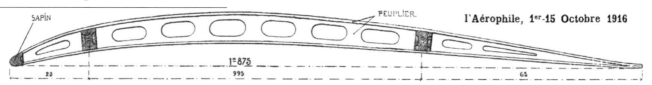

SAPIN — PEUPLIER.

l'Aérophile, 1er-15 Octobre 1916

1ᵐ875

23 · 995 · 65

FIG. 18. — Nervure d'aile d'Aviatik 1914-15 à 1/10ᵉ. Longerons beaucoup plus écartés qu'aux types 1915-16 ; espace beaucoup moindre à l'arrière du longeron postérieur ; longerons pleins, d'une seule pièce en double T, évidés localement à l'extérieur ; ajourements de l'âme moins allongés et plus nombreux.

A rib web of an Aviatik B series biplane displaying pronounced undercamber, narrow depth wings featuring solid spars.

company, as Peugeot held a controlling share in the business. This was an attempt by Albatros to reduce competition in order to secure a government subsidy in return for large aircraft orders. It was later discovered by General Wandel, head of the War Department, that all of Aviatik's shareholders were Alsatian. The attempt by Albatros to monopolize the market backfired: Wandel rejected Albatros's subsidy request for another factory, and refused to eliminate Aviatik from future government contracts. This is but one example of how personal interactions shaped the outcome of Germany's war industry as clearly Albatros felt threatened by Aviatik.

During this early period Aviatik built a variety of different types: the Aviatik "Aero and Hydro" of 1913 was an aircraft reminiscent of its earlier Farman aircraft, with semi-retractable landing gear. The Aviatik Pfeil Rumpf Doppeldecker of 1913, a two-seater reconnaissance biplane with slightly swept wings, was followed in 1914 by a floatplane iteration of this basic design which had a modified vertical fin and rudder. Finally the B.I came out which combined the best features of previous models, but also incorporated aspects inspired by other builders' efforts.

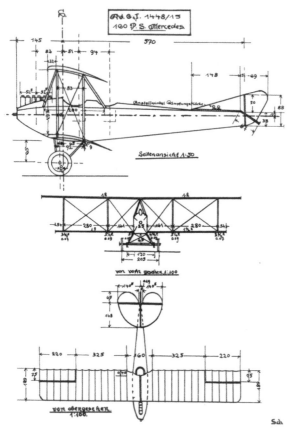

Aviatic B.I of 1915 showing improved interplane bracing, extreme angle of incidence of the wings and a Mercedes 160-hp powerplant. The wings are of constant chord with no sweep, and feature ample ailerons.

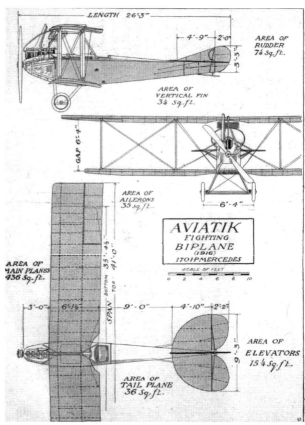

Aviatik B series of 1916 showing slight sweep to the wings, a balanced rudder, ample horizontal stabilizer and streamlined cowling. The drawing notes a Mercedes engine of 170 hp. Wings have a more moderate angle of incidence, likely due to the increased power of the engine. (*Flight* magazine)

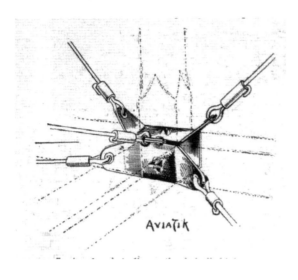

An ingenious folded steel fuselage attachment clip. Note how this entire fixture can be unfolded and laid flat, and that when bent to shape, how the overlapping pieces are activated by virtue of the bracing attachment. Also note the sharp tines bent upward at the intersection of various wooden parts, which were meant to bite the wood to hold the parts in place. (*Flight* magazine)

At the outbreak of World War I in 1914, the company relocated first to Breisgau, then to Freiburg, and finally, in 1916, to the Leipzig-Heiterblick Aerodrome of Leipziger Luftschiffhafen and Flugplatz Gesellschaft at Mackau, where it was managed by Ernest Stoeffler. It was also far enough away to be out of range of Allied bombers. Moreover, the company was sensitive about being construed in any way as French. A subsidiary was created in Vienna—Österreichisch-Ungarische Flugzeugfabrik Aviatik—which would produce the Berg D.I.

The successful C series—C.I through C.IX—had a long run. The most successful was the C.III which was a refinement of the C.I. The principal difference between the two was that the C.III had a reduced wingspan and proportional area than that of the C.I. The nose area of the fuselage of the C.III was more streamlined, including a spinner on the propeller, and the exhaust stack was rotated to lay horizontally to starboard to improve forward visibility. Finally, the pilot and observer positions were switched, so the pilot was forward and the observer faced aft.

The construction of the C.III is described in *Flight* and *L'Aerophile* magazines. They mention that the fuselage was of standard box-girder construction and the steel clips used for securing the stanchions to the longerons were patented such that these clips consisted:

> Of a single sheet steel clip totally surrounding the rail and bolted together where its two ends meet, so as to grip the rail. No strut socket is employed, the strut being prevented from slipping by the simple means of punching the metal of the clip upwards in the shape of four small triangles which project into the end of the strut.

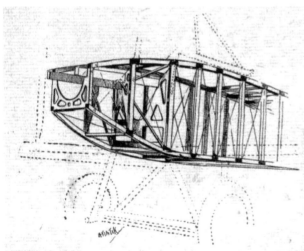

Skeleton view of the fore part of the *fuselage*, showing the ply-wood engine bearer supports on the 1916 Aviatik biplane.

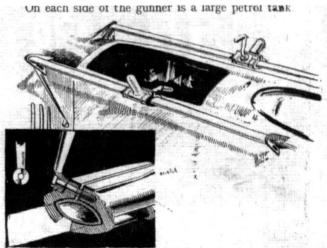

On each side of the gunner is a large petrol tank.

General arrangement and detail of the gun mounting on the 1916 Aviatik biplane.

This illustration shows the composite construction of the 1916 Aviatic reconnaissance biplane. The longerons are attached to the vertical struts by the aforementioned steel clips. The bulkhead formers are of plywood and stamped steel.

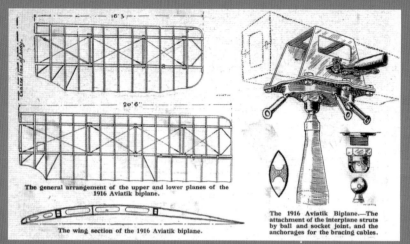

The general arrangement of the upper and lower planes of the 1916 Aviatik biplane.

The wing section of the 1916 Aviatik biplane.

The 1916 Aviatik Biplane.—The attachment of the interplane struts by ball and socket joint, and the anchorages for the bracing cables.

This illustration shows the arrangement of the wing panels, built up from hollow spars, with a long span aft of the aftermost spar. Both spars are braces with compression struts and antidrag bracing wires. The interplane strut attachment points are marvels of efficiency in that the steel staple encloses the wing spar and forms attachment points for rigging as well as an adjustable ball socket interplane attachment point. The interplane struts are comprised of streamline steel tube with spruce cores.

One of the metal clips carrying the tubular compression strut between the spars.

This illustration shows the bent steel clip that forms the attachment point of the compression struts between spars. The strut joint and rigging tangs are integrated into the clip and sandwiched and fastened with bolts.

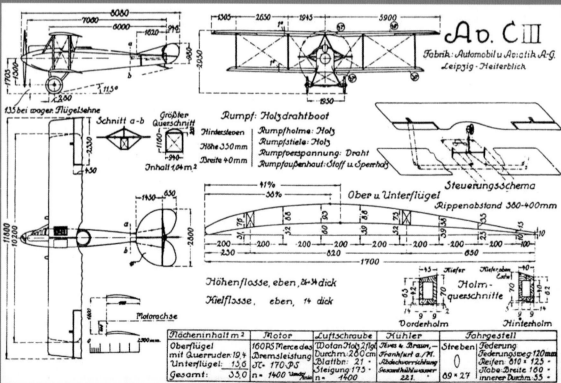

This drawing shows the Aviatik C.III. It features an airfoil of moderate undercamber and both wings are set to very nominal incidence (if not 0). Control of the ailerons was routed through the lower wing and up to the top plane. The fuselage is of box-girder construction with a curved ply turtledeck.

In Profile:
Aviatik D.I

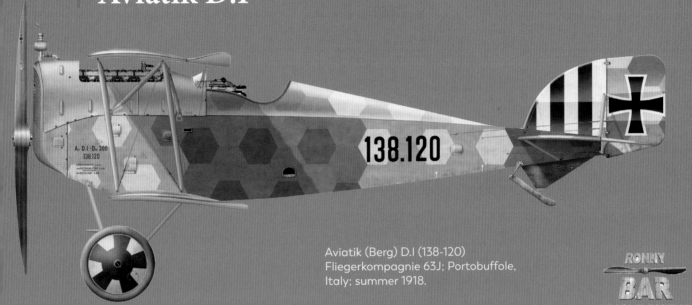

138.120

Aviatik (Berg) D.I (138-120)
Fliegerkompagnie 63J; Portobuffole,
Italy; summer 1918.

RONNY
BAR
AIRCRAFT PROFILES
ronnybarprofiles@gmail.com

An Aviatic, or what appears to
be, in Italian colors. (NARA)

A³ 20173

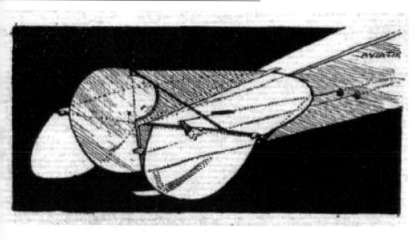

The unusual balanced rudder of the Aviatik C.III. If the vertical fin is omitted, the shape of the Fokker E, D, and Dr.1 series becomes evident.

So in terms of production, this clip had small "teeth" that gripped the strut, temporarily securing it until it could be permanently fastened—much as metal joist hangars do today in house construction. Another metal purpose-made fitting to aid in production was a stamped steel plate that accepted all the longerons at the nose, and is described as "having lightening holes cut in it. On this end plate, and two more further back, rested the two longitudinal ash engine bearers, further rigidity being obtained by bracing the engine bed with steel tubes from the body rails."

The wings were of standard construction with the exception that the spars were hollow, being made from two pieces of hollowed spruce and spliced and glued together. These were in turn reinforced by compression bar fittings that enclosed the finished spar (at various points) as well as providing attachment points for antidrag rigging and the compression bars. The empennage was somewhat different in that "With the exception of the ribs of the fixed tail plane the control organs are made of steel throughout." Of particular interest is the balanced rudder, which resembled a Fokker "comma" rudder inset into a fixed vertical fin—perhaps the inspiration for Fokker.

While the main factory produced the B and C series reconnaissance planes, the subsidiary in Vienna—Österreichisch-Ungarische Flugzeugfabrik Aviatik—created the D series or "Berg" fighter. The D.I was designed by Austro-Hungarian Julius von Berg, and was the first fighter that was not derived from a German design. Its genesis began in 1916 with the Aviatik 30.14, an awkward-looking aircraft, with little known about it. Some sources claim that Professor Richard Knoller had a hand in its design as at this time he exerted great influence over the Austro-Hungarian aircraft industry, with Aviatik contracted to build 24 of the ill-fated Knoller C series two-seaters.

Von Berg next developed the 30.21, which was a closer relative to the Berg D.I. It was completed in late 1916 and tested at Aspern in early 1917. A group of test pilots under the leadership of Lieutenant Colonel Fekete thoroughly tested the D.I and the two-seater Berg C.I. The 30.21 differed from the D.I in its lesser amount of stagger, and minor rigging differences in the aileron and elevator control cables. Fekete and his team liked the new fighter and, upon their recommendation, it was ordered into production for the Austro-Hungarian air force.

The Aviatik Berg D.I at the Museum of Flight. This is one of the few original D.Is in existence. (Public domain)

Like the 30.21 the early production D.Is were equipped with the 185-hp Austro-Daimler engine, but the majority used in combat had the 200–210-hp A.D. engine. In the summer of 1918 a 225 hp was fitted to the same airframe which proved too much for it, resulting in the strengthening of the fuselage and the wings. The D.I. had a Jaray propeller which had unusually narrow blades. The D.I. featured the car-type, frontally mounted radiator, most of which had a rounded top. Cooling was to plague the D.Is to such an extent that many frontline aircraft had sections of the cowling removed to improve airflow over the engine.

A closeup of Museum of Flight's Berg, showing the jaunty forward facing radiator, plywood sides and interesting camouflage scheme.

Due to shortages of skilled craftsmen in Austria-Hungary, Berg was designed as an easy-build. It incorporated aspects of all types of construction

A view of the Aviatik Berg D.I at the Vienna Technical Museum. Note the shape of the airfoil: the aftermost portion of the wing ribs terminate in a very sharp point. This was known to flex, giving the plane's wings a built-in shock absorber. Also evident is the simple construction of the fuselage, formers and ply skin. (IdFlieg.com)

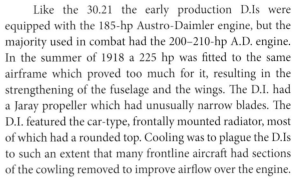

A closeup of the cockpit of the D.I. Compared to other German aircraft like the Albatros and the Pfalz, the Aviatik cockpit appears crude. (IdFlieg.com)

techniques: it had four longerons notched into plywood bulkheads near the engine compartment; spruce struts aft of the cockpit were unbraced owing to the strength provided by the plywood sides; steel struts provided additional strength near the engine and wing root; and the engine was cowled on top with curved aluminum panels. The pilot sat high in the cockpit which resulted in turtle decking of higher aspect than most aircraft. This contributed to the distinctive look of the Berg profile.

The D.VII, which was intended to participate in the third D-type contest at Adlershof in October 1918, was essentially similar to the D.VI apart from having completely redesigned vertical and horizontal tail surfaces. Like its predecessor, it was powered by a geared Benz Bz IIIbm eight-cylinder engine driving a four-bladed propeller. Armament comprised the standard twin 7.92mm synchronized machine guns. Only one prototype was completed.

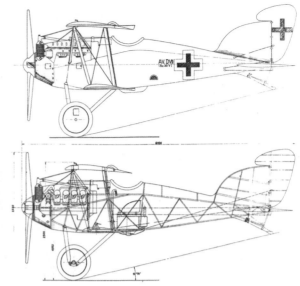

A closeup of the D.I at the Vienna Technical Museum. Note how high the engine is mounted, thus blocking a good portion of the pilot's forward view, although the pilot did sit high in the cockpit. The shape of the wing rib webs is very clear in this image. (IdFlieg.com)

A drawing of the Aviatik D.VII which featured a welded steel fuselage framing, elevators, rudder and ailerons, and a high aspect and interesting rudder and vertical fin arrangement.

What is interesting about this aircraft is Aviatik's attempt to synthesize many different construction aspects. There was a tube steel fuselage (as made popular by Fokker), topped by a plywood turtle deck. The somewhat oversized rudder and fin looks similar to earlier Aviatiks, as well as Siemens-Schuckert aircraft; perhaps this was in reaction to the earlier D.II which had a seemingly undersized rudder and fin. The wings are sesquiplane in plan, and the ribs are closely spaced as in the Pfalz D.VIII, D.XII and, by extension, the Spads. The ailerons are balanced, and what is unique about the rib webs is that near the tips they "cant" or are angled instead of being perpendicular to the leading edge, which would have made production all the more difficult. As with the Spads, S.E.5as, Fokker D.VIIs, and Pfalz D.XIIs, the Aviatik D.VII had its radiator all the way forward.

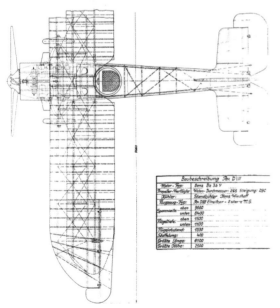

The Aviatik D.I.

Left: The planview of the D.VII wings showing canted rib webs near the tips—a carryover from *Taube* framing. Also, the tail plane looks very similar to the Pfalz D.XII. (NARA)

The Halberstadt D.I. This was a breakthrough for the company as others were preoccupied with *Eindecker*-type monoplanes. The D.I featured ailerons on the upper wing (no wing-warping), four sets of interplanes, a nicely cowled engine area, and the distinctive Halberstadt rudder. (Public domain)

3

Halberstadt Flugzeugzelte

Halberstadt Flugzeugzelte was formed on April 9, 1912 as the Deutsche Bristol Werke Flugzeug Gesellschaft mbH, with an initial capitalization of 200,000 marks. The shareholders of the new company were Hermann and Gustav Behrens, Kurt Stockhausen, and Eduard Schnebel, who were at the same time owners of the Oscherslebener Presstuckerfabrik factory, not far away. There they produced, among other things, aircraft tents and portable airship halls, having already realized the economic possibilities of the growing aviation industry. The Deutsche Bristol Werke was formed on the basis of a demonstration flight of a Bristol Prieur by Howard Pixton at Döberitz. Pixton had been in Madrid undertaking demonstration flights before being sent to Germany, where he flew No. 74 at Döberitz to demonstrate its capabilities to the German army—resulting in the formation by Bristol of a German subsidiary: the Deutsche Bristolwerke Flugzeuggesellschaft mbH. The object of the company was the "manufacture and sale of aircraft, according to the system [used by] Bristol (Note: British and colonial aeroplane company)." Initially, the joint German–British venture produced the Bristol "Boxkite" biplane and the Bristol Prieur monoplane, before modifying their own replicas.

The Bristol, a derivation of the successful Blériot XI model, was quick to assemble and had excellent flight characteristics. These early Bristols had a fabric-covered, wire-braced wooden fuselage and constant chord wings that employed wing-warping for roll control, although differing in rigging details from the Blériot XI. The full-flying "stabilater" was triangular and mounted in a mid-position between the upper and lower longerons. The undercarriage had a pair of wheels on an axle mounted onto a pair of forward-projecting skids. It was powered by a 50-hp (37-kW) Gnome rotary engine. The first aircraft built (works No. 46) was for the Gordon Bennett Trophy race, but it was not ready in time. A two-seater version was developed to capitalize

The Bristol "Boxkite" was aptly named. Companies that built this type of aircraft quickly realized that aside from being obsolete, with regards to other models that were emerging such as Blériot monoplanes, the production costs of such aircraft were prohibitive if the company wanted to stay in business. (Public domain)

on the training schools that were popping up all over Britain and Europe. By October 1911 the two-seater had been thoroughly tested, and put into production. Six airframes were started (nos 71–76), the first of which was carefully built for demonstration and for exhibition at the 1911 Paris Aero Salon where it was the only British aircraft on display. Bristol No. 74 made demonstration flights over Paris during the Aero Salon, and was also the aircraft demonstrated in Russia and Germany, ultimately ending up at the Halberstadt flying school.

The site for the new company was a few miles from the town of Halberstadt near the Thenkenbergen mountains. The site had a newly built road connecting it to town and an empty building that would serve as a temporary storage/work space. In early 1912, Eduard Schnebel, engineer and co-founder of the company, travelled to England to familiarize himself with the associated components and construction of the Bristol monoplane and biplane. He then visited the Henri Farman aircraft company at Mourmelon, Reims, where the Bristol biplane was being built under license. In May 1912, an aircraft school was founded at the factory site as well, as pilot instruction was the focus of the German military more so than construction at this time. Moreover, instruction could begin at once, while the permanent factory buildings and aircraft hangers were being completed.

The first aircraft from England, a Bristol *Coanda* monoplane, (named after the designer), arrived on June 19, 1912 in Halberstadt. With the assembly of the machine, the Deutsche Bristol works began operation. A week later, on June 26, 1912, English pilot Howard Pixton took off with the machine at 9 o'clock, reached an altitude of 60 meters and landed comfortably after a seven-minute flight. This plane was soon followed by the second, a Bristol "boxkite" biplane with the English pilot Kent at the controls. Shortly after that, aircraft construction began. The original anticipated order of four Bristols for the army was reduced to one in April, because the army had no experience with this foreign company and needed to proceed cautiously.

At about the same time, the first group of flight officer students arrived, and began training on July 1. The students, culled from the ranks of flying troops, were initially taught by the two English flight instructors, Pixton and Kent. Their first flights, each lasting almost seven minutes, took place early on in the training. A third plane arrived on July 6, while at the same time flight instructor Pixton returned to England after teaching Deutsche Bristol employees the basics of flight instruction on the *Coandas*.

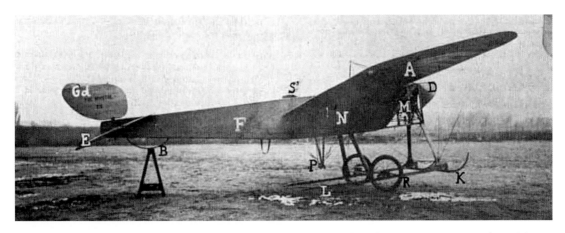

The Bristol Prieur monoplane featured fully flying stabilator and rudder, wing-warping, and an old-style ski and wheels undercarriage. (Public domain)

As flight instruction proceeded at Halberstadt, construction of the aircraft plant continued apace, and on July 22 the first buildings were finished. Because of the large number of students, a dormitory was built soon after. With the military sending increasing numbers of students—48 in the first few months—and in spite of the fact that, being a private venture, the flying school was seen as a gamble, the school became more and more important and was completely separated from the aircraft factory.

The school was named Halberstadt Military Flying School GmbH at the end of 1912, under the command of four officers. The expansion of the school was finished by the end of March 1913. After a year's operation, on July 1, 1913, the school boasted 17 aircraft, all Bristol monoplanes and biplanes, with eight flight instructors and 67 enrolled students. It is estimated that 700–800 pilots were trained there during the war, including Oswald Boelcke—Halberstadt's most famous student.

The Deutsche Bristol plant also made progress, with almost 100 workers employed and 42 aircraft completed by November 1913. Bristol monoplane or biplane parts were delivered or replicated under license, with 29 Bristol aircraft allegedly built in total. In the summer of 1913, the company began building *Taubes*, with 20 finished by the end of the year. The engineer Hans Burkhard, who had arrived at Halberstadt from the Rumpler aircraft works in 1912, having been caught up in the "*Taube* fever" mentioned earlier, designed several biplanes for Deutsche Bristol Werke before moving across to the Gotha factory in October 1914. He was succeeded by Karl Theis. Before his departure, Burkhard finished several lightweight two-seater biplanes which came to be known as the B series—the plane that laid the groundwork for the subsequent fighters.

Karl Theiss, born on July 27, 1887, attended the Munich University of Technology from 1907 to 1911, where he studied mechanical and electrical engineering; by 1910 he was already attending lectures on aerodynamics, aircraft engines, and propellers. During his studies at Munich, he built an experimental biplane with a 50-hp Argus motor. From October 1, 1911 to May 16, 1913 he worked as a designer at the

The Bristol *Coanda* was a refinement of the earlier *Prieur*; it featured a tandom pair of cockpits for instructor and student, and, instead of skis, had two very small "training wheels" up forward. It retained the full flying rudder but had a warping elevator and fixed stabilizer arrangement, the former being too sensitive for students. (Public domain)

Oswalde Boelcke was a student at the Halberstadt Military Flying School, who perhaps developed an affection for the company at this time and most likely kept in touch. Boelcke may have been the source for Halberstadt's shift to biplane development that led to the successful D.II. (Public domain)

Albatros aircraft works in Johannisthal. There he worked on their *Taubes,* led the construction of the Bregeut Albatros apparatus and designed the three-stemmed Albatros biplane with collapsible wings. In May 1913, he moved to Halberstadt as a designer.

With the outbreak of the war, the company changed its name, in September 1914, to Halberstadter Flugzeugwerke GmbH to sever ties with Britain and Bristol. In addition to a few remaining Bristol types and *Taubes,* the company concentrated on the B series biplanes which were used primarily for their flying school. The B types borrowed from a variety of sources: their box-girder fuselage was common with both Allied and German manufacturers, and the tail was of the full-flying type popularized by Morane-Saulnier, Fokker, and Pfalz. Halberstadt B.II trainers powered by 100-hp Mercedes engines were employed in small numbers as basic trainers at the Halberstadt flying school and in the German air service.

During 1915 the new firm built a speedy biplane scout, with a Morane-Saulnier-type body and Oberursel motor, and being, in fact, similar to the Fokker biplane of the same year. The first German biplane to achieve combat service was built by Halberstadt. 1915 was also the year the Fokker Eindecker appeared at the Western Front, giving Germany the edge due to its synchronizing gear, which was in turn shared with all German aircraft companies, including Halberstadt. Modification of the B.II to take a forward firing synchronized machine gun was not a stretch, and although precise details are unavailable, it is known that the Halberstadt D.I flew in the fall of 1915.

By late spring of 1916, the Fokker Eindecker was being eclipsed by the Nieuport 11s and Airco DH.2s of the French Air Force and Royal Flying Corps (RFC) respectively. Boelcke was disparaging of the Fokker E.IV as he felt it was hardly an improvement over the E.III. He was not alone in his recommendation for a "light biplane fighter" similar to the Nieuport 11, that was too swift for the E.IV to catch, as the ideal fighter weapon. When the E.III was at its zenith, it inhibited innovation into biplane design (something the French and British did with tight-lipped efficiency), as it was thought that sheer numerical superiority would achieve air superiority. Grosz pondered why Halberstadt had ventured into biplane design and production when the monoplane ruled

The Halberstadt *Taube.* Note the similar undercarriage system to that of the *Coanda.*

The D.I featured a forward-facing, car-type radiator which foreshadowed later trends in placement of this component. However, it was discontinued in the D.II in favor of the Teves and Braun in wing radiator which afforded better forward visibility. (Greg VanWyngarden)

the roost—especially when much larger firms were not doing it. Wilhelm Siegert and Oswalde Boelcke may have been pivotal figures in effecting change, especially since Boelcke had learned to fly at Halberstadt, and now made his wishes known.

Oberstleutnant Wilhelm Siegert of IdFlieg made the following observation:

> The start of the Somme battle unfortunately coincided with the low point in the technical development of our aircraft. The unquestioned air supremacy we had enjoyed early in 1916 by virtue of our Fokker monoplane fighters had shifted over to the enemy's Nieuport, Vickers, and Sopwith aircraft in March and April.

Rudolf Berthold had commented that "we had too few qualified monoplanes; we lacked an aircraft that was easily maneuverable in combat. We had fallen asleep on the laurel wreaths that the single-seaters in the hands of a few superlative pilots had achieved. It was not the monoplane itself, but the pilots who were responsible for the success. One need but compare the number of Fokker fighters at the front with those few pilots who had victories. I had already requested a new type of aircraft in January 1916—a small biplane. People laughed!"

The Halberstadt D series put the company on the map. The D.I prototype (w/n 155) was powered by a 100-hp Mercedes D.II engine, and underwent static load tests at Adlershof on February 26, 1916. The second prototype (termed D.III) with a 120-hp Argus engine appeared in the February 1916 frontline inventory. It was the first German biplane fighter assigned to the front. On March 8, 1916 (ten days after 155 passed the load tests) Halberstadt received an order for 12 D.I fighters (100–111) powered by the Argus 120-hp engine.

It is useful to briefly describe the Halberstadt D series relative to the Eindecker that was apparently so successful: it had the pinched (as viewed in profile) tail area that was characteristic of the Eindeckers and Moranes. It also had the full-flying stabilator arrangement; in plan form identical to the E.III's. It had a similar tail skid arrangement as the E.III's and a similar full-flying rudder, although it featured a sturdy inverted V-strut structure. Instead of the problematic rotary and resultant gyroscopic effect, it had an inline engine, the direction of future design trends. Its exhaust stack vented over the top wing, thus nominally sparing the pilot from breathing exhaust more so than if it were placed off to one side. It also had a frontally mounted radiator that would become standard with the D.VII, the Pfalz D.XII, and others. It had a braced biplane cellule structure with moveable ailerons instead of the flimsy and sluggish wing-warping of the monoplanes and early Fokker D series. It used box-girder construction but the longerons were hollow, thus saving weight while not sacrificing strength. It was covered with a mixture of materials: linen aft of the cockpit, and ply forward, just like the Nieuports, with a small sheet metal cowling over the engine and front. It featured the same streamlined steel

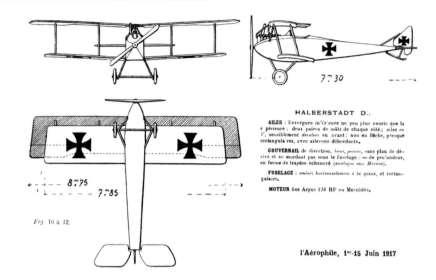

HALBERSTADT D..

AILES : Envergure in'er'eure un peu plus courte que la
« périeure ; deux paires de mâts de chaque côté ; ailes en
I', sensiblement décalées en avant : non en flèche, preeque
rectangula'res, avec ailerons débordants.

GOUVERNAIL de direction, haut, pointu, sans plan de dé-
rive et ne mordant pas sous le fuselage ; — de pro'ondeur,
en forme de trapèze échancré (analogue aus Morane).

FUSELAGE : aminci horizontalement à la queue, et rectangulaire.

MOTEUR fixe Argus 120 HP ou Mercédès.

l'Aérophile, 1er-15 Juin 1917

A three-view drawing of the Halberstadt D series from *L'Aerophile*. The aircraft had much to recommend it with moderate undercamber and stagger of the wings, an easy fuselage to build from a production standpoint, and the full flying rudder and stablilator which was a carryover from the *Eindecker* monoplanes. It also featured an inline engine marking a shift from the rotaries used on the E series monoplanes of Fokker and Pfalz.

tubing for struts that the Eindeckers had. Finally, it had a modern undercarriage similar to the Nieuport 11 (and for that matter some of the *Taubes*) and a unique mechanism to actuate the ailerons, that in part would be adopted by Albatros (ailerons on upper wings were actuated by cables running to lower wing). Finally its synchronization gear was on the outside of the cowling, making it easy to fix but also easy to damage. A few early-production machines had extended aileron balances, but later models were delivered with unbalanced ailerons.. The series of inverted struts, cooling pipes leading to the in-wing radiator and massive exhaust stack contributed to poor visibility forward. On the D.II and D.III the single machine gun was mounted on the starboard side.

In terms of the production/construction of the D.II/ III a number of clues emerge from descriptions in

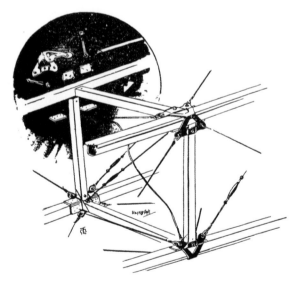

Fig. 16. — Fuselage d'Halberstadt. Assemblage par des équerres
sans percement de longerons. A gauche, en bas, vue du
côté intérieur et des taquets en place ; en haut, montants et
traverses, prêts à être assemblés par les pièces détachées
(sur fond noir) : équerre, 2 boulons, 4 taquets cloués, baguette.

An illustration from *L'Aerophile* magazine showing the production-oriented system of steel clips and cleats on the longerons to aid in alignment and assembly of the vertical and cross struts.

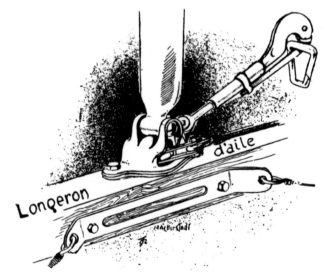

Fig. 13. — Base de mât d'Halberstadt. Tendeur à déclic (sauterelle)
Attache de haubans. Attache de croisillons intérieurs.

This illustration from *L'Aerophile* explicates the quick-release system for the landing and flying wires relative to the interplane struts. The interplanes pivoted spanwise, allowing the wings to collapse flat for transportation.

In Profile:
Halb D.II

Halberstadt D.II (Han) (810/16
Lt Eric Schutze, Jagdstaffel 25; Prilep, Macedonia; Early 1917.

RONNY
BAR
AIRCRAFT PROFILES

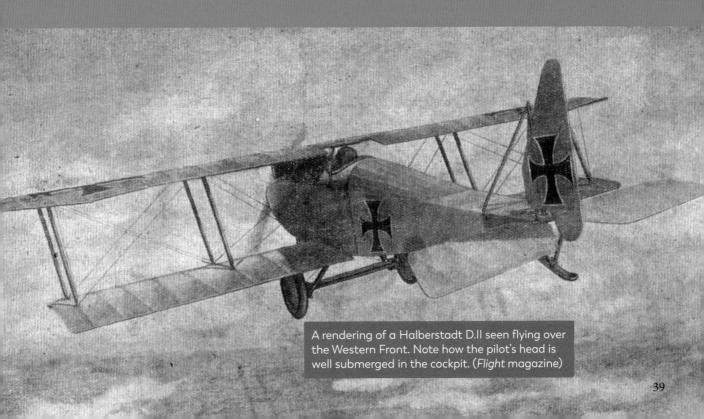

A rendering of a Halberstadt D.II seen flying over the Western Front. Note how the pilot's head is well submerged in the cockpit. (*Flight* magazine)

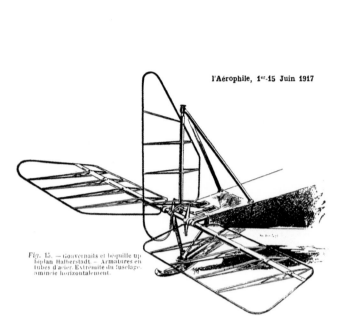

l'Aérophile, 1er-15 Juin 1917

Fig. 15. — Gouvernails et béquille du biplan Halberstadt. — Armatures en tubes d'acier. Extrémité du fuselage amincie horizontalement.

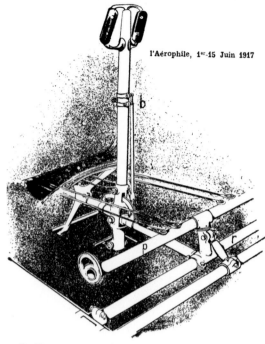

l'Aérophile, 1er-15 Juin 1917

Fig. 17. — Levier de commande de l'Halberstadt pour la profondeur et l'équilibre. — B, mécanisme de blocage de la profondeur. — P, palonnier aux pieds, pour la direction R. son tendeur pour le réglage de sa position.

Another *L'Aerophile* illustration showing the framing of the tail feathers for the D series, the full flying stabilator coopted from Fokker's E series and by extension the Morane-Saulniers. In fact, except for the unique tripod system of supporting the full-flying rudder, the entire tail area is very "Eindeckeresque."

Another nod to Fokker is the control stick of the D series, which features the characteristic double handlegrip of the Fokker E series, as well as the cam lock to mitigate stabilator sensitivity. (*L'Aerophile* magazine)

Flight magazine. Firstly, small rectangular plates were nailed to the longerons' top and interior faces to facilitate alignment of both the vertical struts and the horizontal cross pieces. This may have been done at predetermined spacings on the strip stock (longerons) before it was sprung to molds or a jig. Once the timbers fitted and were temporarily held or clamped, the sheet steel fittings were likely fitted to the intersection of longeron, strut, and cross piece. The aircraft featured a spring-loaded, metal-covered "toe step" which would spring back flush after the pilot boarded the aircraft. It also featured "quick release" pins on the attachment points for the lower planes, a feature seen repeatedly with German aircraft of this period. The wings, although of standard spar, rib web, antidrag rigging construction, featured hinged attachment points for the interplane struts such that after slackening the landing and flying wire (by means of a quick release hook, the wings folded down on themselves, moving either inboard or outboard, such that they could lay flat atop each other for ease of transportation. This too explains the necessity of two sets of interplane struts per wing, because with only one set, this would be an awkward and flimsy affair.

The ailerons featured built-in washout and were actuated in similar fashion to Albatros aircraft, and the rigging was led through pulleys that featured inspection doors. The stabilizer was very similar to both the Morane-Saulnier and by extension the Fokker Eindecker, being full-flying. Both the rudder and stabilator were made from welded steel tube. The control column was referred to as the "Fokker type," lending credence to the assertion that Fokker may have supplied these to various manufacturers. There was a cam lock on the pitch control to mitigate sensitivity of the stabilator.

Specs for the new fighter included a useful load of 331 lb, one synchronized machine gun with 500 rounds, top speed of 90 mph, and rate of climb that was 13,124 feet in 40 minutes—the D.II exceeded these specs. The order of 12 planes was small, but, like other new aircraft companies, IdFlieg was conservative with an untried

An early Halberstadt D.II that put this company on the map so to speak, as well as proving the efficacy of the biplane to IdFlieg and pilots. It had one synchronized machine gun and an excellent rate of climb. (Greg VanWyngarden)

Camouflaged D.II 818/16 with engine running in a winter landscape. The wide spacing of interplane struts allowed structural integrity when the wings were collapsed for transport. Also note the exhaust manifold is led aft of the cockpit as Spads and S.E.s would late employ on their fighters. (Greg VanWyngarden)

A forward view of the D.II showing the modest dihedral, and compactness of the fuselage. Note the pronounced droop to the trailing edges of the wings, which was a washout technique uniquely employed by Halberstadt. The landing gear is minimal and clean—an obvious nod to the Nieuport 11. (Public Domain)

A closer view of the cockpit area showing the exhaust manifold, plywood sheathed forward areas and fabric-covered aft area. The pilot is wearing a padded helmet so is obviously a trainee. Also it appears the tachometer is placed directly in the pilot's forward line of sight just below the top plane, which must have been annoying. (Greg VanWyngarden)

The Halberstadt D.IV at the Omaka Aviation Heritage Centre, New Zealand. This aircraft although not placed in production due to alleged unsatisfactory cabane arrangement, served as the inspiration for the very successful Cl. II series of two-seaters. (Image Creative Commons; Bernard Spragg)

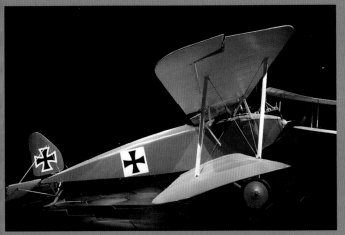

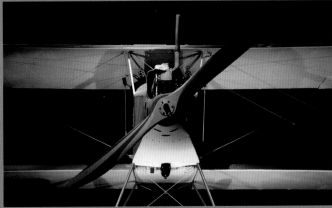

company, and even Albatross only received an order for 12 of its biplane fighters in June 1916. It seems likely that given the input of Boelcke, IdFlieg probably wanted input from other top pilots as to which fighter was better before placing a large order; it could also gauge which company could turn out a given quantity of aircraft in the shortest period of time with consistent quality. Fokker, a tried and tested supplier, received an order for 80 biplane fighters in May.

Response to the new fighter was very positive. Boelcke, writing from Douai in June, 1916, had this to say:

> One evening I flew the new Halberstadt biplane, the first appearance of this machine at the front. Because it had a slight resemblance to the British BE, I was able to completely surprise an Englander. Undetected, I got within 50 m and shot his jacket full. But since I was too fast and did not have my machine in hand like my Fokker [was not as familiar with the Halberstadt as his Fokker], I had to dive under the Englander.

Boelcke must have been impressed as the rate of climb was nearly twice that of the specs. The early success of the D.II was reflected in the following report by IdFlieg:

> The Halberstadt with the 120-hp Mercedes engine has flown with good results and is well regarded; especially praised are its ability to climb and maneuver. It is decidedly preferred to the Fokker E.IV. In addition, where the Eindeckers had to be flown continuously, the Halberstadt was much more stable. Moreover, the Halberstadt would readily spin, which could be used as an escape maneuver.

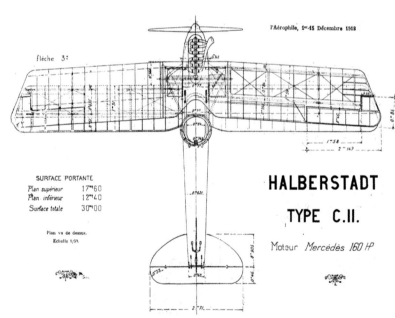

An illustration from *L'Aerophile* of the Halberstadt C.II two-seater. It featured a semi-monocoque fuselage, good streamlining with efficient cowling of the engine, and a modernized vertical fin and balanced rudder. The wings were slightly swept on the top plane which included balanced ailerons, and straight on the lower wing. It featured Nieuport-style bellcrank and pushrod activation of the ailerons, and an unbalanced elevator. (*L'Aerophile* magazine)

An image of the C.II "Martha" in the winter. Note that the characteristic Halberstadt trailing edge "droop" is still present, as well as a candy-striped paint scheme on the fuselage. (NARA)

Boelcke also noted: "However, everyone urgently requests twin machine guns but this will lead to a subsequent reduction in performance." Idlfieg ordered 24 Halberstadt D.IIs and 80 Fokker biplanes in May 1916, and 266 D-type fighters (from various companies) in July—a number that would steadily escalate throughout the remainder of the war. However, the transition from the Eindeckers to the new Halberstadt biplanes took time; by the end of August the conversion from one to the other had begun.

In an effort to keep pace with the orders, Halberstadt licensed construction of the D.II to Aviatik—the Halberstadt D.II (Av)—which began arriving at the front in early November 1916. The D.IV was an elegant aircraft, well streamlined and fitted with single bay wing cellule to reduce drag. It was armed with twin machine guns and powered by the 150-hp Benz Bz.III engine. In October 1916 IdFlieg rejected this design ostensibly over the cabane arrangement. Although this design was never produced, it morphed into the Halberstadt CI.II two-seater which was wildly successful. Jagdstaffeln (Fighter Squadrons, or "Jastas") 21, 22, and 30 had Halberstadt fighters until late spring 1917 when they were replaced by the more powerful Albatros D.III. Most units had a mixture of planes; for example, on October 16, 1916, Berthold wrote that Jasta 14 had three Fokker Eindeckers, seven Fokker biplanes, and one Halberstadt.

In the latter half of 1916, increasing numbers of D-type fighters were supplied to the 2nd and 6th Armies (Somme) and the 5th Army (Verdun). The new Fokker, Albatros, and Halberstadt D-types were encountered with growing frequency by Allied pilots; however, by the fall of 1916 the Nieuport 17 and Spad VII were at the forefront, pressuring Germany to once again modify the equation for success.

A Halberstadt D. II either about to take off or having just landed. Note the streaked camouflage scheme as popularized by the Fokker Dr.1 and the "drooped" trailing edge of lower wing. (Greg VanWyngarden)

A D.II being scrutinized by various military officials—some German and some appear to be Turkish.

43

By the end of December 1916 German squadrons began exchanging their Halberstadts for Albatros D.IIs. On the Western Front Halberstadt fighters were gradually phased out by the summer of 1917 but were retained in rear areas as advanced trainers.

The Halberstadt fighter had earned its place in history; it was the pivotal aircraft upon which favorable opinion of the biplane resulted. Germany would not revisit the monoplane until very late in the war and largely by Junkers and Fokker only.

When German aircraft production was prohibited according to the Treaty of Versailles in 1919, the company, renamed Berlin-Halberstädter Industriewerke AG, resorted to the production of agricultural machinery and the repair of Reichsbahn railroad cars. Insolvency proceedings were opened in 1926. The Halberstadt factory premises were later utilized by Junkers in 1935.

A captured Halberstadt D.II as evidenced by the cockades on the underside of the lower wings and faintly visible are those on the top of the upper wings. This aircraft appears to be covered in doped linen. (NARA)

In this image of a D.II the box cellule structure of the wing is clearly visible; once the rigging wires were disconnected and wings detached from the fuselage, the wings could collapse on themselves by means of hinged interplane attachment points.

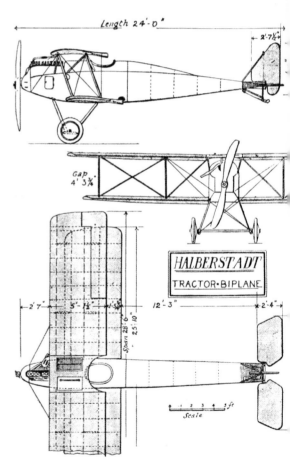

A drawing from *Flight* magazine of a Halberstadt D.II.

This image shows a lineup of Fokker D. VIIs and potentially SE5as further down the line seen after the war. (NARA)

4

Fokker Flugzeugwerke

Anthony Fokker was born April 6, 1890, the son of a Dutch coffee planter who had retired in Haarlem to oversee Anthony's education—the completion of which was a trip to Germany in 1910 to study engineering. Tony had shown an interest in all things mechanical from an early age. He had enrolled in an auto engineering school when he noticed the institution also offered courses in aviation. Although his academic accomplishments were not noteworthy, he did conceive of the foundations that along with Jacob Goedecker and Franz von Daum would develop the *Spin* (Dutch for Spider). In 1909 Goedecker had founded Flying Machine Company J. Goedecker in Mainz-Goosenheim, and was a competent aircraft designer. Fokker learned much from him. He also taught himself to fly at this time. On May 16, 1911 he passed the Federation Aeronautique Internationale test, receiving aviator's certificate number 88, awarded in Germany.

Johannisthal Berlin was home to more than 20 German aircraft builders. Fokker, Frits Cremer, and Bernard de Waal initially planned to set up shop in Johannisthal and offer flight instruction which made good business sense: it meant that Fokker airplanes would more likely find customers, as freshly licensed pilots usually ordered the type of plane they had learned on. A number of companies had their base at Johannisthal, such that two Berlin investors, Erich Schmidt-Choné and Adolph Borchard, (and not Anthony Fokker) signed the founding documents of Fokker Aviatik GmbH (Fokker Aviation Ltd.) on February 6, 1912, with Borchard listed as Director.

Following the popular business model of training pilots instead of construction (initially), as advocated by government, Fokker's school had become one of the most attractive flying schools in Germany, featuring high success ratios. Fokker by this time had become a skilled aviator. By the end of 1912, Fokker Aeroplanbau GmbH was formed at Johannisthal near Berlin.

A young Anthony Fokker in the cockpit of his *Spin* (Spider). Note the very exposed cockpit, maze of rigging and control cables, and the gravity-feed suspended fuel tank. (NARA)

45

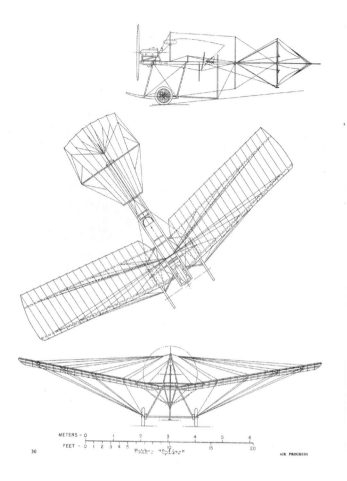

METERS - 0   1   2   3   4   5   6
FEET - 0 1 2 3 4 5   10   15   20
Fokker "Spider"
AIR PROGRESS

A line drawing of the Fokker *Spin*—it was aptly named as the fuselage is a skeletal framework with very little depth to it, and spars extend upward to accept the tail rigging. It featured wing-warping and elevator-warping, and a hinged rudder, as well as an Argus four-cylinder inline engine mounted on brackets.

The Chamber of Commerce listed Fokker's new company as being registered at Johannisthal's shed number 10 at the Alte Startplatz (old start-up grounds)—one of 16 companies located there. "Fokker Aeroplanbau" (Fokker Airplane Construction) was painted on shed 10 to differentiate Fokker from his competitor Aviatik, who was already there. Initially, Fokker assembled planes ordered from Goedecker in Mainz, which arrived in pieces packed in crates. This is most likely how Fokker began to think of aircraft as a product that could be taken apart, and shipped as compactly as possible. Between 10 and 15 planes were built this way.

During the summer of 1912, feeling his company growing, he moved to a larger building (#6) at Neue Startplatz (new start-up grounds). The new building measured 45 square feet, had double doors, could accomodate four to five planes, and was inexpensive. In 1913 his business expanded further as demand increased for flight training. Fokker hired three more sheds to park planes overnight. A few Fokker *Spiders* were ordered by the German government, as Fokker began his long tradition of lobbying key officials, even teaching some of them to fly.

Many aircraft companies were founded in Berlin due to encouragement by the Nationale Flugspende (National Air Subscription), in addition to being close to heart of the politics of the nation, which could mean favorable government contracts. The German army, headquartered in Berlin, was the target client. In 1911 it bought 28 new aircraft, which increased to 461 in 1913. The two main types the army was interested in were the *Taube* monoplanes, and more agile biplanes—production of each was more or less equal in 1912. The army awarded contracts to ten different producers, including Fokker's immediate competitors at Johannisthal: Rumpler, Albatros, and LVG (Luftverkehrsgesellschaft). These firms built about 500 machines between them, mostly for pilot training. Johannisthal was becoming crowded with aircraft companies all vying for the same government contracts. Fokker was seen more of a flier or possible instructor than a builder at this point, such that he was awarded a government contract to train military pilots. Favorable conditions at Schwerin, the need for space to learn his craft, a government contract in hand, and the desire to make a clean break with Goedecker, all coalesced to convince Fokker to move his company to Schwerin, Mecklenburg, in June 1913.

Schwerin, the sleepy capital of the state of Mecklenburg, surrounded by lakes and marshes, was not an industrial hub like other cities. It was dominated by the imposing palace of the Grand Duke, situated on a small island at the water's edge. Otherwise, the main products from Schwerin were bricks, furniture, and pianos,

In Profile:
Fok E.III

Fokker E.III (246/16)
Lt Max Immelman, Kampeinsitzer Kommando
Douai; Douai, France; June 1916.

In Profile:
Fok Dr.1

Fokker Dr.1 (138/17)
Vzfw. Josef Mai, Jagdstaffel 5;
Cappy, France; May 1918.

In Profile:
Fok D.VII

Fokker D.VII (Alb) (638/18)
Jagdstaffel 53; Vivaise, France; August 1918.

The Grand Duke's palace in Schwerin, the capital of Mecklenburg, Germany, where all of Fokker's best aircraft were conceived and produced. (Public domain)

produced in small quantities by craft guild artisans. Schwerin was a perfect setting for Fokker, away from prying eyes of other aircraft manufacturers in Berlin, and which also gave him space and privacy to experiment. The flat landscape around Lake Schwerin was ideal for an airfield. Moreover, the Schwerin Airfield Society came up with a generous offer to rent the entire facility— Görries airfield—to Fokker for a modest fee.

Schwerin was a small town and as such had a more close-knit personal feel. People walked instead of using trams; they knew each other by first name, and local politics were simpler and more accessible; this was all good news for the young Dutch ex-patriot. Fokker also loved the water and boats, so it was not surprising that his first aircraft was a floatplane; his factory was right on the edge of Lake Schwerin which made testing convenient.

Pilot training at Görries airfield remained Fokker's main income, employing 25 mainly young, enthusiastic people by April 1913. The school was teaching eight officers and three private customers at this time. He supplemented this income with demonstration flying, leaving the training to his friends Frits Cremer and Bernard de Waal when he was away.

The German army showed renewed interest in the idea of a plane that was easy to disassemble and move by road or rail. Designs by Albatros, LVG, and Fokker were evaluated. To the great surprise of the aviation community, it was Fokker who landed the sales order on June 11, 1913. His design was found to be more robust and easier to move by motor vehicle than his competitors'. He was contracted to deliver four M.2 reconnaissance aircraft (military version of the *Spin*) before August 15, with the accompanying vehicles to be built by Daimler.

The Fokker M.2, the military version of the *Spider*, featured a fully streamlined fuselage in contrast to the earlier skeletal version, and could be disassembled efficiently per the German army mandate. (Fokker Team Schorndorf)

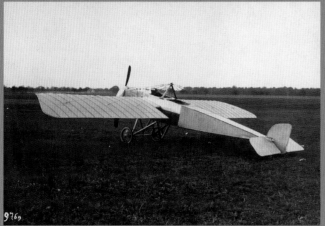

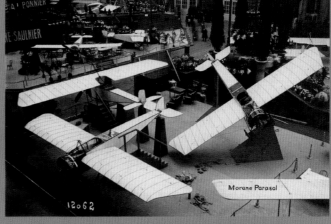

The Morane-Saulnier type H was a revolutionary French aircraft that featured wing-warping, a simple box-girder wooden fuselage braced with wire, a full flying stabilator and rudder, and a 50-hp rotary engine; it was the inspiration for Fokker's Eindecker series.

The Morane-Saulnier type L was a "parasol" aircraft, and was not as popular in Germany as the H. The type L had excellent downward visibility for the pilot. Pictured is an exposition in Paris and display of Morane-Saulnier aircraft—both the H and L are shown. (Greg VanWyngarden)

The airplane had a 75-kW (100-hp) Argus or Mercedes engine and was capable of 97 kph (60 mph). The M.3 and M.4 were next up, but neither of these was successful due to their instability and difficulty to control. Fokker's chief constructor at the time, Carl Palm, was replaced by his assistant Martin Kreutzer at the conclusion of 1913. Fokker's flying school at Görries aerodrome near Schwerin was ultimately where his main factory would evolve—with the war and his ideas—to become Fokker Flugzeugwerke GmgH.

In July Fokker made a close inspection of a Morane-Saulnier type H flown by Leon Letort—a rival for the affections of a girl with whom he was infatuated. With its 50 hp, air-cooled rotary engine, the Morane was the latest in aeronautical technology, far surpassing anything Germany had; this would be the spark that would lead to the Fokker M.5. Instead of seeing Fokker as perhaps the shrewd, opportunistic, and inventive young man that he was, author Marc Dierikx wrote that "In the early days of aviation, copyists were just as important as people with original ideas." This is somewhat of a revisionist perspective, but it contains some truth: variations of the Morane appeared as aircraft types with four different German manufacturers, and if they had not learned by copying, the next steps in innovation might never have been taken.

Fokker knew that he needed a Morane at Schwerin to study further. He struck a deal with Alexander von Bismarck to buy a Morane type H in France, whereupon Fokker and Hans Haller would travel to Paris to pick up what turned out to be a damaged Morane for only 500 marks. By the end of 1913 many Germany aircraft manufacturers began producing single-seat monoplanes similar to the Morane-Saulnier type H.

Fokker rebuilt and repaired the type H and in so doing, learned enough about the plane to develop his own iteration, importantly with an eye toward series production; something about which he and other manufacturers had been hearing with increasing frequency from German authorities. In January 1914, Anthony and his design team scrutinized the Morane in their hangar at Görries. Gradually a new version of the design took shape: the fuselage was stretched by about three feet and constructed from welded steel tube that would be easy to mass-produce and become a Fokker hallmark moving forward. Fokker also lengthened the wings.

By May 11 Fokker sold the M.5 to Bismarck for 8,452 marks and 95 pfennig ($1,998.34). He also built one to serve as a model to take future orders against, which resulted in several orders from private parties with a few for military evaluation as well. The M.5 represented a toe-hold for the small Fokker company,

Anthony Fokker in flying gear posing by the nose of the Fokker M.5 monoplane. The M.5 was an instant success due to its excellent and proven roots (the MS H). It featured a breakthrough for Fokker however, as it had a welded steel framed fuselage as opposed to the wooden braced one of the Morane. (Fokker Team Schorndorf)

A closeup of the M.5 doing a flyby. (Fokker Team Schorndorf)

An M.5 after making a steep dive, zooms skyward and about to kick the rudder and do a stall-turn or hammerhead. A *Spider* sits in foreground of this image, with the Fokker hangar in the background. (Fokker Team Schorndorf)

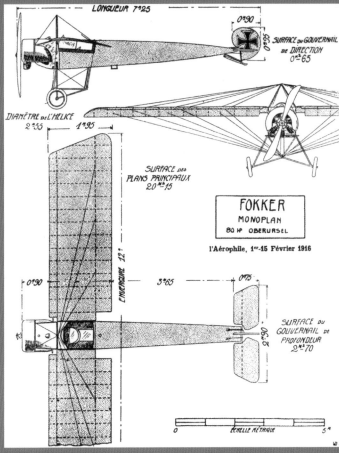

A three-view drawing of the Fokker M.5 from *L'Aerophile*. The M.5 was very maneuverable to the point of being unstable, and was easy to mass-produce.

as well as the birth of a fighter that was maneuverable (to the point of being unstable) and relatively easy to mass-produce. By May 14, 1914, the company had officially moved to Schwerin. The sheds at Johannisthal were gradually emptied and transferred to the Zentrale für Aviatik. Fokker Aeroplanbau GmbH (Fokker Aircraft Construction Ltd.) was registered with the Schwerin Chamber of Commerce number 1069 on July 7, 1914. On the eve of the Great War, the young Dutch upstart had a viable company, a lucrative flying school with 24 aircraft, a cutting-edge design (M.5), and 55 employees. Three weeks later Europe was consumed by its first world war.

Outbreak

The German high command and aircraft industry did not envisage the course or nature of the war in August 1914. From vague, unsure, and nascent views on aircraft as an extension of artillery (spotting) to a mechanized weapon in its own right, the industry was influenced by the views of those doing the fighting. From a production standpoint, most factories were used to an artisanal, hand-crafted approach to aircraft, producing them one at a time, with most factories set up to produce around two dozen planes a year—if that. Making the transition to series production proved difficult for all factories (some more than others) as there was no extant model to follow. Fokker's 56 employees worked to not only build the first of a series of 40 M.8/A.1 reconnaissance aircraft in October, but to do it in a systematic way; in spite of their efforts, at most 23 M.8 aircraft were completed by the end of 1914.

Other, larger manufacturers, such as Rumpler, were also underperforming on production goals. As a result, a series of meetings occurred between representatives of the army, the aircraft industry, and the government. The uneasy outcome was to attempt to raise nationwide production to 200 aircraft per month. Factories needed to implement initiatives to prove they were attempting to increase productivity and production; at Fokker a time clock was introduced to improve worker punctuality. German engine manufacturers could not produce more than 170 engines per month, such that in 1914 and 1915 several dozen Fokker aircraft stood idle at Görries awaiting engines.

The Fokker M.8 shown as the engine is tested. Note the mechanic holding the tail down. It is painted with German military insignia, and is presumably undergoing testing. Twenty-three M.8s were completed by the end of 1914.

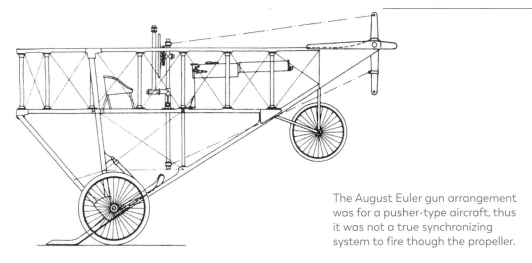

The August Euler gun arrangement was for a pusher-type aircraft, thus it was not a true synchronizing system to fire though the propeller.

Fokker's initial factory buildings were also ill-suited for series production. Fokker bought and erected several standardized wooden prison barracks to serve as factory sheds. These were inexpensive and of a temporary nature, feeding the notion shared by everyone that the war would not last long.

As the war entered its second year, aircraft designers and manufacturers turned their attention to the development of a "point and shoot-type" pursuit tractor aircraft with a forward-firing gun. The problem had always been how to fire forward and not hit the propeller.

In May 1912 August Euler registered a patent—D.R.P. 248,601, dated July 23, 1910—but this was just a proposal to mount a fixed, forward-firing gun on a pusher aircraft; this was not a synchronizing system. "Euler's idea was briefly exhibited at the 1912 DELA Show in Berlin but, at the request of the Germany military authorities, the gun was removed after only a few hours. Apart from the Euler patent, a second patent was later issued that specifically dealt with the issue of synchronization: Franz Schneider, chief designer for LVG, had designed an engine-driven cam mechanism that allowed the machine gun to fire between the rotating

blades of the propeller—giving rise to the term "interrupter gear." Schneider was granted a patent (D.R.P. 276,396) for his design in July 1913, and a description of his apparatus was published in *Flugsport* magazine at the end of September 1913. A. R. Weyl believed that this article was used by Saulnier to spur his experiments in June 1914 with an interrupter gear but these failed due to the rate of fire of the Hotchkiss gun he was using which was incompatible with the revolutions of the propeller at variable speeds.

A simple sketch of the Schneider-patented interrupter gear that was published in *Flugsport* in July 1913. In Figure 2 the cam system is drawn, the notch in the cam wheel represents the point at which the propeller is in line with the gun, thus the gun is "interrupted" at this moment.

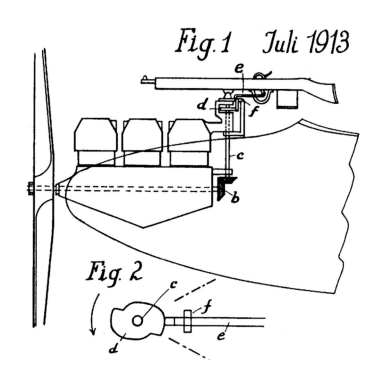

He then resorted to fitting metal plates on the aft side of the prop of an MS type L as a stop-gap solution to the problem. Roland Garros was flying this plane in the French Escadrille MS 23 when he was shot down on April 19, 1915, forcing him to land near Ingelmunster. The aircraft was taken by the Germans to Iseghem for examination.

Fokker may have known of Schneider's device due to his informants in LVG, or he may have read of it in *Flugsport.* In any event, during May Fokker and several other German aircraft constructors who were known to have experimented with fixed forward-firing synchronized arms were invited to Döberitz to review Saulnier's invention in practice. Fokker and his chief mechanic Heinrich Lubbe left Döberitz with the Saulnier armored propeller, a Parabellum machine gun and ammunition. It seems likely that Fokker had little to do with the development of the interrupter gear as developed at Schwerin—it was most likely Luebbe, Fritz Heber, and Leimberger—that was then fitted to M.5K (no. 216) and successfully demonstrated at Döberitz shortly thereafter. The Fokker synchronizing gear was a variation on the Schneider patent, and functioned by allowing the engine to control the firing of the gun once the trigger was pulled. It was immediately accepted by IdFlieg officials at Döberitz and was issued the nomenclature E.I/15. An initial order of the E.I was placed immediately, with instruction by IdFlieg to build them as quickly as possible—something every aircraft manufacturer would hear with growing intensity as the war progressed. Numerical superiority, it was thought, would provide any given (good) weapon the edge in making a decisive difference—an idea taken directly from von Clausewitz.

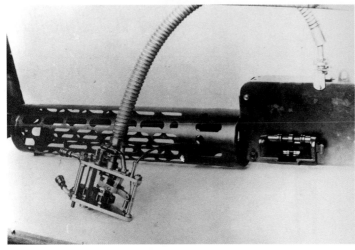

The plywood disc Fokker used to gauge where the rounds were hitting relative to the propeller. He could thus adjust his interrupter gear to fire the gun with a margin of safety for the propeller blades. The other image shows the Fokker interrupter gear attached to an LMG 08/15 machine gun. (Fokker Team Schorndorf)

The new mechanism was tested and refined in front of the Fokker factory at the edge of Lake Schwerin, utilizing a plwood disc to track the pattern of the bullets. Using this system the propeller could be oriented relative to the firing pattern. Since the military demanded trials at the front, a second M.5K (no. 258), E.II/15, and E.III/15 were all fitted with an LMG/08 machine gun and taken on a tour of frontline jastas starting May 23, 1915. Fokker concluded his tour on July 12, 1915 at which time 11 pilots were flying E.Is including Oswalde Boelcke who was flying E.III/15.

To provide the pilot with the ability of looking down on his prey, a viewing hatch was inserted into the floor of the Eindeckers which could be actuated using a lever. This was either an original Fokker invention or it was taken from some of the earlier Taubes where viewing ports were incorporated into wing root structures. As Fokker Eindeckers became more numerous, their successes grew. Despite some shortcomings in the armament installation, the Eindecker proved to be a deadly instrument in the right hands, namely von Althaus, Boelcke, Buddecke, Immelmann, Parschau, and Wintgens.

The Fokker was not at first wholly successful. In July 1915 some were sent to the flying school at Döberitz. On July 27 one crashed fatally, and a second pilot was killed four days later. After a third pilot was killed on August 29, IdFlieg disbanded the Döberitz Fokker unit, and sent the planes back to Schwerin, and grounded all planes at the front. However, such was their success that IdFlieg allowed resumption of training, but stipulated that this was to be done at Schwerin, with the first group of trainees dispatched in October 1915.

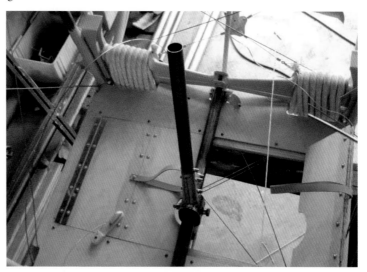

An E.I covered with what has been described as "cellulose sheeting" which was an effort to try and make the E.I invisible and to improve overall visibility for the pilot. It was a failed experiment, but is a testimony to the degree of experimentation practiced by the Fokker design team.

The viewing hatches in the cockpit floor of the Fokker Eindecker replica built by Achim Engels. With the hatches open, the pilot could gauge his distance to the ground for landings, as well as be able to sneak up on unsuspecting prey below the aircraft. (Fokker Team Schorndorf)

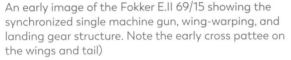

An early image of the Fokker E.II 69/15 showing the synchronized single machine gun, wing-warping, and landing gear structure. Note the early cross pattee on the wings and tail)

An E.II with wings detached and folded next to the fuselage for transport. Also note the engine has been wrapped to prevent moisture and debris from contaminating the engine, especially the valve structure. (Fokker Team Schorndorf)

Fokker E.I was covered with a "kind of cellulose sheeting" due to the desire to make the Eindeckers "invisible," and to improve visibility looking downward. While the initial batch of E.Is were being built in the shop at Schwerin, Martin Kreutzer redesigned the aircraft to accept a 100-hp Oberursel rotary, which was termed the E.II.

The Spartan cockpit of the E.II, with its distinctive Fokker stick grip, machine gun offset to starboard with attendant ammo feed and dump, canvas pouches for flares, fuel gauge offset to port. At the top of the image, the apex of the inverted rigging V-strut shows the turnbuckles used to harden the cable supports for the forward topsides of the wings (at the forward spar), as well as the double sheave that was used to allow the wing-warping top cables to transit to port and staboard, thus contributing to the wing-warping which was actuated via the stick from below the fuselage on a separate strut structure. (Public domain)

The major differences between the Fokker E.I and E.II was the lesser wing area on the latter, reduced to around 14 square meters with the intent of increasing airspeed. However, the E.II was more difficult to fly. New wings were then fitted that had a 9.52-meter span which became the E.III.

The first E.III arrived at the front in August 1915; thus E.I through III were simultaneously in service for a time. The E.III was the most successful and as such the most numerous.

Airframes were produced far more quickly than aero engines, lending credence to the statement that many Fokkers waited for their engines, which was the case with the E.III. This also raises the question of how they were produced. Absent from the many photos of the Fokker factory at Schwerin is any evidence of a production system for rapidly building Eindeckers. If the steel tube fuselages were to be produced with repeatable results on a swift timeline, jigs would have almost certainly been employed.

A Fokker E.III replica built by Achim Engels and flown by Andrew Carter at The Vintage Aviation Society in Australia. Carter commented it was a challenging but rewarding aircraft to fly. (Fokker Team Schorndorf)

An E.III captured by the French. Note the swirling worm pattern on sheetmetal, and the modernized cross insignia. The workers at left are removing the starboard wing panel, and the worker in the foreground is removing the cable rigging in preparation for removing the port wing panel. Numerous cables lay on or around the undercarriage structure near the ground.

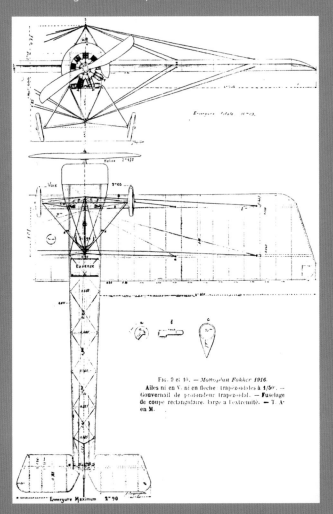

FIG. 9 et 10. — *Monoplan Fokker 1916.*
Ailes ni en V, ni en flèche trapézoïdales à 1/5°. — Gouvernail de profondeur trapézoïdal. — Fuselage de coupe rectangulaire, large à l'extrémité. — T. A. en M.

A drawing from *L'Aerophile* depicting some of the construction and rigging details of the Fokker E.III.

A closeup of the E.III's cockpit. Note the padded clock mounted on the leathered coaming, the gauge that appears to be mounted to the stick, and the flare holders mounted to the starboard side of the cockpit coaming. (Fokker Team Schorndorf)

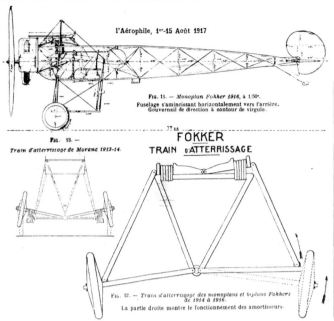

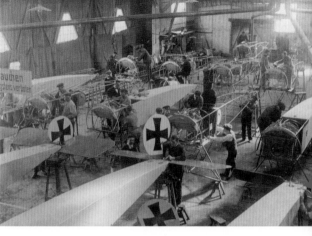

A construction drawing of the E.III from *L'Aerophile*, showing the welded steel tube fuselage, rigging, fuel tank, and, of particular interest, the landing gear shock absorbers and how they work. This was a unique Fokker design and unlike practically all other aircraft during the war, the bungees were up in the fuselage instead of down by the wheels.

Fokker Eindecker fuselages being fitted with various pieces of equipment and rigging, then covered (note fuselage at the far left); finally, stabilators and rudder are attached and rigged. Presumably they were then rolled into another shop for fitting of wings, sheetmetalwork, and engines. (Fokker Team Schorndorf)

It is unknown whether the fuselages were built as two sides (port and starboard) that were then connected with crosspieces on a jig, or if the whole structure was built on a jig from the outset. This would have likely involved a jig of durable and heat-proof material i.e. metal. Fortunately, thanks to Achim Engels, we can glimpse at least one method of building the Fokker aircraft. His approach to building the E series fuselages called for a steel jig to weld the port and starboard panels, which were then aligned on another jig to weld the cross pieces.

Alternatively, but not ideally, wooden molds could have been used between welding stations with metal clips or attachment points. Perhaps station molds were erected to which tube steel longerons were thus fitted (via retractable or adjustable metal clamps), temporarily clamped to the molds until all the struts and cross pieces could be welded into position. Intermediary jigs may have also been fitted to the planar regions for alignment of the various pieces of short steel tube stock. Of utmost importance was that the completed fuselage needed to be easily removed from the building jig.

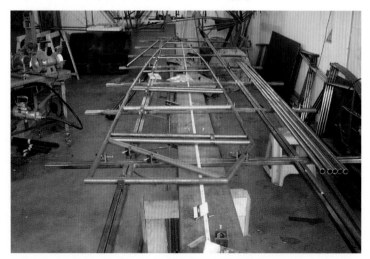

Welding jig used by Achim Engels to fabricate E.III fuselage side panels. Note the multitude of U-shaped clamps that hold the tube steel stock securely during welding. Fokker must have employed something similar to produce the E series in quantity. (Fokker Team Schorndorf)

Engels next erects the two side panels on another jig for welding the cross pieces. He uses rigging wire to plumb the sides as he works forward to aft. How Fokker did it is unknown; whether he relied on the skill of his welders to intuitively and quickly weld the fuselages and with repeatable results, or if removable molds were used—erected perpendicular to base framework/jig like that employed by Engels—is also a matter for speculation. (Fokker Team Schorndorf)

The forward section of Engels's E.III has been welded—that portion that is parallel to one another and flat on the top. The aft portion of the fuselage is still unfinished; Engels mentioned that the sides are brought together on the centerline working carefully fore to aft and welding the cross pieces working aft.

Finished E.III fuselages are hoisted out of the way in Engels's workshop which is fashioned after the actual factory building used by Fokker at Schwerin. (Fokker Team Schorndorf)

A mostly completed replica E.III fuselage outside of Engels's workshop in Schorndorf. In the closeup the fine craftsmanship and attention to detail is evident.

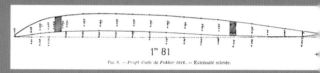

1ᵐ 81

Fig. 8. — *Profil d'aile de Fokker 1916. — Extrémité relevée.*

This airfoil drawing of the E.III indicates that the forward spar may have been solid, whereas the aft spar appears laminated from three pieces. This spar would flex quite a bit due to the wing-warping; laminating a spar together would make it stiffer and less subject to flaws existing in only one piece of wood.

This archival image of an E.III fuselage shows the complex metalwork required to accommodate the rotary engine.

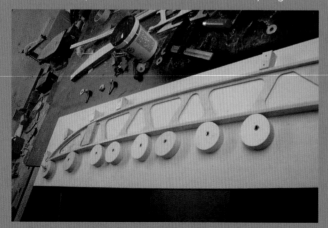

A clever method of clamping the lower cap strip to the rib web; the ovoid pieces of plywood are drilled and fastened off-center, thus allowing the precise amount of pressure required to clamp to be attained by rotating the shape until snug against the cap strip. (Fokker Team Schorndorf)

This rib is being shaped using a flush cut bearing bit on the shaper table; the bearing follows the master template and cuts the stock under to an identical profile. This is a very efficient method of producing identical rib webs and could have been practiced by Fokker. (Fokker Team Schorndorf)

The completed rib webs are slid over the spars and the leading edge is fitted into a fork formed by the intersection of the cap strips forward. The wingtips are made from laminated pieces of wood that are then hollowed out on the interior face to save weight. The spars taper down to meet the rounded tips and are wrapped with fabric to prevent chafing. (Fokker Team Schorndorf)

A completed E.III wing panel outside of Engels's shop. Note the wrapped rounded portions of the wingtips and the grey (steel) compression bars bolted to the spars. (Fokker Team Schorndorf)

This was not such a simple task as it might appear and would have required much advanced planning. Molds could have been designed for easy removal from inside the completed or at least stabilized airframe, or the whole airframe could have been maneuvered off the jig in a specific direction (e.g. upward). Once this was worked out, production could be done systematically and with repeatable and identical results.

The wings of the Eindeckers were of traditional solid/semi-solid spar and rib web construction so the time spent building and fitting this structure was most likely a straightforward affair. The rib webs would have been made in quantity from templates, then the "flanges" or cap strips of spruce would have been glued and nailed

Once the ribs were assembled they could be slid onto the spruce spars (held parallel by steel compression bars or a jig), spaced, and fastened.

A novel feature of the Eindecker's wings was the attachment points for the rigging. Specially shaped apertures allowed the rigging to be secured when taught, but also allowed it to quickly release when slacked; this allowed rapid setup and breakdown of the airframe.

Since the rudder and stabilator were also of welded steel, it seems highly likely that these too were built/welded over a steel jig. There may have been specialized radiusing jigs and tubing benders to shape the tube steel to the various curves that formed the planview of these control surfaces.

The engine area was sheathed in sheet aluminum, and had additional observation windows that were covered by sliding panels for improved downward visibility for the pilot.

The Eindecker featured a unique twin grip control stick, a component that would carry through all subsequent Fokker aircraft, and was utilized by other aircraft manufacturers as well, such as Albatros and Junkers.

This image reveals a wealth of interesting details. The keyhole steel fitting that encloses the spar is so that the rigging can be slid out and detached in one direction only: outboard. Thus the rigging is led inboard. This allows the rigging to be quickly detached from the wings for disassembly. Also note the antidrag rigging, and antitwist cloth strips that keep the ribs from twisting too much under load. (Fokker Team Schorndorf)

Two images of one of Engels's completed E.III airframes, missing only covering, wheels, engine, cowling, and dummy machine gun. It is a thing of beauty! (Fokker Team Schorndorf)

Pictured is a bending for an E.III rudder; the perimeter tube steel is curved using a tubing bender, then placed over the jig to achieve the final shape. Once securely seated in the jig, the other components can be fit to this framework. The pieces are then placed and clamped in a metal jig for welding, similar in method to how the fuselage was framed. (Fokker Team Schorndorf)

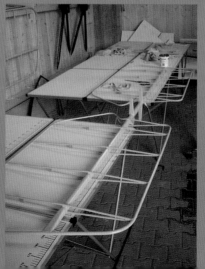

The stabilator was made in a similar fashion, with the main tube forming the foundation for this surface. The tube is pinched at either end to make it fit the diameter of the perimeter tube, and the ribs use the tube as the point of maximum depth of the surface. The stabilator is a symmetrical airfoil. The archival image shows the entire tail group attached to the fuselage. (Fokker Team Schorndorf)

The cheek panels for Engels's E.III. Note the sliding doors that allow the pilot to look diagonally downward from the cockpit under the wings. These doors were used in conjunction with the trapdoors in the floor to yield improved visibility for the pilot. (Fokker Team Schorndorf)

Alternative engines were tried in the E.III; e.g. the 80-hp Le Rhône which worked out to be superior to the unreliable Oberursel. As a result a Le Rhône-equipped E.III was a better aircraft especially with regards to rate of climb and ceiling. However, using captured Le Rhônes was not a sustainable production model. Other German engines were tried but nothing satisfactory was found. The first Fokker captured by the Allies was E.III no. 210/15 on April 8, 1916, which was tested at Upavon on May 30, 1916. The report stated that the top speed was 83 mph at 6,500 feet, with a ceiling of 11,500 feet.

Lastly, the E.IV was conceived as an attempt to achieve good performance with twin guns. The E.IV had a 160 Oberursel twin-banked engine which proved difficult to cool. The span was increased to 10 meters, with a turtle deck behind the cockpit. Max Immelmann, the first German ace, wanted more firepower and suggested three guns. He tried this on January 16, 1916, but ended up shooting away his propeller. The Eindecker's decline began as early as January 5, 1916 with the appearance of the first Nieuport 11 which was delivered to Escadrille N3. Four and a half weeks later the first DH.2s appeared.

At about this time Halberstadt began working on their D.II biplane in response to complaints about the Eindecker, as discussed. Immelmann would die on June 18, 1916, sinking the final nail into the Eindecker coffin. From here on out the biplane was preponderant until very near the end of the war.

During the summer of 1916, Professor L. Prandtl at the University of Gottingen circulated among the aviation industry his theory that thick airfoil sections possessed drag properties that were no more deficient, in comparison with the great amount of lift generated, than thin airfoil sections (lift/drag ratio). This was nothing short of an epiphany for those paying attention, and Fokker was one of them. Junkers had known this for some time.

In parallel to his successful E series, Fokker conducted clandestine experiments in emerging technologies: the most important one for German aircraft during the war was plywood. The research department of the Fokker company conducted many innovative experiments behind a securely locked door.

Villehad Forssman had convinced his employer, J. Bruening & Sohn AG, to build aircraft wings out of plywood to supply major aircraft companies. Bruening initially felt he wanted to simply supply all major aircraft companies with his high-quality plywood but Forssman persisted and finally convinced him of its efficacy. Forssman had discussed his ideas concerning the possibilities of using plywood with Fokker in Berlin at the end of March 1916—one favorable outcome for Fokker was free samples of two test wings. One was to be tested to destruction, the other for a Fokker prototype monoplane: the M.20. Forssman only requested external

By the time the Fokker E.IV appeared, the popularity of this design was already on the wane. The E.IV featured the double-banked Oberursel engine, which due to the layered cylinders (some of which blocking the airflow), tended to overheat. (Public domain)

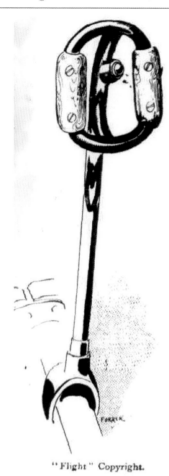

"Flight" Copyright.

This line drawing describes the control stick for the E series. Although this design would vary with subsequent Fokker aircraft, the basic idea was used throughout all his designs. It also seems likely that this component may have been produced by Fokker for other aircraft companies such as Junkers and Albatros. (*Flight* magazine)

dimensions of the M.20 wing, details of the spar root fitting to the fuselage, and airfoil sections used. He kept his internal structure proprietary, which, knowing Fokker's shrewd nature, was wise. Fokker quickly sent plans for the M.20.

By early summer 1916 Fokker was forced to turn his attention to producing biplanes due to the rise of the Halberstadt D.II and the fading popularity of his E series. These biplanes would be based on his Eindeckers but also included aspects of the successful Nieuport and Halberstadt that had captivated IdFlieg's attention. Occurring simultaneously, cantiliever wing experiments continued, with some being fitted to fuselages of the emerging D series (e.g. M.17 which had a set of Forssman/Bruening wings fitted to the basic fuselage of the D.II).

The Fokker D series

With the ascendancy of the Halberstadt D.II and its subsequent success came the reaffirmation of the biplane as the preeminent aircraft type, which was not lost on Fokker, or IdFlieg who asked all major aircraft manufacturers to submit designs similar to or better than the Halberstadt, and by extension the Nieuports. Fokker, putting his experiments with cantilevered wing monoplanes on the backburner, responded by immediately urging his design team to quickly come up with something similar—which they did. The result was the M.18 or D.I and D.II—the latter being basically an E.III turned into a biplane and rushed to the front in July–August 1916 to compete with the Halberstadt.

After the decline of the E series and the popularity of the Halberstadt D.II, Fokker responded with his D series. The D.I, pictured here, owes much to the E series—the rudder is the same except with a vertical fin, it too has a fully flying stabilator, and yes, it was a biplane with wing-warping! (Fokker Team Schorndorf)

The D.I had an inline engine, and the D.II a 100-hp rotary Oberursel U.I. Perhaps the most unusual feature of both models (verging on bizarre) was the fact that it was a biplane with wing-warping. This cannot have been easy to build, although the if two wings warped at the same time roll rate could be increased—much as double ailerons would. Still, based on Fokker's track record with his E series, 90 D.Is were ordered for Germany, and 16 (as the B.III) went to Austria-Hungary. Although 177 D.IIs were ordered for the German army, they were really not much better than the outmoded E series and definitely eclipsed by the Nieuport 11s and 17s.

The D.III was similar to the D.II except with a more powerful 14-cylinder, double-banked Oberursel U.III engine. It had a twin-bay cellule structure similar to the D.I. Boelcke found it sluggish and the engine suffered from the same problems as the E.IV: overheating and poor compression at high altitudes. In October 1916 it was found to be poorly made, the result of Fokker's ongoing problems with series production that would continue through his Dr.1 series. There were 210 D.IIIs built, and some later models abandoned the awkward wing-warping in favor of ailerons. Both the Fokker D.I-III and the Halberstadt D.II were outclassed by the Albatros D series which was becoming available in the fall of 1916.

The construction of the D series would have been much like the E series as previously described, with similar fuselages and wing structures so further explanation of these types of structures is needless.

The Fokker D.II featured a rotary Oberursel U.I 100 hp, with the rest of the aircraft being similar to the D.I except the engine area was reworked to accommodate a rotary; the vertical fin was deleted, leaving just the comma-shaped rudder which would endure through the Dr.1.

Fok. D II 2387/16

The cockpit area of the D.II. Note the four sheaves at the aft edge of the upper wing cutout; these served the same function as the double sheave at the top of the inverted V structure with the E series; they assisted with the wing-warping of the lower wing. The upper wing "echoed" the warping of the lower wing by virtue of the interplane struts. The upper wing was situated at around an average pilot's eye level, so that even if the line of sight forward over the turtle deck was limited, the pilot could simply look over the top wing. (Fokker Team Schorndorf)

IdFlieg had wanted an armored ground support aircraft since the Verdun and the Somme offensives and solicited bids from Junkers, AEG, and others in November 1916. Junkers won the competition but IdFlieg felt it needed someone with proven production skills. So began the infamous partnering of Junkers and Fokker in December as mandated by IdFlieg. On December 18, 1916, a few days after negotiations between Fokker and Junkers began, Fokker asked the Junkers engineers to explain nearly everything there was to know about the construction of the J 1 and J 2. After consulting with his staff at the Hotel Bristol, Fokker quietly decided to use this information for further development of the wooden cantilever wing that he and Forssman had been working on, instead of building aircraft, although he continued with negotiations.

A rare flight shot of the Fokker D.II. The severe oil-staining of the underside of the fuselage is readily apparent, as is the "laced" seam running the length of the after underside of the fuselage which joined the fabric envelope covering the fuselage aft of the cockpit.

On December 22, Junkers filed patent applications for his cantilever technology, and the the fuse was lit. Early in 1917 Fokker and Franz Moser had developed their own cantilever wing, made out of wood. Both types were lightweight and strong. This was a secret endeavor that was informed by the discoveries of Junkers, which will be discussed in detail in the next chapter.

The Fokker D.III was basically the same as the D.II except for the 14-cylinder, double-banked rotary that was also used (unsuccessfully) on the E.IV. Pictured is Oswalde Boelcke's aircraft; he found the D.III sluggish. (Public domain)

On the production side of Fokker's business he received some good news: in July 1917, he received notice from the commander of the German Air Corps to deliver synchronizers for all German fighter aircraft, plus several thousand extra for the Austro-Hungarian Air Corps. This was a major financial and production coup, as it would provide extra security for the company as well as establish Fokker as a leading manufacturer. However, the downside was that once Schneider found out about Fokker's success with his synchronizer, he (through LVG, his employer) filed suit against Fokker for breach of patent. This legal battle would last until 1933 as Fokker's strategy was to hire top lawyers to keep the issue tied up in the courts interminably.

Once German aircraft were armed with Fokker's synchronizer and were actively engaged in combat, this technology had to be kept secret for as long as possible. Hence German pilots received specific instructions not to cross Allied lines in their Fokker aircraft, for fear of this technology falling into enemy hands.

Fokker Dr.1

The genesis of the Fokker Dr.1 was a complex and multifaceted story that overlapped the evolution of the E and D series. A variety of influences contributed to the final design of what would become the Dr.1, including input from Fokker, Moser, Platz, Forssman, Bruening, the Fokker team of engineers, and Junkers. The inception of the Dr.1 dates to the cantilever experiments conducted by Fokker, Forssman, and Bruening in 1915.

These experiments were successful and yielded the cantilevered monoplanes—these were all related to Junkers technology (when Junkers found out he was furious, and filed a lawsuit that would drag on until 1940). After Fokker realized that thick wings were practical—and knowing that bigger box spars could be used—he increased the height and width of his box spars: more height made wings stiffer longitudinally, and more width made antidrag rigging obsolete, or so he thought. The Forssman system of construction was adopted and modified by Fokker, with the important and weight-saving substitution of fabric instead of plywood for covering. The basic concept was used on all his subsequent World War I aircraft.

The "V" designation stood for "Verspannungslos" meaning without external bracing or, more simply—cantilevered. Fokker instructed Reinhold Platz, and likely the Fokker team of designers and engineers to build a prototype (fuselage) using the cantilevered wings, the result being the V.1 which was just barely a biplane with a large cantilevered top plane

The Fokker V.1 was represented a quantum leap in aircraft design, and definitely design and construction shift at Fokker; it featured cantilevered wings that would endure in one form or another throughout Fokker's career, as would the airfoil spreader used on the landing gear. (Public domain)

The framework of the V.1 tells a very interesting story: the fuselage is made up of steel formers and longitudinal stringers which must have been very labor-intensive. The wings have double spars of full depth (relative to the rib webs); it is easy to see the roots of the D.VII wings here. It appears as though the bottom of the wings are partially sheathed with plywood.

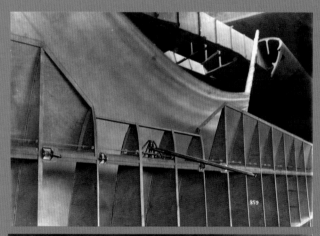

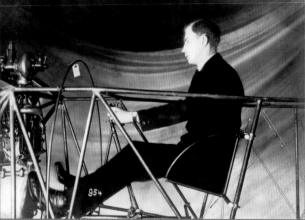

Another closer view of the framing of the V.1 wings. The mechanism on the aft side of the cutaway could be the adjustable incidence device, or it is a component of the aileron actuation system, the cables for which are seen running along the after side of the aft spar. The wingtip of the V.1 wing is seen with the very thin ply sheathing removed to show the convergence of the wing spars and the laminated and rounded wingtip structure.

The identity of the man pictured in the seat of the skeletal V.1 is unknown, but he is in a suit and not workclothes so he could be one of Fokker's design team or senior engineers. He is testing the elevators of the V.1. (Fokker Team Schorndorf)

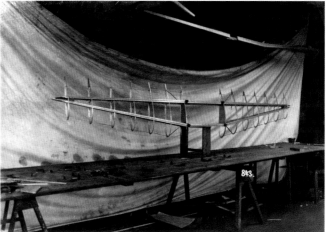

The spars for the V.1 wings undergoing load tests. Although crude and not representative of compound forces of the wing in flight, the sandbags and strapping was a simple way to gauge static strength of wooden component. The other image shows an all-metal, lower wing prototype presumably for the V.1. (Fokker Team Schorndorf)

that was hinged such that it had a variable angle of incidence, and stub—almost vestigial—bottom wings of fixed incidence. It featured a rotary engine, and the wings were sheathed in plywood and the fuselage was completely streamlined—similar to a Morane-Saulnier parasol monoplane, which should not be discounted as a major influence.

Fokker and ostensibly Forssman experimented with several different wing types for the V.1 incuding one made out of ply sheer webs and metal. In the end, the Le Rhône 110-hp engine was underpowered for IdFlieg standards, and poor visibility on landing made it unsuitable for military use; although with the V.1 we see the first use of what would become the characteristic Fokker airfoil spreader between landing gear struts. The V.1 weighed a total of 563 kg, had a top speed of 180 kph., and it could climb to 1,000 meters in 2.5 minutes—this was significant as the Albatross D.III and D.V could only climb to 3600 meters in 30 minutes.

The V.2 was the next iteration and it featured a more powerful 160-hp inline engine, thick cantilever wings, and a similarly streamlined fuselage. It had wingtips that pivoted (full flying) instead of ailerons, and the rudder and stabilizer had a similar design. The lower wing was of pronounced stagger and was also cantileverd. Imrie wrote that according to film footage taken at the time, Fokker was producing the wings for the V.2 on site, not subcontracting them out to Forssman who worked for J. Bruening & Sohn. However, in aggregate, the performance of the V.2 was inferior to the original V.1.

The Sopwith Triplane made its incandescent debut over the Western Front in February 1917—Germany scrambled to develop an equal. In April 1917, Anthony Fokker examined a damaged Sopwith Triplane while visiting Richthofen at Jasta 11 before it was taken to Adlershof for examination. He also observed the Sopwith Triplane in flight near the front. Richthofen commented that the triplane was the best plane the allies had due to its superior rate of climb, maneuverability, its ability to hold

The V.2 employed the basic airframe of the V.1 except with an inline engine. The V.2's performance could not match that of the V.1. The hallmark tripod-forward cabane strut has emerged on the V.2—something that would continue on the D.VI, D.VII, and D.VIII. Note the extreme thickness of the airfoils, and the pivoting rudder and elevator sections. (Fokker Team Schorndorf)

The V.3 followed the V.2, and it featured an Albatros-style tail assembly, an almost vestigial lower wing, and strange radiator assembly in the leading edge of the upper wing; the pivoting wingtips serving as ailerons were also continued. The variable-incidence top wing was discontinued in the V.3. (Fokker Team Schorndorf)

altitude in a bank, speed, and its ability to dive straight down. The Red Baron and others in Jasta 11 wistfully acknowledged that the Sopwith Triplane was better than their Albatros D.III. Fokker most likely knew what IdFlieg would be demanding next.

Back at Schwerin, Fokker told his design team and Reinhold Platz to build a "Dreidecker" (three wings) fighter, powered by a rotary engine, giving him only nominal details about what he had seen at Jasta 11. Fokker insisted on the rotary due to shortages of inline engines, and his controlling share in Oberursel engines, which could be produced with no limitations. Platz found the idea of a *dreidecker* abhorrent; preferring instead to continue working on high-winged monoplanes—a natural outgrowth of the V.1 and V.2 aircraft he and the Fokker team had been working on. The V.3 followed which included an Albatros-type tail, and the variable incidence of the upper wing was eliminated—and the increase of wing area from 17 to 22 m² on the V.2 was retained on the V.3. Still, the V.3 was better than the V.2 but could not match the V.1, most likely due to the overweight nature of the plywood wings, and streamlined fuselage (921 kg and 938 kg for V.2 and V.3 respectively). That being said, the V.2 and V.3 were better than the operational Albatros aircraft then in use.

Fokker, aware that in June 1917 IdFlieg would announce triplane contracts to three different firms, leveraged the Fokker designers and engineers to produce a triplane. They responded with the V.4, a small, rotary-powered *dreidecker* with a steel tube fuselage and thick cantilever wings. The V.4 had an upper wing of longer span, and a shorter middle and lower wing of equal span. The fuselage was of steel tube construction like the E and D series, and the rounded formers and stringers were abandoned. It also had welded steel tail feathers. Fokker tested the V.4 himself, and after the flight Fokker instructed Platz to modify the next version to include balanced ailerons and elevators, and to add two sets of interplane struts—as the cantilevered wings flexed a bit too much for comfort—this resulted in the V.5 prototype.

The birth of the Dr.1 is evident in the V.4, a triplane version that incorporated much of the work done in the V.1 through V.3. It featured three cantilevered wings, a simple box-type fuselage similar to those used in the E and D series, a rotary engine, and the comma rudder has returned. The stabilizer featured a rounded leading edge. (Fokker Team Schorndorf)

The V.5 followed the V.4, the most noticeable feature being the addition of the interplane struts. Fokker flew the V.4 and noticed the wings flexed a bit too much for his liking, such that the interplane struts were added which linked all three box spars together. The V.5's stabilizer had a straight leading edge.

Instead of submitting the V.5 for testing, the aircraft was rushed into production; however, Fokker did his own internal tests on the V.5 wings at Schwerin. An initial order of 320 aircraft was placed which included three prototype F.1s. On July 14, 1917, IdFlieg issued an order for 20 preproduction aircraft. The prototype, serial 101/17, was tested to destruction at Adlershof on August 11, 1917.

The first two F.1 prototype triplanes were serials 102/17 and 103/17, and were the only machines to receive the F.1 designation and were distinguishable from subsequent aircraft by a slight camber of the horizontal stabilizer's leading edge. These two F.1s were sent to Jastas 10 and 11 for combat evaluation, arriving at Markebeeke, Belgium, in late August 1917.

Richthofen first flew 102/17 on September 1, 1917 and shot down two enemy aircraft in the next two days. He was very enthusiastic about the new triplane and told the Kogenluft (Kommandierender General der Luftstreitkräfte, or Commanding General of the Air Service) that the F.1 was superior to the Sopwith Triplane—how he could know this without flying a Sopwith is perhaps wishful thinking. Richthofen recommended that fighter squadrons be reequipped with the new aircraft as soon as possible. The forward trajectory for the *dreidecker* was halted

The V.5/Dr.1 sits patiently in front of a hangar. A beautiful modern interpretation of the Fokker Dr.1 built by Mikael Carlsen is seen completed except for covering. (Mikael Carlsen for top image and NARA for bottom image)

when First Lieutenant Kurt Wolff was shot down in F.1 number 102/17on September 15, and Lieutenant Werner Voss, squadron leader of Jasta 10, was killed in 103/17 after an epic dogfight on 23 September 23. McCudden and Rhys David claimed credit for shooting him down.

The remaining preproduction triplanes—now designated Dr.1—were delivered to Jasta 11. IdFlieg ordered 100 Dr.1 triplanes in September, then an additional 200 in November. The Dr.1s had straight leading edges on their horizontal stabilizers, and lower wing skids, the need for which became apparent after numerous instances of ground looping. In October, Fokker began delivering the Dr.1 to squadrons within Richthofen's Jagdgeschwader 1 (fighter wing).

Extensive load tests were conducted on the box spars used in the V.4 and V.5; the system that Fokker engineers finally settled on included two boxes within a box, which proved very strong indeed. (Fokker Team Schorndorf)

The construction of the box spar is pictured: two tapering boxes (taper increases moving toward centerline) are joined using spacers and H-shaped fillers to withstand the compressive forces of the cabane attachment bolts. In the second image, the completed box spar minus top and bottom sheathing is seen. The final image shows the webbing that joins the two sub-box spars; it is scarfed together. (Fokker Team Schorndorf)

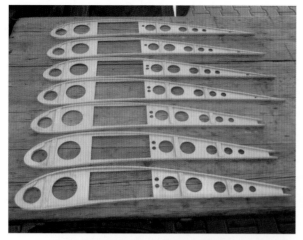

The completed rib webs for the Dr.1 complete with flanges, lightening holes, ailerons cable holes, and vertical stiffeners that were added after early wing failures of the Dr.1. (Fokker Team Schorndorf)

A description of the noteworthy construction aspects of the Dr.1 is useful at this point. The fuselage would have been in a similar fashion to the E and D series which has been described.

The cantilevered wings were revolutionary and, although influenced by Junkers, capitalized on plywood technology. It is difficult to ascertain who actually devised this system but it seems likely that Fokker, Forssman, Moser, and Platz all provided input. These wings required no bracing wires or interplane struts due to the two parallel box spars (although tapering to thicker toward the centerline on the inside faces only) joined with plywood webbing to form boxes within a box.

The depth fore and aft of these box spars eliminated the need for drag wire rigging which was found on every other wing of the time that had smaller solid-wood spars.

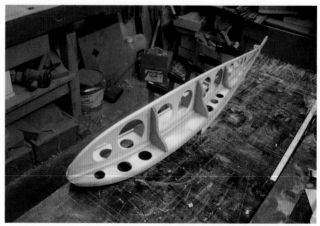

The rib webs are slid over the completed box spar and are cleated into place using joiners (triangular in section) to increase glue surface between the ribs and the box spar. The wingtip is formed by rotating a rib web profile 90°, flattening the bottom edge, and is joined using ply "knees." The completed lower wing of the Dr.1 includes leading edge sawtooth ply sheathing, antitwist fabric strapping, and auxiliary spar just forward of trailing edge (another improvement after early wing failures). (Fokker Team Schorndorf)

An interesting detail is the laminated and hollowed "scallop" that defines the cutout on the middle wing. (Fokker Team Schorndorf)

The metal attachment hardware for the lower wing skids and bottom attachment point for the interplane struts. Also visible are the adjustable attachment bolts for the middle wing, and the middle wing joined to the fuselage using this hardware. Being adjustable, the precise incidence and lateral alignment could be controlled. (Fokker Team Schorndorf)

The height of the box spars kept the wings stiff over their span. The box spar's outside dimension was constant so ribs could be used interchangeably (in most cases) and slid into place, and secured with triangular cleats.

All three wings were built mostly the same way, although the middle wing required a few extra details to achieve the scallop near the fuselage and canting of the inboardmost rib to fair in with the cowling. All of the box spars provided a solid foundation for attachment hardware; the interplanes and cabanes joined the three spars to make a very robust structure, and the attachment points for the fuselage also were fastened to these spars.

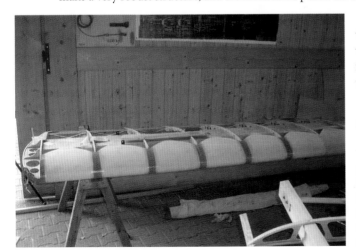

Finally, the rib noses were wrapped with thin plywood; the sawtooth pattern on the top was tacked to the box spars. The tail feathers (full flying rudder, stabilizer, and elevators) were, like the fuselage, built over a steel jig and welded.

The airfoil spreader for the main landing gear was built in a similar fashion as the wings;

The attachment of the leading edge ply sheeting was reinforced by means of fabric tape that was glued/doped into position over the intersection of the plywood and wing ribs. The tape was led over the ribs moving chordwise and folded over the ribs and affixed. (Fokker Team Schorndorf)

The framing of the Dr.1's horizontal stabilizer was done the same way as the fuselage and rudder: over a metal jig that could hold the steel tubing securely while being welded together. A closeup of the jig's "C-clamp" is seen holding the tubing firmly in place. (Fokker Team Schorndorf)

plywood ribs were used to define the airfoil, and a steel box and two tubes were used to provide rigidity and strength over the span of the spreader. Steel V-struts and specially designed shoes were fitted to the steal rectangular box (through which the axle passed) and had horns facing outboard to accept the bungees (shock absorbers). The steel tubes were flared outward to form a locking joint, and the whole airfoil was sheathed in ply then covered in fabric.

Compared with the Albatros and Pfalz fighters, the Dr.1 offered exceptional maneuverability. Although the ailerons were nominally effective, the rudder and elevator controls were light and powerful. Rapid turns were possible, especially to the right, due to the gyroscopic force of triplane's rotary engine and short-coupled fuselage. Franz Hemer of Jasta 6 said, "The triplane was my favorite fighting machine because it had such wonderful flying qualities. I could let myself stunt—looping and rolling—and could avoid an enemy by diving with perfect safety. The triplane had to be given up because although it was very maneuverable, it was no longer fast enough."

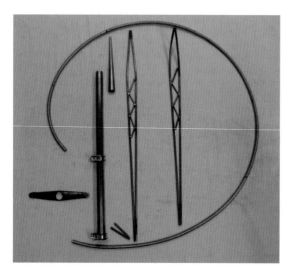

The rudder of the Dr.1 is done in much the same way as that of the E series. First the shape is finalized over a jig then the components are welded into place over a metal jig. (Fokker Team Schorndorf)

The airfoil spreader for the undercarriage has been estimated to generate enough lift to offset the weight of the gear itself. The system for building this component is much the same for all Fokker aircraft from the Dr.1 forward. A set of special rib webs are made with apertures large enough for the steel box that will house the axle. The two V-struts are welded together and meet at a special fitting that includes a slot for the axle and its rebound, as well as twin horns over which the bungees are wound. The fittings on the struts mate over the steel box forming an internal unit that is very strong. When assembly is completed, the whole airfoil is covered with thin ply then again covered in fabric and painted. (Fokker Team Schorndorf)

The interior of the Dr.1 cockpit is clean, minimal and all about functionality. Nothing is frivolous and for the era the ergonomics are not bad. Note the fabric wrapping on the steel longerons and the turnbuckles to prevent chafing of the covering. In the aerial environment the fabric vibrates and, depending on the maneuver, can be pressed against some of the metal fittings which can cause untimely wear and tear. (Fokker Team Schorndorf)

An archival image of a Fokker Dr.1 after suffering a wing failure. Note that the rib webs are completely shorn from the box spar as is the rest of the wing. In post-war testing, it was found that the top wing of the Dr.1 generated more lift than the other two wings which contributed to the stress on this structure. (Greg VanWyngarden)

As Hemer noted, the Dr.1 was considerably slower than contemporary Allied fighters in level flight and in a dive. While initial rate of climb was excellent, performance fell off dramatically at higher altitudes because of the low compression of the Oberursel UR.II—the German version of the Le Rhône 9J 110-hp rotary engine. As the war continued, chronic shortages of castor oil made rotary engine operation increasingly difficult. The poor quality of German *ersatz* lubricant resulted in many engine failures, particularly during the summer of 1918.

The Dr.1 suffered from other deficiencies. The pilot's view was poor during takeoff and landing. The cockpit was certainly utilitarian if not comfortable, moreover, the aircraft was prone to ground looping and nose-overs due to its short wingspan and short fuselage and nose moment. In addition, when the tail dropped on landing, rotating the middle wing downward, it blocked airflow from the tail feathers making ground handling problematic. It was an aircraft that required expert and experienced piloting at a time when Germany was in short supply of same.

Before the Dr.1 could attain widespread deployment at various Jastas, it was plagued by problems with the wing structure. On October 29, 1917 triplane 115/17 came apart while being flown by commander of Jasta 15, Heinrich Gontermann, who was performing aerobatics at 1500 feet over his aerodrome. The *dreidecker* was seen to lose control as the top plane disintegrated. Gontermann was badly injured and died the following day.

Two days later Jasta 11's Lieutenant Pastor perished when 121/17's upper wing fell apart in a similar fashion. At this point all Dr.1s were grounded, and an investigation was ordered by the Sturz-Kommission (crash commission). Richthofen was proactive such that even before inspectors arrived, he personally led an inspection of all triplanes under his command. It was discovered that poor workmanship had been the cause of the structural failures. Evidence of excessive moisture build-up had resulted in softening of glues, and delamination of joinery in box spar to rib joints. IdFlieg demanded that all Fokker triplane wings be modified, repaired, and made sound at Fokker's expense. In addition, tests on the shape and composition of the triplane's ailerons were also instituted by the IdFlieg which were inconclusive.

Another upper wing failure of, again, a Dr.1. This wing shows more ribs still attached which led to the conclusion that not only was the internal structure too weak, but that the method by which the covering was attached to the ribs was insufficient for the stress incurred. (Greg VanWyngarden)

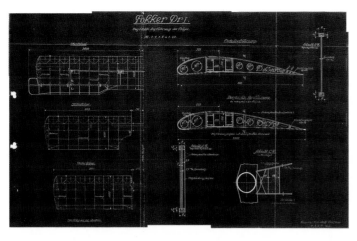

A very telling blueprint showing the Fokker Dr.1 "before and after." The early weaker-type ribs are shown in the upper right quadrant of the plan; the reinforced version showing the vertical stiffeners is shown in the lower right quadrant. The planview shows other reinforcements added to the wings such as triangular gussets joining ribs to aileron spar, intermediary spars, and diagonal struts reinforcing aft all corners of the wings.

In response to the crash investigation, Fokker improved quality control on the wings production line (which was off-site at a repurposed Perzina piano factory in downtown Schwerin), particularly varnishing of the wing spars and ribs, to combat moisture build-up.

Analysis of glues used on the D.VII after the war indicate that a combination of hide (gelatin) and casein glues were used on the D.VII wings. Hide glue is water soluble and heat accelerates this effect. If this adhesive system was also used on the Dr.1, and the weather while these wings were being produced was warm and humid, and stored, transported and hangared in similar conditions, it may have exacerbated this flaw (in fact, Richthofen demanded wooden hangars for his Jastas). Fokker also strengthened the rib structures and the attachment of auxiliary spars to the ribs. He also modified the way in which the fabric covering was attached to the rib webs: originally the covering was nailed, after the crashes it was stitched to the ribs. Fokker paid to have existing triplanes modified accordingly and after testing a modified wing at Adlershof, IdFlieg authorized the triplane's return to service at the end of November 1917, and production resumed in early December.

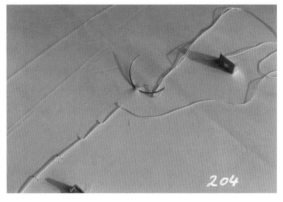

An image showing the fabric wrapping of rib flanges of the Dr.1, as well as diagonal bracing and intermediary spars running spanwise. The covering material was thus stitched to the fabric wrapping the ribs and therein lay the improved strength of this joint. In early model Dr.1s the fabric was simply tacked to the ribs which proved lethally insufficient. (Fokker Team Schorndorf)

An interesting Image of the interior of the Fokker factory. The gentleman with the scowl on his face is reworking a weaker Dr.1 wing with fabric tape and extra stitching to secure the fabric to the ribs; this was mandated by IdFlieg and done at Fokker's expense. To the left women workers are covering a new wing with linen. Note the wing racks in the rafters.

A load test of the newly improved/strengthened rib web. The direction of the weight being applied is upward, in the direction of the lifting force of the wing. Seemingly the designers and engineers knew this was the direction of force to be tested. In the second image, the entire new and improved wing structure is subjected to a load test, again in the upward direction of the lifting force of the wing. (Fokker Team Schorndorf)

However, in spite of the repairs, the Dr.1 continued to suffer from wing failures. On February 3, 1918, Lieutenant Hans Joachim Wolff of Jasta 11 successfully landed after suffering a failure of the upper wing leading edge and ribs.

On March 18, 1918, Lothar von Richthofen, squadron leader of Jasta 11, suffered a failure of the upper wing leading edge during combat with Sopwith Camels of No. 73 Squadron and Bristol F.2Bs of No. 62 Squadron: he crash-landed and was seriously injured.

Postwar research and testing in 1929, by the National Advisory Committee for Aeronautics (NACA) concluded that the upper wing of the Dr.1 possessed a higher lift coefficient than the lower wings: at high speeds it could be 2.55 times as much, which increased the tension on both interplane and cabane struts. This effect combined with quality control issues during production helps to further explain the upper wing failures.

The delay caused by addressing and solving the triplane's chronic structural problems widened the gap between the era of the turn-fighter, and that of the high-speed gun platforms such as the D.VII, Spad XIII, and S.E.5a. Bad timing sealed its fate as something of an anachronism and also eliminated any prospect of large production orders. Production eventually ended in May 1918, by which time only 320 had been manufactured. The Dr.1 too was sidelined from frontline service as the easier-to-fly Fokker D.VII entered widespread service in June and July. Still, in popular culture the Dr.1 was perhaps the most iconic fighter of the war.

Fokker D.VII

Toward the end of war it became increasingly difficult to obtain materials, and factories fell into disrepair. Fokker was no exception. Heat was only allowed to be turned on after 5 pm and could not exceed 64°F. The winter of 1917 was termed the "winter of despair."

Toward the end of 1917, the German authorities invited major aircraft manufacturers to submit designs that would leverage the Mercedes D.III engine to advantage. The prototypes would be rigorously tested by frontline pilots including luminaries such as Richthofen and Tutesch. Emphasis would be on rate of climb and speed in level flight, and aircraft would have to be able to carry a 220-lb load in addition to the pilot. Fokker had a number of prospects for this competition including the V.9, V.11, V.13, V.17, V.18, V.20, and Dr.1 as insurance. The V.11 was the eventual winner at Adlershof between January 20 and February 12, 1918.

The V.11 was the winner of the Aldershof trials between January 20 and February 12, 1918. It combined aspects of the Dr.1, but its wings harkened back to the early V.1 with its dual plywood spars of full depth relative to the wing ribs. (Fokker Team Schorndorf)

A very telling pair of images of the V.11 without covering. The ribs still have the lightening holes characteristic of the Dr.1. The fuselage is welded steel just as all the other Fokker aircraft, the tripod-forward cabanes of the V.1, V.2, and V.3 are evident, as is the integration of the Mercedes straight-six engine.

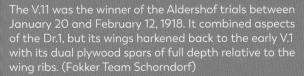

Testing of the D.VII wings was done using sandbags and many different angles to simulate the ever-changing load characteristic in flight. As the ailerons were prone to coming off early model Dr.1s, note the extra care Fokker took to insure that the ailerons would not come off the D.VII. (Fokker Team Schorndorf)

The V.11 leveraged the Dr.1 fuselage and tail feathers (to save time and production tooling costs) but had very different wings. The precise evolution of the design process/path for these wings remains unclear; however, a few observations can be made based on photos and conclusions reached based on the evolution of the Dr.1.

Due to the wing failures of the Dr.1, clearly Fokker was not quick to repeat the single box spar, which left a good portion of the rib webs not well supported—especially in a dive. Since this was a biplane and not a triplane, the chord had to be extended, thus dictating the use of two spars. The design team at Fokker therefore took the two tapered box spars that comprised the vertical walls of the Dr.1 box spar and separated them to a more traditional spacing on the rib webs—these were also tapered vertically to match the diminishing rib heights moving toward the tips.

The spar spacing also aligned with the interplane and cabane attachment points, although the interplanes were largely an afterthought. The rib webs on the V.11 had the lightning holes characteristic of the Dr.1. However, with the final production model of the D.VII the rib webs were solid, perhaps due to the results of Fokker's stress testing of the V.11 wing set.

The V.9 was the rotary iteration of the V.11 and the resemblance to the Dr.1 fuselage is unmistakable. The popularity of the rotary engine was on the wane due to the gyroscopic effect imparted on the aircraft, which translated to more training for fledgling pilots, and shortages of high-quality castor oil as mentioned.

Manfred von Richthofen flew the V.11 and found it tricky, unpleasant, and directionally unstable in a dive. Platz lengthened the rear fuselage by one structural bay and added a triangular fin in front of the rudder. Richthofen tested the modified V.11 and praised it as the best aircraft of the competition. It offered excellent performance from the outdated Mercedes engine, yet was safe and easy to fly. Richthofen's recommendation virtually decided the competition but he was not alone in recommending it. Fritz von Falkenhayn, who represented the General Staff, placed a provisional order for 400 production aircraft from Fokker, which were named D.VII by IdFlieg. Fokker was again asked how quickly he could go into production.

Fokker's factory was not up to the task of meeting all D.VII production orders and IdFlieg directed Albatros and AEG to build the D.VII under license, though AEG did not ultimately produce any aircraft. Because the Fokker factory did not use detailed plans as part of its production process, Fokker simply sent a D.VII airframe for Albatros to copy. Albatros paid Fokker a five percent royalty for every D.VII they built under license. Albatros Flugzeugwerke and its subsidiary, Ostdeutsche Albatros Werke (OAW) built the D.VII at factories in

The V.9 was a rotary engine version of the V.11; it was not as successful as the V.11, due to shortages of high-quality castor oil, and the extra training required to master the gyroscopic effects of the rotary engines. (Fokker Team Schorndorf)

Johannisthal (Fokker D.VII [Alb]) and Schneidemühl (Fokker D.VII [OAW]) respectively. Aircraft markings included the type designation and factory suffix, immediately before the individual serial number.

When Fokker began his factory, he knew most everyone by name; as production expanded and employees increased, he complained that there was an "inhuman accumulation of labor, which as descended upon me as a result of the growth I managed to achieve for my companies." Contracts mushroomed after that with 1,000 aircraft mentioned, so here again, numerical superiority was thought to be decisive and victory assured. What IdFlieg imperfectly understood was that of equal significance to large quanitities of excellent planes, was the capacity and time to train pilots to fly and fight effectively: more time than Germany had to turn the tide of the war.

Fokker had a huge contract in hand for what many viewed as perhaps the best fighter of the war, but now he had to deliver in quantity with no production problems. As with his E, D, and Dr.1 series, the fuselages would be made from ¾ mild steel tubing and likely built over jigs.

Flight magazine wrote in October 1918 that:

As in the case of the triplane, the body of the Fokker biplane is built of steel tubing throughout … the four corner tubes or longerons vary considerably in section as one progresses from nose to stern. Their outside diameter at any point is indicated in the drawings … Apparently the tubes are of very light gauge, and are joined, a larger to a smaller, at the points where occur the body struts. The struts are attached to the longerons, as in the triplane, by welding, the joint being particularly well made. As a matter of fact it is only this excellent workmanship that makes this construction feasible. Whether the welding has been done by the oxy-acetylene method, by oxygen and hydrogen, or by electricity is impossible to say. The construction points unmistakably to the body framework having been welded in place over jigs, and as one spoiled joint

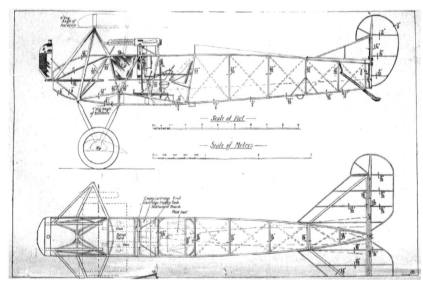

A D.VII being built in Achim Engels's shop in Shorndorf. As with the E, D, and Dr.1 the side panels are welded first over a jig, then the two sides are joined via the cross pieces. It is unknown how exactly Fokker did this in a production context. The drawing from *Flight* magazine shows the basic construction details of the D.VII. Note how the stresses transmitted through the V struts of the landing gear are transferred and offset by the arrangement of the steel framing. (Fokker Team Schorndorf)

would ruin the whole framework it appears probable that a considerable amount of control of the temperature of the flame used would be an advantage. Possibly therefore, the welding has been done by electricity. Whatever the method, there can be no doubt that the welding is excellently done, and, unless an entirely new method has been evolved by the enemy, could only have been entrusted to highly skilled workmen.

Clearly Platz was the most likely man responsible for the superiority of the welding operations at Fokker. Although by this time it was questionable if he was actually welding airframes, it is more likely that Platz was charged with designing and overseeing the mass production of welded components on a progressively grander scale, including training and oversight of Fokker's welding team. Although appointed chief constructor after Martin Keutzer's death, it is unclear what could readily be attributed to him, given his background, versus other engineers and designers in Fokker's talent pool. The airframe of the D.VII, although similar in style to his previous aircraft, was different in its engine area and tripod cabane strut structure which was devised for the V.2. It is interesting to ponder the nature of the jigs used at Fokker; which would include key control points such as the cabane to wing attachment points, lower wing lug holes on the fuselage, engine bearers and their appropriate attachment lugs, and tail feathers. Likely there was an initial tacking of fuselage tubes followed by addition of cabanes, landing gear, and other key attachment points. Of all the Fokker photos that are extant, none show a main welding shop as this would largely have been proprietary. It also begs the question—exigencies of wartime secrecy aside—if Fokker employees had to sign a confidentiality agreement for at least this portion of the works.

The tail feathers were built just as the others were, with the notable inclusion of a vertical fin to aid directional stability. The fin's forward point is slightly offset to port, probably to counteract a tendency, caused by the torque, to turn to the left. "This offsetting of the fin would probably result in a tendency to turn to the right with the engine switched off, noted *Flight* magazine.

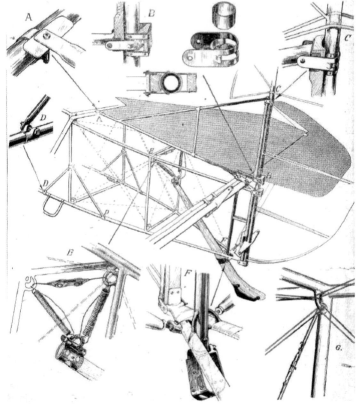

The tail feathers of the D.VII assembled in Engels's shop. These were built much as the other Fokker tail assemblies were built, using steel tubing over jigs. In the series of illustrations from *Flight*, note the judicious use of wood within the steel structure of the stabilizer and vertical fin. Also note that the forward tip of the vertical fin was adjustable and could be slightly offset to port or starboard. (Fokker Team Schorndorf)

Mikael Carlsen's D.VII with all fuselage systems installed during an engine test. Note the excellent use of space moving from the radiator to the pilot: engine, oil, fuel, and ammunition are all situated such that there is very little wasted space. (Sven Stridsberg)

Carlsen's Fokker D.VII. (Sven Stridsberg)

In Profile:
D.VII Wings

The wings of the D.VII were different from the V.11 in that the ribs were solid three-ply wood (about 1.5 mm) with vertical stiffeners. They were pierced only to allow passage of antidrag rigging and control cables. The pine flanges of the ribs were attached in two strips flanking the top of the ply, and according to a patent filed by Fokker in January 1918, were clench-nailed spanwise.

The spars for the upper and lower planes are made in a similar fashion; there is s thicker one that is just forward of the thickest part of the airfoil, and an aft one that is just over 2/3 the way aft of the leading edge. All four are hollow box spars, and are made from laminated (quarter sawn) solid spruce with filler pieces shaped like an elongated H turned on its side.

These pieces coincide with the attachment points for cabanes and interplanes and provide (compression) support for the bolts that pass through the spars (fore and aft). The spars are sheathed

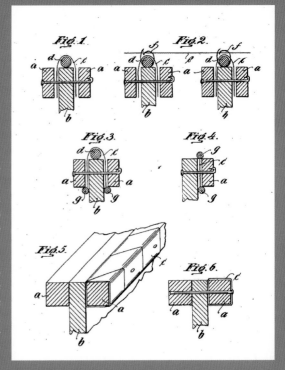

A patent award to Fokker dated August 1924 regarding attachment methods for wing fabric to the rib webs, presumably for the Fokker D.VII as it was filed in January 1918 in Germany.

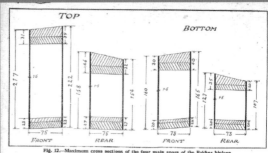

Fig. 12.—Maximum cross sections of the four main spars of the Fokker biplane.

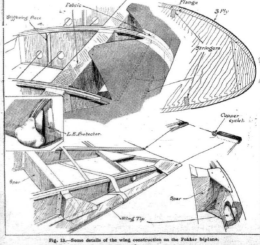

Fig. 13.—Some details of the wing construction on the Fokker biplane.

1162

The spar benches at Schwerin for the D.VII. (left) Note how the solid stock is firmly butted up against cleats that are fastened to the bench, which insures repeatable and identical results. The compression filler blocks for the interplanes and cabanes are clearly visible. The color image depicts two spars (missing plywood sheer webs) built by Engels at his shop. The line drawing describes the various construction details of the D.VII wings. Note how the solid stock portion of the spars is laminated, to afford increased strength and dimensional stability. (Fokker Team Schorndorf, *Flight*)

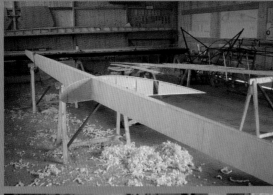

The construction of the D.VII wing at Fokker Team Schorndorf. Note how the spar depth is almost that of the rib webs, thus allowing maximum support. From a production standpoint, because the spars taper (and the ribs gradually decrease in height moving outboard) there is only one "right" spot for each rib outboard of the cabanes. This self-alignment aspect must have speeded up and aided construction. Also note the use of intermediary stringers, and stiffeners on the ply rib webs. (Fokker Team Schorndorf)

with 3-ply plywood webbing which is scarfed to make up the necessary lengths. Presumably the glue used was casein. The shape of the spars is noteworthy, as they taper in planview, as well as on the bottom (if viewed from the front) outboard of the cabane attachment points moving toward the tips. The spar is almost the full height of each respective rib, and the joint was reinforced by means of triangular (in section) fillets

that provided enough glue surface between spar and rib web.

It should be well noted that since the spars were tapered, two directions (outboard of the cabane attachment points) the ribs will/would have fitted properly in only one location; this could have helped alignment of the wings such that each rib goes in a specific spot on the spar making assembly a bit more

Two images of D.VII wings being assembled on trestles at Schwerin. (Fokker Team Schorndorf)

Unlike the Dr.1's leading edge sheathing, the D.VII's leading edge was sawtoothed top and bottom and was tacked to the box spar. (Fokker Team Schorndorf)

self-evident. With labor becoming a problem toward the end of the war, designing assembly sequences that required perhaps fewer skilled workers would have been advantageous to any industry. Obviously the wings were built from the centerline working outward due to this taper; the presence of two (well-spaced chordwise) box spars made this wing very rugged. Additional stringers were added at the midpoint between spars and between the aft spar and trailing edge at the tops of the ribs on the top wing only. In addition, on both the top and bottom wing a stringer passed through the ribs very near the trailing edge. In theory if the spars and ribs were free from warps, due to their self-aligning nature they could be built using no jigs on trestles, which is what factory images of Fokker depict.

The leading edge, as in the Fokker triplane, is in the form of very thin three-ply wood, which extends back to the front spar, where it finishes off in a sawtooth edge having its points tacked to the spar—on both top and bottom—unlike the Dr.1 which only

had the sawtooth on the top. A piece of fabric tape was glued/doped over the joint of the ply leading edge where it met the rib running fore and aft.

The trailing edge was formed by a piece of piano wire passed through a metal clip at the end of each rib, as on the Dr.1. After the wing was covered, the doping/shrinking process pulled the wire inward imparting the characteristic scalloped look to the trailing edge. Between trailing edge and rear spar, the ribs are strengthened by tapes running alternately over and under the ribs to prevent twisting.

The attachment of the lower wings to the fuselage was effected by four staple shaped plates through which bolts passed in mating holes in lower fuselage framing.

The upper wing is attached at the fuselage by means of the tripod steel structure on either side forward, each of which attaches to an adjustable bolt and staple fitting (port & starboard) that passes around and is bolted through the forward spar. The landing gear and airfoil spreader is similar to the one previously described for the Dr.1. The cockpit is also similar to the Dr.1, except there is more instrumentation due to the Mercedes D.III engine.

The D.VII's fuselage was mated to the lower wing by means of four staple-shaped tangs that accepted gusset plates welded to the fuselage, and were then through-bolted. The top wing was bolted to the tripod cabanes via a long staple-shaped pair of tangs that wrapped around the box spar, and was through-bolted fore and aft. (Fokker Team Schorndorf)

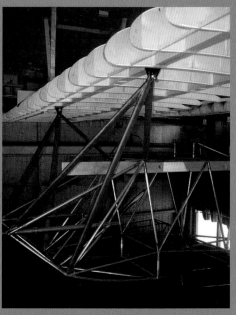

Fokker D.VIII

The D.VIII began with the early V.1–V.3 experimental aircraft, all of which had plywood-covered wings, and tapered not only like the D.VII's rib heights moving toward the tips, but also in planform. The Fokker design team was dismayed to have to go backward and build a triplane after the cutting-edge V.1 and V.2. J. M. Bruce wrote that "It can't be confirmed that the V.17 was Platz's first monoplane; what is indisputable is that was the first Platz design to be built and flown." However, where and how Bruce obtained this information remains a mystery as there is no extant documentation to support this assertion. In any event, the V.17 was powered by a 110 Oberursel UR.II and was rolled out in late 1917. It was virtually a V.4 fuselage with a cantilever mounted just under upper longerons. Its wing was ply-covered, so likely this was a variation on one of the Forssman and Fokker wings, perhaps with additional influence from Junkers. A new production technique emerged of making the ailerons as part of the wing and cutting them out of the main structure just before skinning. Fokker liked the V.17 and flew it in the Adlershof trials in January 1918; its engine was underpowered, but Fokker asked his team to use a 160-hp engine which became the V.20—which was built in six and a half days such that it could be flown during the trials. It was unsuccessful and was followed by the V.23 which was also unsuccessful due to poor pilot visibility. The V.25 was built and was a clean airframe and very contemporary due to its low wing mounting, but the 20, 23 and 25 all suffered from poor downward visibility. V.26–28 were parasol monoplanes so featured improved downward visibility.

The V.26 and V.28 were identical airframes; the V.26 had the 110 Oberursel UR.II, the V.28 the 11-cylinder 145-hp UR.III and 160-hp Goebel Goe.III (two V.28s took part). V27 was inline iteration with the 195-hp Benz Bz.IIIb watercooled V-8 and was a bit larger. The Fokker design team realized the ideal in the V.26/28 design— as it was very simple. The fuselage was welded steel as all other Fokkers; it had the twin tripod cabanes forward; it had a similar if not identical engine mount as the Dr.1, which was also blended into the slab-sided fuselage with triangular ply fairings (like the Dr.1). The cantilever wing was wooden, and it tapered in planform and vertically. Each wing spar was a full-span wooden box with upper and lower spanwise members composed of five 10-mm laminations; the flanges were joined by vertical webs of 2-mm plywood; the forward spar was one-fifth of the root chord from the leading edge; the rear three-fifths chord.

Like the D.VII, the spar decreased in depth as it moved toward the tips. The ply covering was 1.5-mm thick that was glued and nailed to the ribs and spars. The tail feathers were typical Fokker welded steel, struts

The spars for the D.VIII are similar to the D.VII, here seen with their sheer webs about to be installed. The structure of the D.VIII wings was/ is similar to the D.VII, except there are a few more stringers running spanwise to support the thin ply sheathing, as plywood will not shrink drumtight as with fabric covering. (Fokker Team Schorndorf)

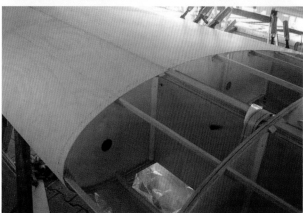

The wingtip framing and aileron framing of the D.VIII. The ailerons were of mostly wooden construction built around a steel tube that was in turn set in bearings in the appropriate ribs. Since the aileron was being skinned with ply, the framing had to be of wood to insure a good glue joint. The final image shows the ply sheating being carefully glued and nailed into place. The holes in the ribs are to allow air circulation throughout the entire structure which reduces contraction/expansion of gases as well as reducing the chance of moisture being trapped in the various "cells" of the wing. (Fokker Team Schorndorf)

were all similar to the D.VII as was the airfoil spreader between the V-struts of the gear. The V.28, powered by the Goebel Goe, climbed to 19,700 feet in 16 minutes. It weighed 1,380 lb and the climb was record-setting. IdFlieg was impressed and placed a production order provided use of the UR.III and the 200-hp Goebel Goe. III, but since these engines had not been fully tested, the Le Rhône 110 hp served as an intermediary engine. With structural tests completed on the V.28, an order of 400 parasol monoplanes was placed with the official designation of Fokker E.V (the version with the UR.III was the E.Ve); they were supposed to build 80 per month.

Twenty E.Vs were delivered by the end of July, 1918. The production differed from the prototype in planform, as the tips were more rounded which increased the span to 8.4 meters. Cabane and tail feather supports were more robust as well. The internal differences in the wings of the E.Vs and the V.26 and V.28 did not present themselves until the aircraft were tested at the front. Six E.Vs were delivered to Jasta 6 on August 7, 1918, and 12 days later the E.V flown by Lieutenant Rolff suffered a wing failure in flight, crashed, and Rolff was killed. Two more crashes followed during the next week, all due to wing failures. So the same unpleasant drama that surrounded the Dr.1 repeated itself: the Sturz-Kommission headed by Friedrich Mallinckrodt began investigation at the end of August. However, they repeated the assessment they made for the Dr.1, saying that the wing failed due to torsion under high load conditions, rather than performing a thorough autopsy of the wing which was finally done at Adlershof.

It was found that the craftsmanship of the wings was substandard: the spar wood was inferior and water was found in the wing, as well as rot. Obviously a high humidity content in the wings could have caused the casein glue to soften and fail. The plywood was found to be acceptable but the fastening schedule was haphazard, most of the fastenings missing their mark. Some wood was found to be green, and some dry-rotted, gluing was sloppy and insufficient clamping pressure was noted. Finally, the spars were found to have insufficient flanges; the glue joint had slipped, resulting in most of the structural integrity of the spar being planed off to bring the spar to its proper profile.

IdFlieg fumed and mandated that if two more wings were tested (via sandbag tests) and found to be faulty, that all wings would be returned to be corrected at Fokker's expense. Testing was done on the September 3 and 5, 1918—both failed. An E.V wing that was not built at the ill-fated Perzina factory was sent to Adlershof on September 7 and passed with flying colors. Due to the exigencies of war, it was decided that the E.V wings would have cable bracing (flying wires) to augment what might be questionable construction; however it seems unlikely that any with flying wires were operationalized. IdFlieg had reached their limit with Fokker's production problems and took a very harsh view of the failures of the E.V wings. The result, according to Bruce, was that Platz was asked to oversee production at Perzina. Production was resumed in late September 1918 of the E.V wings with the stipulation that wing spar flanges be increased by 2 mm. These new aircraft were to be called the D.VIII, and they did not appear at the front until October 24, 1918; the Armistice was signed 18 days later.

To give a brief overview of notable construction traits, the fuselage, tail feathers, and landing gear were all similar to either the Dr.1 or the D.VII; only the wings differed materially so I will confine my description to these. The rib webs are similar to the D.VII in that they were solid (no lightening holes) 1.5-mm-thick ply. They were reinforced with vertical stiffeners of pine, and also had flanges of pine. The ribs were pierced only for control cables. This raises an interesting question: once sealed with ply, there would have been very little ventilation that produced an environment susceptible to rot—with anything wooden.

The spars were made in a similar fashion to the D.VII as well, but with increased flange depth and the aft spar was canted forward, outboard of the cabane attachment points. As with the D.VII, the structure was fairly self-aligning—perhaps even more so than the D.VII as the D.VIII wings tapered in planform as well which visually would have aided alignment. The spars were exactly the full height of the rib at their intersection, thus affording maximum strength. A series of spanwise stringers were next installed to aid in providing extra stiffness to the ply skin, and to give an additional gluing point. This is where problems arose during production at Perzina, as casein glue requires adequate clamping pressure to achieve a good bond, a function that can be aided by using small brads/nails which serve to hold the wood firmly until the glue cures. However, without careful layout lines on the exteriors of the ply skin, it would be difficult to know where the substrate is located once the ply skin is applied to the framing. One could presume that this step was not strictly enforced at Perzina, or was at least not as carefully overseen as it should have been. It should also

A D.VIII replica created by Fokker Team Schorndorf is nearing completion.

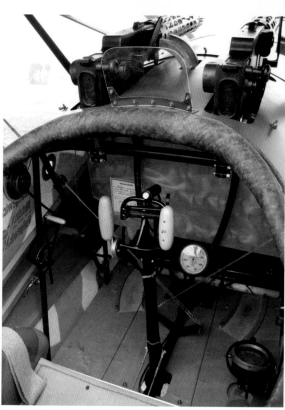

Flight shots and cockpit of Achim Engels's Fokker D.VIII replica—a beautiful and accurate job! (Fokker Team Schorndorf)

be remembered that casein is not a gap-filling structural adhesive as is modern epoxy. In any event, if carefully glued and nailed, the wing of the D.VIII was/is very strong indeed.

The ailerons were of the modern type, unbalanced and inset into the trailing edge just as modern aircraft are. Bruce mentions that the wings were framed in the entirety first then the ailerons were "cut out" afterwards. This does not seem to be a system efficient in a production context and would in fact be more difficult to achieve good results with than planning the shape of each rib to accommodate the ailerons. The ailerons were different from the D.VII in that they were steel tubing at their pivot point, but had wooden riblets to form their shape. They were attached by means of welded flanges that were then fastened to the wooden parts, the steel tube passed through bearings in the ribs to give frictionless movement.

As with the D.VII, the cabanes were attached to U-shaped straps that fitted over the spars almost in their entirety, and were then bolted fore and aft (with compression fillers). The control cables were led through sheaves, the location of which was accessible by means of hinged inspection plates Thus cable wear could be examined, and sheaves could be periodically greased. The cowling was also identical to the Dr.1.

Although it was deemed very maneuverable (more so than the D.VII), had an excellent rate of climb, and a wing that presaged the next generation of combat aircraft, the D.VIII arrived too late to make a tactical or strategic difference in the German air campaign.

The *Ente* built by Professor Hans Reissner utilized corrugated-steel wings produced by Junkers. (Public domain)

29.5.12.

5

Junkers Flugzeugwerke

Hugo Junkers was born in Rheydt in the Prussian Rhine Province, the son of a well-off industrialist. After taking his Abitur exams in 1878, he attended the Royal Polytechnic University in Charlottenburg and the Royal Technical University in Aachen, where he completed his engineering studies in 1883. At first, he returned to Rheydt to work in his father's company, but soon attended further lectures on electromagnetism and thermodynamics held by Adolf Slaby in Charlottenburg. Slaby placed him with the Continental-Gasgesellschaft (Continental Gas Company) in Dessau, where he worked on the development of the first opposed-piston engine. In order to measure heating value, Junkers patented a calorimeter and founded a manufacturing company in 1892. Junkers personally introduced the calorimeter at the 1893 World's Columbian Exposition in Chicago, where it was awarded a gold medal. The next year, he patented a gas-fired bath boiler, which he refined as a tankless heater. In 1895, he founded IKO Heating Apparatus Compnay to maximize on his inventions. In 1897 he accepted a position as chair and professor of thermodynamics at Aachen University. Here he collaborated with Professor Hans Reissner in 1907 on the *Ente,* a canard-type monoplane designed by Reissner, which featured corrugated-iron wings, which were made by Junkers' company.

In 1909, the *Ente* successfully flew several times, but after it stalled and crashed on takeoff, killing the pilot, Reissner halted work on the aircraft, not due to the unfortunate crash, but more likely he was unsure as to how to proceed with the new technology—Junkers picked up where Reissner left off. In February 1910, Junkers applied for a patent for fully cantilevered, thick airfoil wings. Next, he built a wind tunnel at Aachen to continue his experiments in aeronautics. He resigned his teaching position at the university in 1911 to allow more time to run his company in Dessau where he also built a wind tunnel. It seems likely that he preferred not to share his discoveries with the academic community until after they were patented. Junker resigned from Aachen in 1912 to continue his experiments under a more controlled environment and free from prying eyes. Junkers also set up the Jumo works to build his diesel engine which occupied his attention until early 1915.

He next founded the Forschungsanstalt Professor Junkers, which was basically his own research institute dedicated to the design and construction of his cantilevered monoplane which would come to be known as the J 1.

This seminal aircraft was the result of a productive collaboration between Junkers, Dr Mader (director of Forschungsanstalt), and Otto Reuter. In spite of the war being in its second year, and the pressure from IdFlieg and other German leadership, Junkers stubbornly saw his J 1 not as a weapon that could win the war, but as the first of series of aircraft that would allow him to continue to refine his theories concerning cantilevered aircraft design, construction, and production of all-metal aircraft. The aircraft was made entirely of steel due to shortages of Duralumin, which was preferred and earmarked for airship construction. The fuselage was tube steel, like Fokker, but was clad in corrugated-steel sheathing and had an integrated wing root (much like Pfalz and Albatros had done). The cantilevered wings tapered as they moved toward the tips, and were made up of short sections of welded steel tube that served as zigzag trusses.

In high load areas, an additional layer of corrugated steel was arc-welded to the inside of these panels (e.g. wing root, engine area). Sixteen workers constructed the J 1 in six weeks, and welding techniques for the new aircraft had to be invented during its construction. On December 12, 1915 the J 1 was successfully test flown at Dessau by Lieutenant Mallinckrodt, who first flew

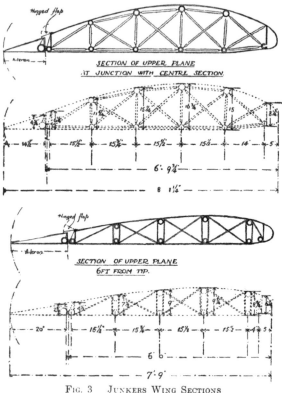

Fig. 3   Junkers Wing Sections

The J 1 was produced in 1915 under the auspices of Junkers' Forschungsanstalt which was in essence his own aircraft research institute. It was an amazingly clean design for its time and featured Junkers' patented cantilever wings with a zigzag of steel trusses and corrugated-steel sheathing. (NARA)

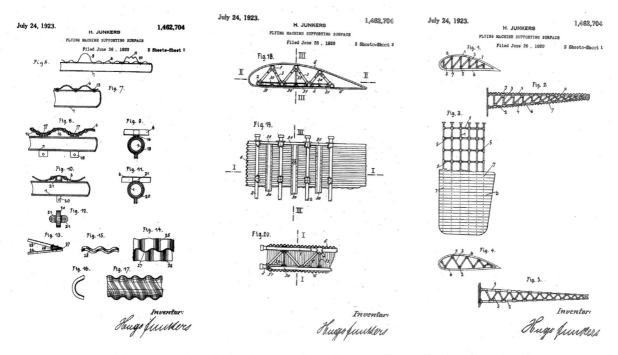

A group of illustrations from Junkers' patented metal corrugation method, and construction methodology for his cantilevered wing that featured a thick airfoils tapering in height and in planview moving toward the tips.

the aircraft over a distance of several hundred yards; he later noted that none of his comrades wanted to fly the plane, all believing it would crash. It was then taken to Döberitz for evaluation. The J 1 could attain 106 mph in level flight but had a slower rate of climb (as compared to the Rumpler C.I, its chief competitor at Döberitz). It also had poor pilot visibility; nobody that flew it or serviced it really liked it, and as such it earned the disparaging moniker of "Tin Donkey" or "Flying Urinal." However, the concept of the J 1 was brilliant; the notion of a cantilevered wing, semi-stressed skin aircraft, that was rugged and fast was not lost on Anthony Fokker at the very least as discussed in the previous chapter. Felix Wagenführ of IdFlieg was convinced of the efficacy of Junkers' direction, and his February 15 communication confirmed that the War Ministry had approved an order for six further aircraft at a cost of 25,000 marks apiece. The order vindicated Junkers' belief in his design, and he immediately began work on the new model, the J 2.

The J 2 was another clean and very modern-looking design, but despite its fine lines, it weighed 308 lb. heavier than the J 1 and could only reach 90.5 mph in level flight, and was not as maneuverable as the J 1 due to the reduction in size of its control surfaces. (NARA)

An image of the construction of the J 2 shows the corrugated sheathing of the fuselage and wing root, the trussing system, and a very modern air-scoop below the wing for the radiator. Note too how the V strut gear is tied into the principal vertical struts inside the wing root. (Public domain)

The J 2 was ordered by the military while still in early design phases, such was the cleanness and beauty of this design. The landing gear of this plane was a nod toward the necessity of takeoffs and landing on grassy fields at the front. However, in spite of its clean lines and slightly smaller size (to the J 1), it was heavier by 308 lb and could only do 90.5 mph in level flight—it had a Mercedes D.II 120-hp engine—and due to smaller control surfaces and reduced wing area, it was not very maneuverable. Junkers built six iterations of the J 2 during 1916 (E 250/16 to E 255/16); only the first two incorporated armament into the design, such was Junkers continued focus on theory over practice. E 251/16 was the first to fly in July 1916, and it was then given to the military for testing in August; its fate was sealed when E 252/16 crashed on December 25, 1916. The J 3 was never tested as it was too similar to the J 2 and all interest in the model ceased after the fateful crash. It served as a display piece in the exhibition hall at Junkers' factory in Dessau. Junkers became convinced at this time that iron was never going to be a suitable metal for aircraft sheathing and general construction.

On November 18, 1916, IdFlieg called for designs from three firms—Junkers, Albatros, and AEG—for an armored ground support/reconnaissance plane: Junkers abandoned steel as his primary material, instead focusing on light metal alloys such as Duralumin; thus while the armored areas would be of steel, the rest of the plane would be of lightweight Duralumin. A meeting was convened with Junkers, Fokker, and Felix Wagenführ (of IdFlieg) December 16, 1916 to decide whose plane would get the contract. The Junkers design won the competition, but differences surfaced between Professor Junkers and IdFlieg officials; Junkers submitted a monoplane design, but IdFlieg wanted a biplane configuration. Idlfieg had by this time mandated integration of Nieuport technology; thus Junkers proposed a sesquiplane design: it had a large

The J 4 featured a 5-mm steel "bathtub" that protected aircrews from fire from below. It was a sesquiplane, and was produced in conjunction with Fokker which proved to be a partnership fraught with contention and acrimony. The only surviving J 4 is in the collection of the Canada Aviation Museum in Ottawa.

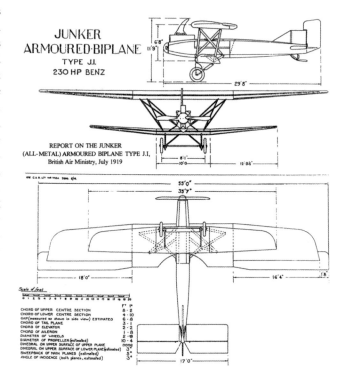

JUNKER ARMOURED·BIPLANE
TYPE J.I.
230 HP BENZ

REPORT ON THE JUNKER
(ALL-METAL) ARMOURED BIPLANE TYPE J.I.,
British Air Ministry, July 1919

upper wing and small lower wing. This new aircraft, designated the J 4, featured a 5-mm armoured "bathtub-type" cockpit. It was also clear that Junkers needed a partner to help him produce his plane. Fokker had a proven track record with his E series, and so began the negotiations between Junkers and Fokker.

Junkers had spent over one and a half million marks of his own money on aircraft research between 1915 and 1916, and his resources were almost exhausted; he could not continue his work independently. Faced with IdFlieg's position that no large orders would be granted without his incorporation with an established producer, he sought to influence the merger with Fokker as best he could. Junkers refused Fokker the right to use the patented wing design in his own aircraft, Junkers demanded that only a new joint-stock company, and not the Fokker Aircraft Works in Schwerin, would be granted this privilege.

On December 18, 1916, (two days after meeting), Fokker asked Junkers' engineers to explain nearly everything there was to know about the construction of the J 1 and J 2. After consulting with his design team in the Hotel Bristol, he decided to use this information for further development of wooden cantilever wing that he and Forssman had been working on, instead of building aircraft by another competitor as described in the previous chapter.

Upon learning this Junkers was furious: he could not find words to describe his loathing for Fokker. On Wagenführ's insistence, a second meeting was set for February 2, 1917; Fokker dodged this meeting, sending Horter instead who delivered the message that Fokker only wanted patent rights for Junkers' cantilever wing. Idflieg supported Fokker in this in that they wanted practical application and production of Junkers' theories, and were tired of waiting around for him to perfect his fighter as there was a war to win. In March 1917 IdFlieg had placed an advanced order for 50 J 4 aircraft (J.I was the military designation).

Dec. 8, 1925.

H. JUNKERS

ARMORED AEROPLANE

Filed June 28, 1920

1,564,354

Fig. 1.

Fig.2.

Fig.3.

Fig. 4.

Fig. 5.

Inventor:

Hugo Junkers

J 4 in the collection of the Canada Aviation Museum in Ottowa. (Public domain)

Patent drawing for the Junkers J 4 showing the armored "bathtub" that protected the pilot and gunner.

A group of Junkers J 4s delivered to the allies as part of the Armistice agreement. Photo was taken just over a week after the Armistice was signed at Tellancourt, France. (NARA)

Feb. 22, 1927.

H. JUNKERS

1,618,536

ERECTION OF THE HULLS AND THE LIKE OF FLYING MACHINES

Filed July 22, 1925

Fig.1.

Fig.2.

Fig.3.

Inventor:
Hugo Junkers
by Kluicharin
Atty.

The challenge for Junkers, like so many other manufacturers, was how to efficiently produce a new design in large numbers. A clue to this is revealed in a patent he applied for in Germany in 1924 which was granted in 1927. Described in the drawing is a building jig for aligning Junkers fuselages in such a way as to be able to rotate the entire fuselage to allow for efficient fastening of the metal panels. Moreover, the jig's elongated pyramidal shape allowed for it to be withdrawn when the framing and sheathing was stable enough. Although the patent was filed after the war, something along these lines undoubtedly was being worked out during production of his aircraft. Alternatively, this may have not been entirely successful during the war, which could account for the relatively small numbers of Junkers aircraft produced. Junkers also embarked on the design for a four-engined R-plane (monoplane) at the end of January, but this would not see fruition before the close of the war; another example of the dilution of Junkers' focus.

After months of negotiations, a verbal agreement was reached on June 16, 1917, where Fokker gained permission to produce and develop aircraft according to Junkers designs (enter the D.VII); the deal included use of the cantilevered wing construction at a cost of 500,000 marks, plus 10 percent of the sales price of every machine Fokker turned out under contract with Junkers until end of war.

By the summer of 1917 production challenges of the J 4 (J.I) were dragging on. This is not surprising due to the toxic negotiations with Fokker, and Junkers' own penchant for distraction and new ideas. He must have seen mass production as an annoying waste of his developmental time. Junkers was also an outspoken liberal (like much of Germany, he did not like the war at this point), making him suspect by conservatives in upper-echelon leadership. Moreover, instead of

Pictured is the patent drawing for Junkers' ingenious fuselage construction jig. This jig was able to be rotated to facilitate ease of sheathing the formers. The jig was also able to be withdrawn from the completed fuselage, enabling production in a very systematic and repeatable way.

The J 7 was another design reflecting ultramodern sensibility. It was flown in September 1917, and was made of lightweight Duralumin. The radiator and anemometer perched on a tripod seem as afterthoughts in this otherwise clean design. (NARA)

buckling down to solve production problems on the J 4 (J.I), Junkers worked between July and September 1917 on a series of low-wing monoplanes that leveraged what Junkers had learned using Duralumin in the J 4 biplane. To increase pilot visibility, a rotary engine design was developed with the engine being near the center of gravity (CG). This allowed the cockpit to be in the nose in front of the engine. Also at this time the J 6 parasol was developed, which was very similar to the later Fokker D.VIII. The J 6 was to have used the powerful Siemens-Halske Sh.III counter-rotating engine (see Chapter 7) which would have given the J 6 superior performance to the Fokker D.VIII.

The J 7 followed, flown in September 1917, was a leap forward; it had the low wing of the J 3 combined with the lightweight riveted metal structure of the J 4 (J.I). It had fully flying or pivoting wingtips instead of ailerons (something Fokker copied in his V series of prototypes) but these proved too sensitive and prone to flutter so were replaced by those employed on the J 6 parasol. Cowan states that the use of the cumbersome radiator was one of the biggest puzzles surrounding the J 7 design which resulted in poor performance. Indeed, both the radiator and the anemometer (perched high on a tripod) seemed like afterthoughts.

In spite of the verbal agreement between Fokker and Junkers, when Junkers refused to grant Fokker's additional demand that he control all operational aspects of the new firm, IdFlieg intervened and ordered the creation of the new joint-stock company with a capitalization of 2,630,000 marks, 630,000 marks of which would be funded by a subsidy from the War Ministry. IdFlieg oversaw the signing of the agreement on October 20, 1917, resulting in the formation of the Junkers-Fokker-Werke A.G. Metallflugzeugbau.

The CL.I two-seater ground-support aircraft grew from the J 8 design, which featured a constant chord cantilevered wing with balanced ailerons (that tapered toward the tips in height), and very good visibility for the observer/gunner.

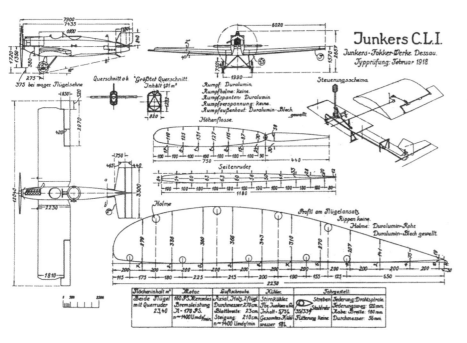

The J 9 (D.I) was perhaps Junkers' most popular and arguably successful design; it incorporated everything he had learned over the course of the war. Unfortunately, they did not arrive at the front in time to make any difference in the trajectory of the war. (NARA)

Junkers provided all fixed assets for the new enterprise: land, buildings, equipment, and raw materials from the Dessau works. Shares valued at two million marks went equally to Junkers and Fokker, and Fokker agreed to buy his stock from Junkers at the rate of 118.5 percent. Fokker received the title of director, with responsibility for production, while Junkers, as chief designer, was responsible for research and development. With the ink barely dry on the agreement, Junkers began designing the J 8, a lightweight two-seater, by the end of October 1917. This would eventually become the successful C series of ground support two-seater.

The protracted negotiations had in the meantime slowed production such that the first two J 4s were not delivered until October; Passchendaele was winding down and the much-hoped-for ground-support weapon had not materialized. IdFlieg was understandably angry at the delay and threatened to pay a much lower price for the J 4s. Thanks to a government subsidy, production facilities at Dessau were improved, and the workforce grew from 200 to over 1,000 by the end of 1917.

The new firm immediately resumed production of the J 4, and by early December Fokker and Wagenführ agreed to try and increase production to have eight J 4s out by end of 1917; in 1918 production would expand further. However, this was in the end posturing as the relationship between Fokker and Junkers was characterized by distrust, ill will, and suspicion. Both designers were out to use the cantilever wing construction, but on their own terms and at each other's expense. In December Fokker wrecked the J 7 on landing. There is no proof that he did this intentionally; however, he had much to gain and was an expert pilot.

A Junkers D.I most likely after the Armistice was signed. Note the lack of tires on the main landing gear and the exceptionally thick airfoil at the wing root. (NARA)

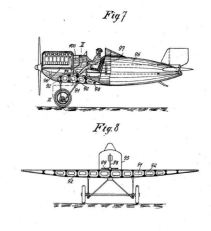

Fig 7

Fig. 8

Inventor:
Hugo Junkers
by
Attorney.

The J 7 was rebuilt using the best aspects of the bigger J 8; both were ready for army trials in January 1918. Fokker at the controls again, broke the propeller of the J 7 during the dead stick portion of the testing and was subsequently retired on January 22. By February 1918, the J 7 had again been modified with the outboard panels of the J 6 which represented the last major modification of this model. This iteration of the J 7 could reach 127.5 mph in level flight. Chief criticism at this point was on its lateral stability resulting in a redesigned rudder area in April; but this problem would not be completely solved until the lengthened fuselages of the preproduction J 9.

During this process IdFlieg had sustained interest in Junkers' designs but the monoplane had fallen out favor with increasing intensity. Such that the military designation D.I (*doppeldecker* or biplane) was issued in spite of it being an *eindecker*, the J 9 emerged at the end of April 1918—it had a 185-hp BMW engine instead of the 160-hp Mercedes of the J 7. Testing continued through the summer of 1918 but by then the war was already lost. In all 41 J 9/D.Is were built but the majority were after the Armistice.

In the end, the biggest fight in which Junkers participated was over his intellectual property with Fokker, and his own stubbornness and myopia in pursuing innovation at the expense of his country's defense.

Patent drawing for a Junkers low wing monoplane—most likely the D.I. The patent was filed well after the war had concluded (June 28, 1920), but Junkers no doubt wanted to protect his inventions created during the war in the post-war market.

148,890. Junkers, H.
March 12, 1918. [*Convention date*].
Planes, arrangement of.—The wing spars 2 of a monoplane extend uninterruptedly through the lower part of the fuselage so as to dispense with external bracing and still leave sufficient space in the fuselage for the accommodation of the engine, pilot, &c. The lower surface of the fuselage merges into the lower surface of the wings.

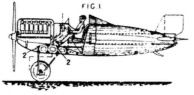

148,891. Junkers, H.
Aeroplanes; planes, arrangement and construction of; propelling; cars and cabins; tanks, arrangement of. — A monoplane with self-supporting wings has the plane structure continuous over the full breadth of the machine, the engines, undercarriage, pilot's seat, &c. being connected directly to it, the fuselage serving only as an envelope. Fig. 1 shows a monoplane structure in which the wings are built up on booms 2, 2ᵃ extending right across the machine and stayed by members 3, 4, and 5. The engine is connected by members 7 . . 11 to the plane structure, and the pilot's seat 33 is connected to the plane structure by a plane 16 . . 21. The engine frame and the frame which supports the seat are connected as shown, and certain members such as 18 and 22 are formed as closed frames

March 22, 1918, [*Convention date*]. *Addition to* 148,890.

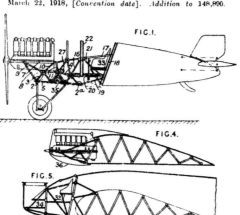

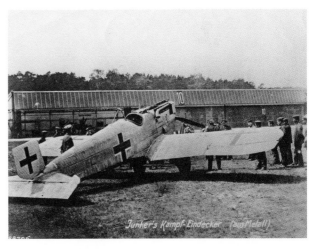

A D.I after the war is seen being inspected by Allied troops. (NARA)

Three patent drawings describing Junkers unique system of joining the wing at the root to the fuselage and how the engine/fuselage framing was tied into the wing; thus forming foundation for the cantilever.

A replica Oeffag D.III built by Craftlab. (Craftlab)

6
Albatros Flugzeugwerke

The Albatros company began with Dr E. Walther Huth (born in Altenburg in 1875), who followed family tradition by serving in the military for 13 years, finally leaving in 1908 to study biology. Like so many others during the first decade of the 20th century, Huth was fascinated by flight.

The fledgling compnay was co-founded by Otto Weiner with an initial capitalization of 25,000 marks. Huth purchased a Levasseur *Antoinette* singler-seater and Farman two-seater. Prescient in his view of military application of the airplane, he offered his planes to the War Ministry in 1909—their response was lukewarm due to ambivalence over the efficacy of the airplane in combat operations. The Wrights had made a similar offer free of charge, so Huth did the same, and offered his chauffeur Simon Brunnhuber as instructor. His intention was to ingratiate himself with those who could award military contracts should war break out. Chief of the General Staff General von Moltke recommended to the war minister that they train officers as pilots. By the end of 1909, von Moltke was well aware that the French were already buying numbers of planes, building their own, and training military pilots. Huth established his company—Albatros Flugzeugwerke GmbH—in December 1909. Negotiations with the Militärbehörde (Military Authority) lasted until March 1910, when they finally accepted Huth's proposal. At this juncture the German high command emphasized pilot training over aircraft production—as opinions varied as to preferred type, cost, and use. Flight instruction began that July at Albatros, and by March 1911 Brunnhuber had trained a half-dozen pilots. Albatros Werke GmbH had its head office in Johannisthal, Berlin. Its subsidiary, Ostdeutsche Albatros-Werke (OAW) was located in Schneidemuhl.

The General Inspectorate of Military Transportation maintained an outwardly impartial stance toward the various aircraft manufacturers. However, for reasons best known to themselves they favored the

Dr Walther Huth, born in Altenburg in 1875, was the founder of Albatros Werke GmbH. (Public domain)

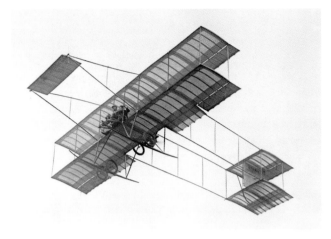

The Albatros MZ 2 was based on the Farman boxkite-type biplane. This was a difficult design to mass-produce due to the many struts and attendant rigging. They were also extremely fragile.

Albatros company. It would appear, like most things where human beings are involved, that politics or economics—or both—may have been the reason. This favoritism soured in 1911 when Otto Weiner, one of the directors of Albatros, urged Colonel Messing of IdFlieg not to deal with Arthur Mueller, owner of LVG, because he had allegedly persuaded Weiner that the army would rather deal with him than Albatros. Weiner maintained that Albatros had the exclusive right to sell to the army, and as such, with Weiner acting as broker, he offered LVG 750 marks for each aircraft sold. Weiner was seemingly a shrewd and unscrupulous businessman, as LVG had basically saved the Albatros company from financial ruin in 1911, after the army rejected their subsidy request. In order to keep LVG producing aircraft, they were forced to buy four aircraft from Albatros at a cost of 100,000 marks. However, the War Ministry sided with LVG in their claim of unfair dealing, and realizing that they could no longer believe that any of the companies were acting in the nation's best interest, mandated that awards of contracts would be contingent upon a given company's ability to mass-produce. It is important to understand the Clausewitzian desire by Germany, and the Allies, for the "decisive weapon." If the airplane could be produced in overwhelming numbers, it might prove to be the elusive "super weapon" that could turn the tide of a war.

Meanwhile, the fledgling Albatros "factory" built Farman-type designs termed Albatros MZ 2. Realizing that the labor-intensive, tedious nature of these early and fragile "stick-style" aircraft was not sustainable, Huth searched for a better, cost-effective and efficacious way to build an airframe. The answer came in the form of the civil engineers Robert Thelen and Helmut Hirth.

Thelen joined the Albatros team in 1912 as chief designer after working for Wright GmbH as a flight instructor. Hirth advocated for the semi-monocoque wooden fuselage designs of senior engineer Hugo Grohmann. Thelen

Robert Thelen's ID card (#2470) for the Johannisthal factory, and (right) Helmuth Hirth. (Public domain)

collaborated with Hirth to produce semi-monocoque fuselages that were a hybridization of Thelen, Hirth, and Grohmann. His first foray into this new construction type was a variation of the Etrich *Taube*—a type Huth favored due to its resemblance to his beloved birds. It was during this period that Albatros made their first foray into semi-monocoque construction, realizing early that if they could master the difficulties of making plywood conform to compound curves in a production context, they might be able to simplify their construction methodology (all wood instead of wood, wire, and hardware characteristic of box-girder construction).

Also in 1912 Rudolf Wiener, Otto's brother, was placed in charge of a new Vienna subsidiary, Oesterreichische-Albatros Werke (OAW). *Flight* magazine reported that during the 1913 Lake Constance race, the Albatros *Taube* had a fuselage of "particularly good streamlining form having no sharp angles in its outline." This aircraft would appear to be the result of the Thelen, Hirth and Grohmann collaboration in semi-monocoque construction. In the photo of the double-wide-cockpit *Taube* built in 1913, Kolomon Mayrhofer stated that the company had some help from a coachmaker in Bremen to build this, which raises an interesting question: did Albatros utilize craftsmen outside of the company to inform the construction and production protocols necessary to produce these aircraft in a timely and cost-effective fashion? In any event, Albatros shelved this construction process during its production of the B series reconnaissance planes; perhaps the techniques and all-important "shortcuts" were not yet in place to produce fully streamlined fuselages efficiently.

Albatros designers Thelen, Grohmann, and perhaps Heinkel abandoned the Farman boxkite-type airframes as it was clear that this direction was a dead end. The *Taubes*, although much sleeker and aerodynamically sound, were slow and sluggish. Thelen and his team next designed an enclosed fuselage-type reconnaissance plane which was more rugged and easier to build, and to maintain parity with other aircraft manufacturers such as Aviatik and LVG.

The Albatros Type DD-1, later known as the B.I, was designed in early 1913 by Thelen and perhaps something was contributed by Grohmann and Ernst Heinkel. Thelen referred to the type as "Albatros DD, system Heinkel-Thelen." Powered by a 100Ps Mercedes D.I engine, the semi-monocoque three-bay DD was a successful design that set several world records for duration and altitude in the months prior to World War I. *Flight* magazine of April 4, 1914 described the Albatros B.I (as well as Thelen's demonstration flight) in England:

> Among the many interesting features the construction of the fuselage is worthy of notice, for it is built up without the use of the ordinary diagonal cross bracing, the necessary rigidity being obtained by the covering, which is of three-ply wood. According to calculations carried out by the Albatroswerke and corrected by Deutsche Versuchsanstalt fur luftfahrt, the factor of safety of the fuselage of the Albatros biplane is about 60, and the bending resistance of this type of fuselage is 2.5 times greater than that of a diagonally wired fuselage of the same outside dimensions and having members of the size usually employed in structures of this type. The Versuchsanstalt also states that the Albatroswerke are justified in concluding that the bending resistance of the veneer type of fuselage is greater than that of a cross wired fuselage of the same weight.

Thelen and his team most likely conducted their own stress/weight tests on the new type of fuselage before abandoning the tried and tested wire bracing of the standard box-girder construction. They must have been delighted not only in the savings in time from the new ply-over-solid stock framing, but to have it actually prove stronger must have been an exciting moment in the history of aircraft design and construction. The description of the fuselage continues:

> There are six longerons of ash, one in each corner of the rectangular section fuselage and one about half-way up each side. The struts are also of ash, and occur at frequent intervals along the whole length of the fuselage. The three-ply covering is tacked to struts and longerons. From the nose up to a point in

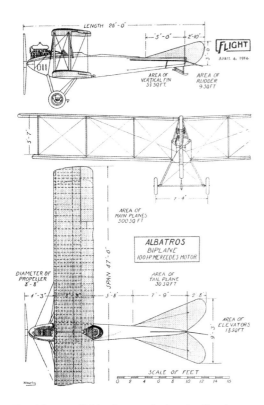

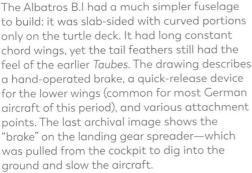

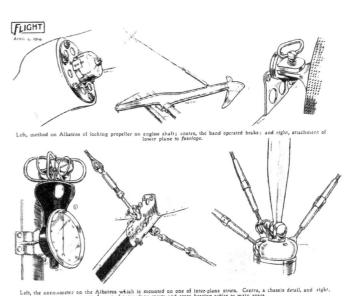

Left, method on Albatros of locking propeller on engine shaft; centre, the hand operated brake; and right, attachment of lower plane to fuselage.

Left, the anemometer on the Albatros which is mounted on one of inter-plane struts. Centre, a chassis detail, and right, attachment of inter-plane struts and cross bracing cables to main spars.

The Albatros B.I had a much simpler fuselage to build: it was slab-sided with curved portions only on the turtle deck. It had long constant chord wings, yet the tail feathers still had the feel of the earlier *Taubes*. The drawing describes a hand-operated brake, a quick-release device for the lower wings (common for most German aircraft of this period), and various attachment points. The last archival image shows the "brake" on the landing gear spreader—which was pulled from the cockpit to dig into the ground and slow the aircraft.

front of the tail fin the deck of the fuselage is given a streamline form by means of a curved turtleback, whilst the under surface is flat.

Thelen likely surmised that the factory could save time and money by building a standard longeron and strut box-girder fuselage with face-nailed plywood which required no tedious and time-consuming rigging. Building it this way would also keep all the struts/longerons in alignment due to the planar nature of plywood. From factory images of the construction of the B.Is, it would appear as though the skeletons were built on jigs, then moved to another area to be sheathed in plywood. This was most likely the beginning of the jig structures that would become crucial to building the D series of fighters, which was well documented in the film on the Albatros factory. The wings are described as such and contain some noteworthy features:

The main planes … have the two main spars comparatively close together, the rear spar occurring about half way along the chord. The rear portion of the wing therefore possesses a considerable amount of flexibility, further increased by having the extreme rear part of the wing single surfaced for a distance of about a foot from the trailing edge. This … provides a form of progressive springing of the trailing edge, to which the machine no doubt owes a considerable amount of its lateral stability. Ailerons are fitted to both upper and lower planes, and the crank levers for operating these are not set at right angles to the planes, as it is usually done, but lie parallel to the planes and work in slots cut in the upper plane. From the end of these crank-levers cables pass round pulleys in the lower plane, and thence to the control wheel. The ailerons on the lower plane are set at a slightly negative angle of incidence, thus probably further enhancing the lateral stability.

The flexible trailing edge would seem to be the inspiration for the later Berg D.I which also had a similar type of "shock absorber" built into the structure of the wings. Also, the method by which the ailerons were actuated survived throughout the D series of fighters. The last sentence describes "washout" as imparted to the lower wing by means of negative incidence. Albatros would incorporate built-in washout in the wing structure of its later aircraft. As an interesting historical footnote, the article concluded with the note that Albatros intended to establish a factory in England—this being only April 1914, the idea of an impending war must have seemed very distant indeed.

On April 9, 1914, the Albatros Militär Fliegerschule GmbH (Albatros Military Flying School Ltd.) was established at Schneidmühl. Like all the other aircraft companies in the years immediately preceeding the Great War, flying schools were seen as baseline income to provide a steady cashflow, as large orders for aircraft were yet to materialize from the German authorities.

After the outbreak of war and once the stasis of trench warfare had been accepted, reconnaissance aircraft such as the B.I and B.II and eventually C series were finally deemed necessary to transit the rough terrain of no man's land as well as surrounding areas that were impossible to navigate from the ground. Fighter aircraft were developed to protect the reconnaissance aircraft and dogfighting grew from have opposing fighters in the same airspace.

As discussed in Chapter 5, the Fokker Eindecker dominated the German fighter type from late 1915 to June 1916. When Immelmann perished faith in the Eindecker began to wane. Occurring simultaneously was the ascension of the newer Allied planes: the DH.2 pusher and the Nieuport 11 scout, that latter being superior to the E.III and E.IV. Oswald Boelcke wrote that "In a climb, [the E.IV] loses speed to such an extent that Nieuport biplanes have repeatedly escaped me." The superiority of the Nieuports compelled German command to decide that biplanes were the future—the emergenece of the Halberstadt D.II galvanized this view. June 1916 was also the month that Albatros, which was doing well producing its two-seater reconnaissance aircraft (B and C series), was awarded a contract for 12 single-seater biplane fighters.

According to Ray L. Rimel, the Albatros D.I (L.15) was built in 13 days, or at least in a very short time, and after tests at IdFlieg it was approved by the Zentral Abnahme Kommission (Central Certification Commission) as fit for military service.

If it was indeed built in this short span of time, it would verify that by this time Albatros had potentially engineered the best way to make a semi-monocoque fuselage—meaning one that could be built quickly, efficiently, and thus could turn a profit. Clues to some of this process exist in the aforementioned film on the Albatros factory, as well as in still photos.

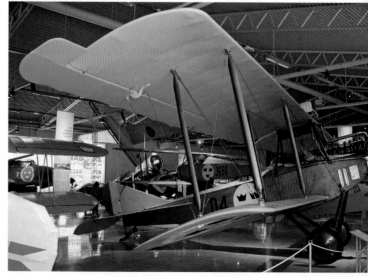

The B.II followed the B.I and differed principally in the amount of interplane struts—going from six pairs in the B.I to four pairs in the B.II. The color image is of the B.II in the permanent collection of the Swedish Air Force Museum. There is also an example at the Polish Air Museum in Krakow. (Public domain)

In Profile:
Alb D.III

Albatros D.III (2182/16)
Oblt. Rudolf Berthold, Jagdstaffel 14; Marchais;
France; March 1917.

In Profile:
Alb D.Va

Albatros D.Va (5787/17)
Jagdstaffel 76b; Habsheim, Germany; Early 1918.

In addition, the superb craftsmanship of Kolomon Mayrhofer of Craftlab lends insight into the construction process. The following images are of Mayrhofer's replicas of D.III airframes but the construction of the D.I would have been similar. It would appear that the plywood formers were shaped to their precise contour, including lightening holes on the bench. All finish sanding and shaping was done at this time as it would be inefficient to do this after assembly.

Next, the finished formers were inserted into the building jig and either clamped or screwed temporarily but securely. Next longerons were inserted into the various notches in the formers; sighting of the various longerons would establish whether the fuselage was truly aligned. The longerons could at this time be beveled to conform to the angle of the intersecting former; then the entire longeron would be faired to form a smooth curve.

Returning to the streamlining of their earlier *Taubes*, the D.I featured a semi-moncoque fuselage, constant chord wings with blunt tips, two LMG 08/15 machine guns, and a Mercedes D.II engine. It was the direction that would occupy Albatros for the rest of the war. (NARA, *Flight*)

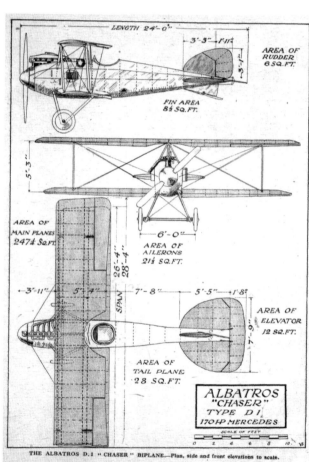

THE ALBATROS D.1 " CHASER " BIPLANE.—Plan, side and front elevations to scale.

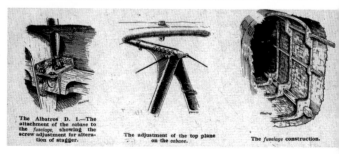

The Albatros D. 1.—The attachment of the *cabane* to the *fuselage*, showing the screw adjustment for alteration of stagger.

The adjustment of the top plane on the *cabane*.

The *fuselage* construction.

Former beveling could have occurred at this time, using the run of the longerons to inform the proper bevel on the edges of the formers.

While this work was being done, simultaneously, another group of workers could have prepared the four main panels (port and starboard sides, bottom and top turtledeck) which were scarfed together from smaller panels off the endoskeleton.

The position of the scarfs on extant D.Vas confirm that these scarf joints did not align with the formers.

Smaller subassemblies like the tail feathers would have been executed first, as the scarfs all needed to run "downhill," moving from nose to tail relative to the airflow over the fuselage; to have the scarfs running in the opposite direction would invite airflow to "lift" the scarfs. After the tail was skinned, the sheathing of the main portion of the fuselage could begin in earnest.

The skinning would have proceeded first with the curved turtle decks to stabilize the framing structure, working from tail to nose area. From period factory photos it appears as though the fuselages were next rotated so that either port or starboard side was facing up to facilitate sheathing.

Once the sheathing had been completed, the fuselages would have been able to be moved about having achieved structural stability/integrity.

Presumably wings and tail feathers were built in parallel with fuselages. These were of standard (non-cantilevered) construction, although the spars were hollow and sheathed with three-ply webs. It is logical to assume that the wing construction would have been standardized insofar as possible with jigs for spar alignment, rib fabrication, and spar construction.

After fuselage, wings, tail feathers, and struts were finished, the aircraft could be assembled, starting with the installation of the engine. After this was completed the wings were most assuredly also done on a jig to speed and aid alignment.

A very telling image—Albatros factory workers setting up formers in a jig. One worker has placed a spirit level on the aftermost former with the vertical fin former, while another is seemingly cutting a notch in a tab on another former to accept a stringer. A wing rib web is propped against the building jig in the foreground.

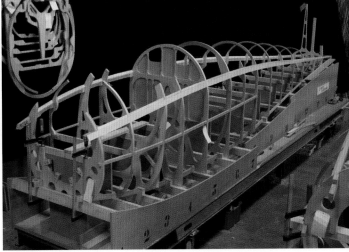

The building jig of Kolomon Mayrhofer's Albatros D series at Craftlab. Building the Albatros in a jig such as this insures the fuselage does not twist or distort during the sheathing process. (Greg VanWyngarden, Craftlab)

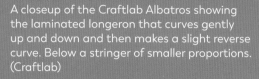

A closeup of the Craftlab Albatros showing the laminated longeron that curves gently up and down and then makes a slight reverse curve. Below a stringer of smaller proportions. (Craftlab)

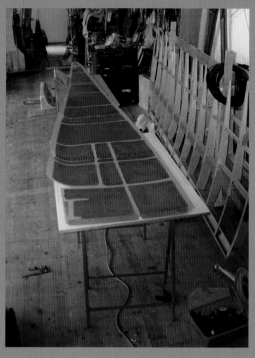

The plywood turtle deck sheathing has been scarfed on the bench, and has a slight curve imparted to it. This is consistent with findings of actual Albatros aircraft (e.g. *Stropp* at NASM) where the scarf joints do not land on the formers. In the next image, this plywood panel has been assembled using butt joints and ply backing plates that are riveted, a characteristic of OAW Albatroses. Note that the areas of ply between the glue joints have been prefinished. (Craftlab)

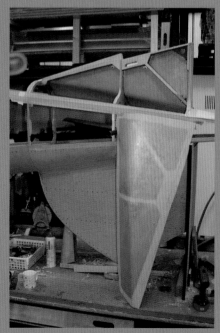

The ply sheathing for the tailskid fin has been prefinished around the gluing areas and is ready for installation. A closeup of the vertical fin for an OAW Albatros, which can be identified by the riveted backer-plates. (Craftlab)

The vertical fin was already built into the fuselage as was the alignment for the horizontal stabilizer. The elevators and rudder were made from welded steel tubing. The precise order of installation of sheet-metalwork is unknown, but likely it would have been done toward the end of the process unless it was easier to do it earlier.

Returning to a general description of the design path of the D series, the D.I combined the streamlined fuselages of the early Albatros *Taubes* with the slab sides of the B.I and B.II reconnaissance planes, resulting in a pleasing fuselage that was apparently cost-effective to build, rugged, and needed no internal wire bracing of any kind—which represented a significant savings in labor and material costs.

Thus the company would have largely needed skilled woodworkers to build the bulk of their airframes, thus streamlining production from a material, tool, and labor standpoint. The system they settled on for the D.I was most likely used through the D.Vas.

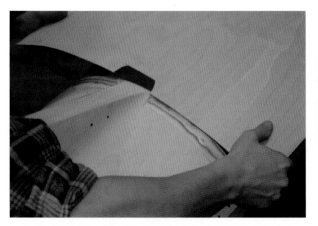

The turtle deck sheathing is installed moving from aft to forward—not the reverse as the feather edge of the scarf could "catch" the edges of the scarf and could cause lifting. (Craftlab)

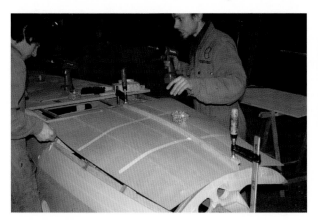
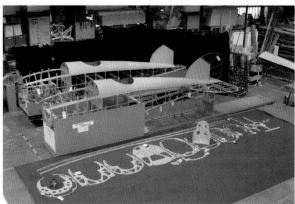

The panel on the underside of the nose just aft of the propeller requires several narrow "gores" to achieve the compound curve. It appears as if these strips are tapered at either end, thus imparting a curve to the finished structure—much the way staves of a barrel perform the same function. Once the turtle deck and all longerons and stringers are installed, the fuselage form can be removed from the building jig to facilitate finishing of the sheathing. (Craftlab)

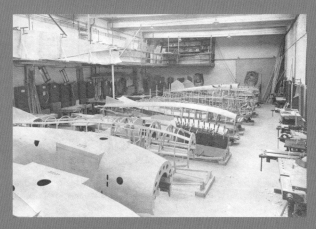

An archival image of the Oeffag factory showing D-type fuselages in various stages of completion; some are upside down, others are on their sides and right side up. The veneers are stored on the mezzanine level of this room, and some appear to be precurved. Benches and tool cabinets line the walls on either side. In this image the Craftlab Albatros replica receives a side panel; band clamps and battens help snug down the panel on the endoskeleton below. (Craftlab)

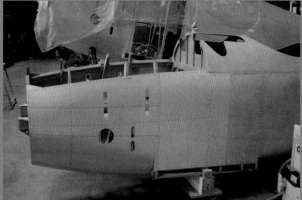

The side panel has been trimmed, glued and nailed to the formers; there is one panel remaining up forward. In the closeup of the engine area, the sheathing has been neatly glued and fastened to the formers, and apertures cut for the various vents and access plates. (Craftlab)

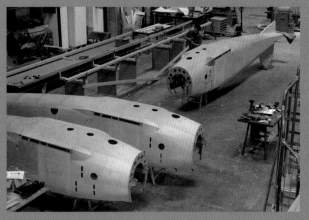

Finished D series fuselages at Craftlab. Note the wing spar jig in the background to facilitate alignment and spacing of the wing spars. There were two types of wing root fairings: one of plywood and the other of formed aluminum, with both pictured here. An archival photo showing the fuselages and wing panels at Oeffag. Note the wings are doped linen with the balkenkreuz painted in black. (Craftlab)

The following is a description of D.I/391 No. 2944 built in 1916, from *Flight* magazine June 28, 1917:

Built up entirely of wood without any wire bracing—and the arrangement of the planes … contrary to Hun practice, have neither sweep-back nor dihedral—the top plane, in fact, being one complete unit. The wing curve [airfoil] is similar to the Albatros "C. Ill," but having a flatter camber, whilst the angle of incidence varies from 3° at the centre to 2° at the left- and right-hand wingtips respectively.

A somewhat novel feature consists of the method of adjusting the stagger of the top plane from 0 to 12 cm, by moving it along the top of the cabane. This is effected in the following manner: In each end of the top horizontal tube of the cabane 638 formed a slot, which receives an eyebolt passing of which—according to the Y-adjustment required—through the main spar of the plane. At each slot are receives the bolt that locks the eyebolt in the cabane – five holes passing horizontally through the tube …

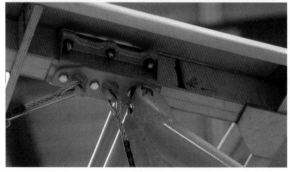

The wing structure of the D.III showing the plywood (and solid stock) lower spar, the rib webs, strut attachments, and enclosed sheaves that house the aileron control cables. Note how the rib flanges taper in width aft of the spar. (Craftlab)

This is an interesting and not to be repeated feature of Albatros D series fighters: that the amount of stagger between the wings could be adjusted, presumably to alter stall characteristics or increase visibility depending on the height/size of the pilot. The streamlined steel tube interplane struts were attached (bayonet socket joint) such that they could be adjusted accordingly. The article continues by describing the wings:

As in other Albatros machines the main spars are located well forward, the front one being some 4 ins. from the leading edge, and spaced 2 ft. 7 ins. from the rear one. They are of the usual Albatros rectangular section, fabric bound, and are bevelled off on the top at the extremities. The ribs … are spaced 16.5 in. [on center]. As on other Albatros machines, the ailerons are given a washout at the tips, and have operating cranks working in slots in the plane. They are hinged on auxiliary spars on the top plane only. The span of the top plane is 28 ft. 4 ins. And that of the lower 26 ft. 9 ins., the chord of both

Finished Oeffag D.III airframes by Craftlab; they look fabulous and display a wealth of information. (Craftlab)

The Albatros aircraft all had welded steel rudders, elevators, and ailerons. (Craftlab)

being 5 ft. 9 in., and the gap 5 ft. 3 ins. The total supporting surface is 269 sq. ft.

The horizontal stabilizer was of semi-elliptical in plan form, was of symmetrical airfoil and 5 inches at its thickest point and was cantilevered and set at 0 incidence; it had no struts or wires which were typical of other aircraft. The single elevator was welded steel as was the rudder.

The tail of the D.I had some unique features, namely the framing for the vertical fin was integrated into an aftermost former perfectly plumb—which represented a significant time savings when one eliminated the need for men to carefully align these surfaces as separate components. The article describes the fuselage composition as such:

> In section it varies from circular at the nose, to a horizontal knife-edge at the rear—being flat-sided, with rounded top and bottom in the center. It is built up of six longerons, three a side, the central ones being of small rectangular section spruce (3/4 x 5/16 in. aft of cockpit, forward of which they are 3/4 x 3/4 in. in L section). The top and middle longerons are placed one above the other, but the bottom ones are closer together. Top and bottom members are, except at certain points, of L-section, and up to the cockpit are of spruce, forward of which ash, 1 3/16 and 1 9/16" employed.

Another noteworthy modification was the transition from spruce to ash longerons: spruce where some strength was needed, ash where the most strength was needed; around the cabanes and engine. The article

The formed cowling and nose area have been painted gray-green and attached to a finished German D.III replica by Craftlab. A view looking forward showing the various metal inspection plates on the tail. (Craftlab)

continues by describing the bulkheads or ply formers that comprise the "endoskeleton" of the D.I, which was built one after another thanks to the building jigs seen in photos and film. Over the skeleton a sheathing of three-ply plywood was fitted, made up in scarfed sheets off the framework then applied by means of glue, nails, and screws. Thus the fuselage could be sheathed in four large pieces (two sides, turtle deck aft of cockpit, and bottom) and various stouter and smaller pieces around the engine area. As with Fokker, the seat was adjustable and mounted on two transverse tubes mounted to short longerons on the side of the cockpit. The engine, described as a 170-hp Mercedes straight-six engine, was cooled using the Windhoff "ear-type" radiators mounted on either side of the fuselage; which was at this time a departure from the cumbersome radiators used on the Albatros B and C series.

One characteristic of the D.I that is compelling is the notation that the "control lever is of the Fokker type, operating the ailerons and the elevator. It consists of a 1 3/16-in. tube mounted on a 1 9/16-in. transverse tube supported on a wooden base. A locking device is fitted whereby the lever may be locked against a fore-and-aft movement enabling the pilot to remove his hands, but operate the ailerons with his knees." This suggests that Fokker may have been supplying other aircraft companies with prefabricated parts such as the control stick, as this type of stick is seen on Albatros, Junkers, as well as Fokker aircraft. Perhaps this was an effort by IdFlieg at cooperation among aircraft manufacturers in the interest of speeding up production and, by extension, winning the war. (Moreover, Albatros's master of works Hedtke had developed a synchronizing gear but IdFlieg mandated in October 1916 that the Fokker synchronizer be tested on the D series; Albatros rejected it on the grounds that it was "prone to malfunction" and as such a reduced rate of fire.)

Static load tests were done June 7–9, 1916, which resulted in the wing depth being redesigned to make them equal and to facilitate better production, and the elevators were balanced to lighten the stick's pitch control. On November 10, 1916, use of Windhoff radiators was banned from frontline units (when punctured they sprayed scalding water in the pilot's face).

The Albatros D.II was built almost simultaneously as the D.I. Its upper wing was lowered by 30 cm to improve pilot visibility, a Teves and Braun radiator replaced the Windhoff, and new cabane struts replaced the inverted V structure which improved visibility forward.

IdFlieg ordered 100 D.Is in August 1916. Both D.Is and D. IIs were manufactured in parallel, which would have presented no problem except that another 100 D.Is were ordered in September 1916, causing Albatros to subcontract 75 out to LVG to produce under license. A total of 50 D.Is and 275 D.IIs were built at all factories. As with other German companies, IdFlieg mandated that Albatros incorporated the best aspects of the Nieuport 17 in some form. Using the D.II as a baseline for development, the D.III was developed by Thelen, Schubert, and Gnadig. The upper wing had what would become the characteristic trapezoidal shape, and the lower wing was of narrower chord like the Nieuports. It too had a V strut and single spar; thus in copying the Nieuport, Albatros also copied its fatal flaw.

The D.III underwent tests in September in parallel to the D.I and D.II; the D.IIIs were successful enough such that IdFlieg ordered 400 of them, the largest order of the war. Along with this order was the suggestion to use strips of ply due to shortages of same. Five planes were ordered for testing, but the results were unsatisfactory

Archival images of the D.II captured by the Allies and repainted with cockades and a tricolor rudder. Note the slight puckering of the slab-sided portion of the fuselage; perhaps this was the reason for the fully curved (oval in section) fuselages of the D.V and D.Va. (NARA)

as the strip-molded fuselages (like Pfalz and Roland) had less strength and the weight was about the same—the idea was abandoned. They were also built at Oeffag at Wiener Neustadt. The Oeffag D.IIIs had some important differences such as no spinners, more rounded rudders, and Schwarzlose machine guns. Also, and importantly, Oeffag corrected the weaker single spar by increasing its proportions and using thicker ribs. This largely solved the lower wing flutter found in the German D.IIIs.

In February and March 1917 two more contracts of 50 planes each were placed at which time the radiator was shifted four meters to port from the centerline, thus sparing the pilot a scalding shower if punctured; the undercarriage was strengthened as well. Since Albatros was again at capacity due to production of fighters and reconnaissance aircraft, in the spring of 1917 the order was given to OAW in Schneidemuhl (present-day Pila). On January 24, 1917, Manfred von Richthofen noticed a crack in the lower wing of his D.III; that same day two other pilots perished due to lower wing flutter and failure in their D.IIIs. Lower wing failure was less common in D.IIIs manufactured at OAW (according to British sources).

"*Vera*" was a captured Albatros D.III and shows the influence of the Nieuport fighters. (NARA)

In March 1917 IdFlieg ordered a lighter version of the D.III from Albatros which resulted in the D.IV. This plane's fuselage was oval in section; perhaps the designers realized that with a compound curve (plywood under tension and compression) the structural integrity of a given area was increased, whereas the flat panels on the sides of the D.III were prone to puckering—this is apparent in many period photos of the D.III. This could have resulted in lighter scantlings (proportions) for interior formers and stringers/longerons. The D.IV was produced with a geared Mercedes 160 hp but it vibrated excessively such that it was discontinued.

The Albatros D.V had the same fuselage as the D.IV but retained the semi-sesquiplane design of the D.III wings. Aileron control cables were routed through the upper wing. The D.V reverted to the standard Mercedes 160-hp non-geared engine. The D.V was 50 kg lighter than the D.III but its performance was only marginally better. In June 1917 the D.V went into production with a huge order totaling 900 aircraft at the Johannisthal plant.

Werner Voss tightening his flying cap before climbing into his D.III. (NARA)

Fantastic flying shots of the Craftlab Oeffag Albatros D.III. (Craftlab)

Albatros D.Vs being built. Note the cradle in which is sits while landing gear is attached, and the pilot head fairing aft of the cockpit. (Greg VanWyngarden)

The first D.Vs reached Jastas during June 1917 and met with some initial setbacks. The new, weaker ferrule that joined the lower wing to the fuselage changed the center of pressure–spar axis arrangement, leading to lower wings tearing away, mostly when recovering from a dive.

The D.III also suffered from this but not that often. Installation of a short strut tangent to the leading edge and about a fifth of the way up the forward V strut helped eliminate flutter, as now the wing could not pivot readily on the single attachment point on the lower wing single spar.

Ernst Udet described how "When I was beginning a steep dive I looked at the lower wing and when I noticed it had started to flatter [sic] I knew it was time to recover or I would lose my wings."

According to German records, Germany lost more Albatros D.Vs due to accidents than combat-related destruction. However, due to the ailerons being routed through the upper wing, if both lower wings were lost,

A dark-colored D.V is being pushed out to the flightline. (NARA)

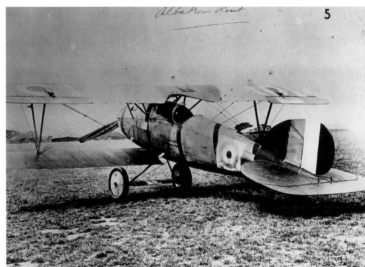

A captured D.V showing the aileron cables feeding into the top wing; a hallmark of the D.V. (NARA)

the newly formed "parasol" could still be landed with one wing. Another flaw of the D.V was the fairing behind the pilot's head that impaired visibility.

The results of these modifications resulted in the D.Va which reverted to the aileron cables being routed through the lower wing, and strengthening of the wings.

An archival image of the D.Va—easily recognizable due to the aileron cables exiting the lower wing to meet the ailerons from below. Also note the short metal strut extending from the lower portion of the forward V strut to the leading edge of the wing, done to reduce wing flutter in a dive. (NARA)

Two images of the D.Va reproduction at the Old Rhinebeck Aerodrome, New York. (Author)

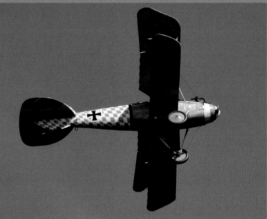

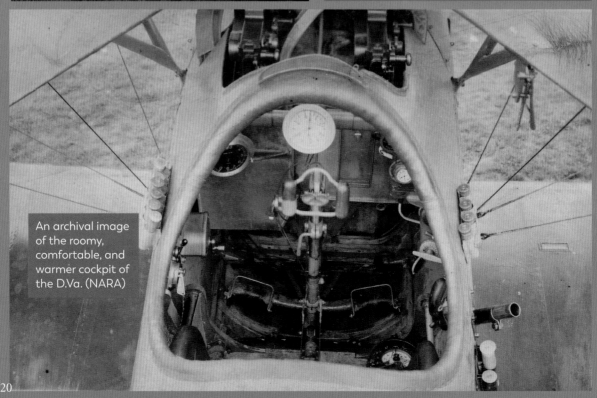

An archival image of the roomy, comfortable, and warmer cockpit of the D.Va. (NARA)

Phonix

Phonix Fluegzeugwerke was created as a surreptitious way of buying Öesterreichisch-Ungarische Albatros (Oest-Ung), a subsidiary of Albatros Johannisthal. This was just another one of the companies that Camillo Castiglioni was intent on obtaining to expand his growing share in the Austrian aircraft industry. Castiglioni was an affluent and powerful financier (some say profiteer) during World War I, and was one of the first to invest in series production of aircraft; thinking that if ordered into quantity production, there would likely be more orders—thus garnering more profits. In 1914 he purchased Hanas Brandenburgische Flugzeugwerke, Ungarische Luftschiff, and Flugmaschinen AG (UFAG), and invested in both Lohner and Aviatik. He also acquired a majority of stock in Austro-Daimler. Speculation over his hegemony relative to the Austrian aircraft market caused concern at the Luftfahrtruppen (Imperial and Royal Aviation Troops, i.e. the air force). In order to obtain the Albatross company, Castiglioni and Prinz August Lobkowitz created the Phonix company. The company then very quietly acquired the majority of shares, thus taking control of Oest-Ung and all their contracts. In order to keep the name of the company Oest-Ung was tasked with design and testing of all prototype aircraft and made part of a subsidiary company to Phonix. The new company searched out the best designers and engineers and found Leo Kirste who had worked for the French Breguet company in London after earning a degree in aero engineering in Paris. He then joined Rumpler in Berlin before being headhunted by Phonix. He was hired and made head of the design department. In May 1916 he was joined by Edmund Sparmann who was assigned to the company by the military to oversee aircraft manufacture. He was a test pilot and builder. He designed the "Sparmann Wing" which was used on some Phonix aircraft. Castiglioni's wartime assets and influence collapsed when the war ended.

A Phonix D.II. Note the strange aft turtle deck that afforded some directional stability due to its shape. (Greg VanWyngarden)

A Pfalz E. II which featured wing-warping, a rotary engine, and a synchronized machine gun that fired between the propeller blades. (Greg VanWyngarden)

7

LFG Roland and Pfalz Flugzeugwerke

LFG Roland

LFG was formed on April 30, 1908 from assets of an experimental airship engine company (Motorluftschiffstudiengesellschaft) and funding from Gustav Krupp and AEG. The company's first project was, not surprisingly, an airship built on the von Parseval design which entered service in 1910. The company had offices in Berlin and a factory in Adlershof near the Flugmaschine Wright GmbH which was established in June 1909 and had acquired the Wright patents (filed in Germany), as well as the exclusive right to manufacture

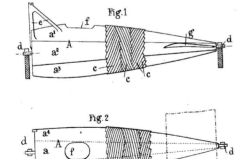

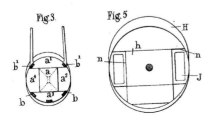

An illustration from the Deperdussin patent dated August 4, 1914 showing the double diagonal strip planking that was used on the Deperdussin 1912 racer, and may have influenced Roland and, by extension, Pfalz construction methodology. (Public domain)

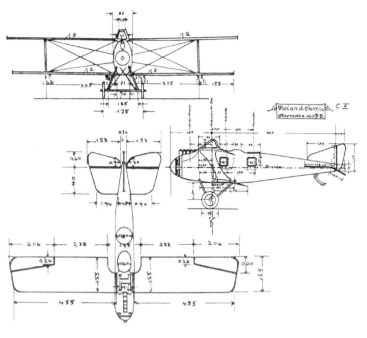

A drawing of the Roland C.II "*Walfisch*" (whale) that featured semi-moncoque construction.

Wright airplanes in Germany, as well as sales rights for Sweden, Norway, Denmark, Luxemburg, and Turkey. The company was not well run, lost money, and was slow to pay the Wrights which resulted in a lawsuit. Flugmaschine Wright Gesellschaft was then forced to liquidate, selling its assets to LFG. In 1912, using existing as well as the Wright equipment, a new aviation department was formed by LFG to construct aircraft primarily of steel tubing. This could have been the influence of Gustav Krupp, who, in addition to bailing out the company, was one of Germany's premier steel industrialists. It was thought that these aircraft would be well suited to Germany's African colonies. Africa was also an ideal testing ground for an untried weapon. Pfalz and Aviatik sent aircraft there as well as LFG, who produced a *stahldoppeldecker* (all steel-framed biplane) to be sent to southern Africa. To avoid confusion with other aircraft manufacturers, especially LVG, the trademark Roland was adopted for all LFG aircraft. The famous statue of Roland in Bremen was chosen as a symbol of strength and reliability.

Pilot Lieutenant von Scheele was the first to arrive in the city of Swakopmund on the coast of South West Africa (now Namibia), in May 1914. He was accompanied by four aircraft mechanics. His plane, an Aviatik B.I, arrived two weeks later. The Roland-Stahldoppeldecker (Roland *Taube*) arrived in late June. The steel framing of the Roland plane was thought ideal for service in the tropics; the pilot was Second Lieutenant (res) Fiedler. The assembly of the Roland aircraft took a long time. Technical problems plagued the tests and in late June the aircraft crashed, possibly due to its low rate of climb. Fiedler was slightly injured and the aircraft was badly damaged. During that time, two German planes arrived in Duala, Cameroon, but unfortunately the pilots and mechanics were still held up in Germany. Thus, when war was declared shortly afterward, the planned air operations had to be cancelled.

A C.II "Whalemouth"— note curtains in the windows. (Greg VanWyngarden)

In early 1915 LFG Roland was awarded military contracts to build Albatros B.II (Rol) and C.II (Rol) two-seaters under license. After building a number of these, Roland engineers, for reasons best known to themselves, began to revisit the idea of cold-molding a fuselage—as was done with some of the *Taubes*, and of course, the Deperdussin racer of 1912 for which a patent had been filed in 1913, that described the double diagonal planking of the fuselage as such: "The construction of the fuselage is effected upon a mold or former 'a' composed of several parts with a view to allowing removal when the fuselage is finished." To translate this, each piece of the mold could be withdrawn one at a time thus reducing the amount of strain on the finished fuselage, as the surface contact between mold and finished skin is less. The patent continued: "In the example represented, this former is composed of a central part 'a' of pyramidal shape upon which are fixed by suitable means cheeks a^1, a^2, a^3, and a^4. These cheeks are provided with grooves b^1 to allow accommodating the ribs b of the fuselage upon which are to be nailed the wooden slats 'c' which form the fuselage body.

The former is mounted preferably upon trunions 'd' which allow revolving it around its axis during construction of the fuselage." So it would seem the "central pyramid" was withdrawn first, then the various formers, now free from this central "wedge" could be easily taken out in pieces. It would also seem that not only Roland, and by extension Pfalz, may have known of the content of the Deperdussin patent, but also Junkers—whose jig also rotated on a longitudinal axis, and could also be withdrawn (see Chapter 5).

For Roland, it was a production challenge: could this type of fuselage be cost-effectively built using available materials and manpower? The man responsible was engineer Kurt Tantzen (a student of Prandtl's) who was aided by senior engineer Cammerer, and engineer Richter. The result was a quantum leap in aircraft design. The fuselage was (presumably) built using thin strips of ply over a fixed mold (like Deperdussin or similar to the one Pfalz used which will be described presently). The next layer was laid at approximately 60° to the first and glued using hide or casein adhesive. When dry the shell was popped off the mold (or the mold was withdrawn) and fitted to ten lightweight ply formers/bulkheads and six spruce longerons. It was ovoid in section, and because of the streamlined shape and relatively high aspect (as the top wings sat atop the fuselage), it was nicknamed the "*Walfisch*" (whale).

The shape of the fuselage resulted from testing a 1:15 scale model in the wind-tunnel at Gottingen, the development of the final structure was the work of Richter. On October 7, 1915 a patent was granted for the C.II "*Walfisch*" design.

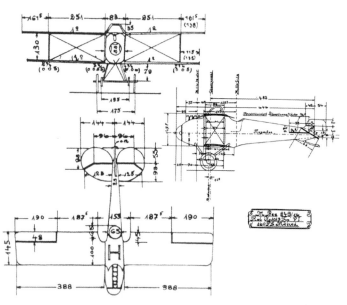

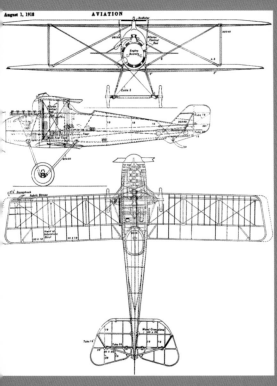

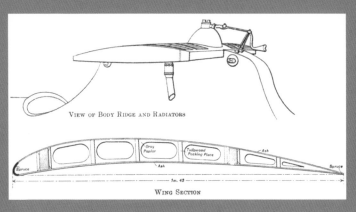

VIEW OF BODY RIDGE AND RADIATORS

WING SECTION

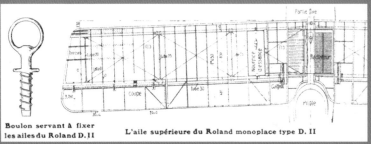

Boulon servant à fixer les ailes du Roland D. II

L'aile supérieure du Roland monoplace type D. II

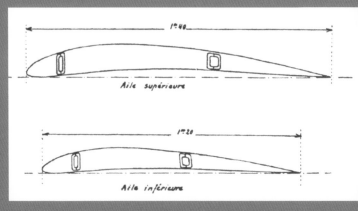

Aile supérieure

Aile inférieure

The D.II was an improvement over the D.I in that it had better visibility and functionality for the pilot. The attachment point for the top wing was pinched to allow the pilot better forward and downward visibility. The pilot sat deeper down in the fuselage which was also slimmer than the D.I The D.II featured hollow wing spars, and Nieuport-style bellcrank and torque tube aileron actuation. (Greg VanWyngarden)

The Roland D.III was similar to the D.II except it had stubby cabane struts that improved visibility better still. (Public domain)

The signature fighter for Roland: the D.VIa. This aircraft abandoned the smooth-skinned, laminated monocoque construction in favor of "lapstrake-"or "clinker-style" construction—much as small boats were built. It has been written that this was due to wood shortages such that a new system had to be developed. Note the "finger-jointed" strakes near the cockpit, alluding to the notion that long pieces of ply were not available. (Greg VanWyngarden)

A closeup of the cockpit of the D.VIa. Note the bellcranks inset in the upper wing that were ostensibly joined to torque tubes running through the wing, and also unusual is the tachometer mounted to the upper wing at the cutout. (Greg VanWyngarden)

This line drawing shows the method of planking overlap:the top edge of each strake was planed to a feather edge to facilitate a snug fit against the formers. (Flugsport)

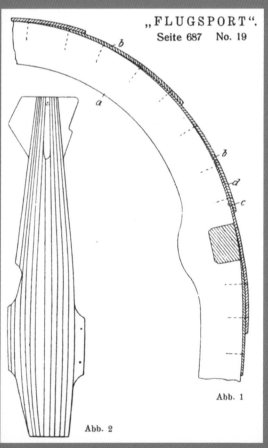

„FLUGSPORT".
Seite 687   No. 19

Abb. 1

Abb. 2

The cold-molded style of fuselage construction was termed *Wickelrumpf* (wrapped body). These fuselages were popular with aircrews as they withstood crashes better than standard box-girder construction. This method was introduced to Pfalz when they built the Roland D.I (Pfalz) under license.

The wings were of standard design using ply rib webs and spruce spars. Grosz claimed that the low-drag advantages of cantilever wing construction under investigation by Junkers, was virtually unknown. After testing, problems were found in its directional stability due to the thinness of its wings, which tended to distort after long flights.

Grosz also stated that the cold-molded fuselage was expensive to build and this is why more were not made. Perhaps an efficient method of doing this had not been fully realized yet, or perhaps the learning curve for factory employees took too long. In contrast, Pfalz was to use this method in both of their most successful fighters: the D.III and the D.XII, so presumably they (at least) had worked out a way to do this in a cost-effective and efficacious fashion. The exact number of LFG Roland C.II "*Walfisch*" that were built and supplied to the army is not known, but it is believed to be several hundred. The Linke-Hoffman company built a number of these under license.

An improved model of the C.II was built in 1916, powered by a 200-hp Benz Bz.IV engine. However, only one was built and was destroyed along with the factory by a "mysterious fire" on September 6, 1916, said to have been caused by the British secret service! The company then moved to Charlottenburg, where the company decided to build the D.I, a single-seater fighter. Looking like a slimmer version of the C.II, the D.I was powered by the 160-hp Mercedes D.III engine, giving it a top speed of 105 mph. It was named "*Haifisch*" (shark).

The D.II was built shortly thereafter, and was very similar with only minor differences. An article on the D.II appeared in *Flight* magazine in July 1918 that described the D.II fuselage as being built in two halves; thus we know that at least by this time that this was the method of construction being used. Over 300 of these were built, but the majority were constructed by Pfalz under license. Both aircraft were armed with twin fixed Spandau machine guns.

In October 1916, the D.III appeared as a replacement for the D.IIa. Unfortunately its emergence coincided with the superior Albatros fighters, so only a handful were built. Presumably at this time sheet plywood was becoming scarce (at least for Roland), which mandated a shift in production methodology.

One of the best fighters from LFG Roland that incorporated this new construction method was the D.VIa that featured a distinctive "clinker-built" or lapstrake construction, with strakes overlapping each other by two-thirds.

The D.VIa had a large horn-balanced rudder and balanced ailerons. It borrowed from the Albatros D series in the configuration of its cabanes, its tailskid, and Teves and Braun in-wing radiator offset to starboard in the upper wing – which had hollow spars and an interesting bellcrank to actuate the ailerons. It was powered by the Benz Bz.IIIa engine, giving it a top speed of 114 mph.

It featured an airy cabane structure that gave good visibility and the stub that had supported the D.II's top wing was flipped and positioned on the bottom of the D.VIa's fuselage to anchor the lower wing. The lapstrake or "clinker" method of building the fuselage is interesting indeed as it speaks to what would appear to be extreme shortages of medium to large sheets of plywood, as each strake is also "finger jointed" together which is a production form of scarf that makes many small segments into a long one. An example can be found today in production millwork for residential construction.

The lapstrake construction also signaled a different way of sheathing the fuselage, as the strakes had to be applied directly to the formers and nailed—just as clapboards are nailed to studs on a house, in strident contrast to the method of strip-planking over reusable molds as with the C.II, D.II and the aircraft built by Pfalz. This

The Roland D.VIb was similar to the D.VIa except that it had a Benz Bz.IIIa 200-hp engine. According to one flight report, the D.VIb handled in a similar fashion to the Fokker D.VII, although the Fokker was easier to build and had a more reliable engine. (Grey VanWyngarden)

would have required that each strake be planed to a feather edge to lie correctly under the successful planks, after which the finished strake could be applied to the already built endoskeleton of formers, longerons, and stringers. Presumably the delicate skeletal structure was held firmly in a jig while planking proceeded until structural integrity was achieved.

The D.VIb evolved from the D.VIa, and this version was similar to its predecessor but had a more powerful Benz Bz.IIIa 200-hp engine. A performance test of the D.VIb was performed in August 1920. The pilot's report by Louis P. Moriarty had the following to say:

> The flying qualities of this airplane are very similar to those of the Fokker D.VII. Its controls have about the same degree of effectiveness but operate more easily. Its maneuverability is well above that of the average single seater. The balance is normal, tail heavy with full engine and slightly nose heavy at slow speed with engine throttled. In a normal glide it will balance without the use of the controls. The lateral balance is good. The airplane takes off quickly with a very short run. It lands rather slowly without rolling very far, but has a tendency to ground spin. The rudder is not very effective in taxiing.

From a maintenance point of view the airplane is well designed. Engine parts which require attention are accessible, with the exception of the water pump, which is somewhat difficult to reach. In order to remove the gas tank, it might be necessary to take out the engine. The oil tank is easily removed. It is very difficult to keep the engine from overheating at low altitudes. Even in moderate weather it is impossible to fly with the upper engine cowling in place. In addition, there are no radiator shutters, making it difficult to keep the engine warm on glide.

So it would appear as if the D.VI was a good flying airplane but was subject to a few maintenance issues, and had an engine prone to overheating. The additional comments about this engine were "performance good

The notion that the D.VI was prone to breaking in half near the cockpit is supported by these two crash pictures. The thinness of the plywood is readily apparent. (Grey VanWyngarden)

but not exceptional. Not recommended as a service type." Final comments about the aircraft's visibility noted that it was "exceptionally good. The design is such that all the totally blind spots are eliminated except that below the lower wing. The pilot is perched high above this wing and his cockpit is designed to give him considerable freedom of movement, both of which factors tend to reduce the blind areas to a minimum."

The Polish Aviation Museum in Krakow has an original D.VIb fuselage in their permanent collection. Their description of their D.VIb states that it was outperformed by the Fokker D.VII which was easier to build and had a more reliable engine. They also note that on hard landings, the fuselage of the D.VI was prone to breaking in half behind the cockpit!

Most likely due to the thinness of the ply, insufficient substructure, and perhaps the finger-jointed stock, which, as indicated from archival images, was located around the cockpit in area. Moreover, unless the overlapping edges of the strakes were glued and sufficiently clamped, this joint could have cracked under extreme load, as there is no evidence of these joints being riveted—as one would see in the maritime version of this construction. In all, a total of 359 D.VIs were built by the war's conclusion.

Variations on the D.VI followed such as the D.VII which featured a 185-hp Benz Bz.IIIbo engine; the D.VIII with a geared-drive Benz Bz.IIIbm; the D.XIII which had a 190-hp Körting Kg.III water-cooled V-8 engine; and finally the D.XIV which had the 160-hp Goebel Goe 11-cylinder rotary engine. One of each of these variants was built, and all were largely unsuccessful due to perennial engine problems. The problems with the engine overheating mentioned in Moriarty's report were seemingly addressed without success in the subsequent models.

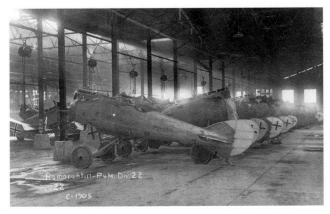
A group of Roland D.VIb fuselages are lined up like cordwood at Romorantin; also visible is a row of Fokker D.VIIs in the next bay. (NARA)

The Roland D.VII and D.XV. Both suffered from engine troubles, thus condemning them to obscurity.

In Profile:
Pfalz D.XII

Pfalz D.XII (2454/18)
Lt Fritz Kieckhafer, Jagdstaffel 32b; Gosselies,
Belgium; October 1918.

In Profile:
Rol D.VIa

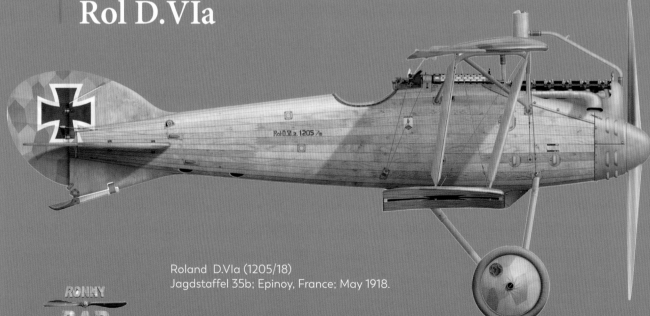

Roland D.VIa (1205/18)
Jagdstaffel 35b; Epinoy, France; May 1918.

RONNY
BAR
AIRCRAFT PROFILES

Pfalz Flugzeugwerke

Bavaria was second only to Prussia as the largest state in Germany. It had its own armed forces, including the air service Königlich Bayerischen Fliegertruppen (KBF) (Royal Bavarian Flier Battalion). The Bavarian government wanted its pilots to fly Bavarian planes, hence its interest, through subsidies, in having Bavarian cities promote and cultivate aircraft production—the city of Speyer was one such example. Alfred Eversbusch obtained a subsidy from the Bavarian government for an aircraft factory, and as a result tried to lease land at the newly established Speyer airfield in March 1913. In addition, the Bavarian Flying Service enlisted the help of financier Gustav Otto to help Pfalz hammer out a business plan. Eversbusch procured a draft contract for the lease, which outlined 2,000 square meters at 10 pfennigs each. In addition, the flying association's shed could be leased for 50 pfennigs a day, and the nearby festival hall could even be used free of charge. Alfred by this time had involved his brothers and a few investors, including Otto who also provided licensing rights for his pusher biplane.

On June 13, 1913, three brothers—Alfred, Ernst and Walter Eversbusch (leader)—founded an aircraft company in Speyr on the River Rhine. There is also reference to Ernst's brother-in-law Willy Sabersky-Müssigbrodt as also being involved at the company's inception. The capitalization was provided by Richard, Eugene, and August Kahn (unrelated). On July 12, 1913 it was entered in the commercial register at the Ludwigshafen county court, the entry reading: "The purpose of the company is to construct aircraft and train pilots as well as to exercise all operations which are suitable in furthering the company." Alfred Eversbusch and Richard Kahn were appointed managing directors; initial assets comprised 30,000 marks, a flying machine, an aircraft shed, an Opel aircraft engine and various tools and drawings. The flying machine was likely designed by the Eversbusch brothers in 1912/13. Alfred Eversbusch was a nominally trained pilot.

The start-up factory began preparing for licensed production as this was the quickest way for any newly formed company to get in the game. Moreover, Willy Sabersky-Müssigbrodt was the only one with technical training in aircraft, and realizing the amateurish nature of the fledgling company, left in 1914 to work as a design engineer for another company. After this setback, Alfred Eversbusch negotiated with Albatros in Berlin-Johannisthal for licensed production of their aircraft. However, the shrewd managers at Albatros would only grant a license in exchange for a piece of the company. Pfalz was desperate and drew up documents for Pfalz-Flugzeugwerke Licenz Albatros GmbH, but the deal was called off by Albatros on August 5, 1913, for reasons unknown. After a few legal skirmishes the cancellation was finalized in December 1913 and the company reverted to Pfalz-Flugzeugwerke GmbH.

A Pfalz-licensed Otto pusher biplane is pictured on an African expedition.

Pfalz-Flugzeugwerke immediately started manufacturing and repairing Otto pusher biplanes in the Speyer festival hall. The first aircraft designed by Pfalz was ordered by the Rudolf Hertzog company, a renowned clothing business in Berlin. After this first Pfalz aircraft was built, it was used to promote future orders at events. For example, as a publicity stunt the plane was flown cross-country and landed at Tübingen, on October 25, 1913, which was noted as the "first aircraft landing" in the town.

On February 6, 1914, the Speyer city council granted Pfalz's request for the purchase of 7,000 square meters on the corner of the old Lussheimer Strasse for a new aircraft factory, which after being built featured a large sign: "Pfalz-Flugzeugwerke Speyer am Rhein." To offset the cost of the new building, Pfalz immediately began producing Morane-Saulnier L and H aircraft under license.

The terms of the license were favorable, including a large deposit from MS to cover start-up costs. Walter went to Paris where he learned to fly at the MS flying school, and came back as the Pfalz company test pilot. The MS Pfalz copies were built simultaneously with the Otto pushers.

At the time of the outbreak of World War I, they had built three each of the Otto pusher, Pfalz A.I (MS L), and Pfalz E.I (MS H).

The two Pfalz aircraft were powered by Oberursel U.0 rotary engines (80 hp). Production increased after the war began. The Bavarian government was under the Kaiser's command in times of war, so the fighters produced by the factory were not only sent to Aviation Department combat units but also to pilot training schools. A total of 61 Pfalz aircraft were built with numbers from P.1 to P.61. A turning point occurred when Pfalz and other manufacturers were invited to a demonstartion of a synchronization gear by Fokker.

The gear was installed on a Fokker M.5 as discussed in Chapter 4, and was similar to the MS H and, by extension, the Pfalz E.I. The Fokker was slightly faster, maneuverable, and rugged. The synchronization gear was installed on the Pfalz E.I. The E.II had a larger engine, greater wingspan, a longer fuselage, and three sets of wires to induce wing-warping, whereas the E.I only had two—presumably this improved roll response. 130 E.IIs were built between September 1915 and February 1916. The Pfalz A.II (parasol) was identical to the Pfalz A.I, except it was powered by an Oberursel U.I engine. With the addition of a synchronized machine gun, the Pfalz E.III was born, which was similar in speed to the E.II but less maneuverable and with a reduced rate of climb.

A.Is and A.IIs serving in Flying Company 9b were fitted with bomb racks which held 10 4.5-kg Carbonit bombs, and were used on the Italian front (Tyrol) as part of the German aid package to the Austro-Hungarian monarchy. The Pfalz E.IV was fitted with an Oberursel U.III 160-hp engine, and had a longer fuselage to balance the heavier engine. It had two synchronized machine guns. The double-banked U.III caused cooling problems— as it had with the Fokker E.IV—and was only marginally better than the E.II. Only 46 were built, and only a handful saw action.

During 1915 and 1916 experimental A.I biplanes were built, inspired by the LVG B.I. The Pfalz E.V was a version of the E.IV with an inline Mercedes D.I engine; the performance was better than the rotary-powered planes, but due to the increased weight, only one gun was installed. The E.V passed the *Typenprufung* flight tests in July 1916. Fifty were ordered but by this time D-type fighters had entered the war, resulting in only three E.Vs being sent to the front. Pfalz built one more E type—the E.VI with an 80-hp engine and reduced roll rate, but these went to flying schools instead of the front. The E and A series used many captured Le Rhône 110 engines that were fitted at the front. They suffered from the combination of a larger engine without sufficient reinforcing of the original box-girder wood and wire fuselage.

In the spring of 1916 IdFlieg suggested that the main aircraft producers build biplanes with twin synchronized machine guns. The first to respond were Halberstadt, LFG Roland, Fokker, and Pfalz. By the

The Pfalz A.I (MS type L) and the Pfalz E.I (MS type H); the parasol design would eventually be discarded by the E.I series and led to a slew of variants, including the popular E.II (pictured) and E.III. (Greg VanWyngarden, Fokker Team Shorndorf)

summer of 1916 Pfalz began working on their D series that bore a strong resemblance to their Es: wooden box-girder construction and top wing based on Roland D.I, attached to fuselage. The Pfalz D.4 featured an inline Benz Bz.III engine; which was completely cowled and featured a front-mounted "car-type" radiator—something Pfalz would return to with the D.XII. The fuselage and top wing had cutouts to improve visibility but it was a squat, ugly duckling. The flight performance was far worse than either the Hablerstadt D's or the Albatros D's., and as such was hastily discarded.

Roland's D.I featured a semi-monocoque fuselage that would provide a crucial and pivotal turning point for Pfalz. The LFG company burned down on September 6, 1916, and as a result of the fire, a new factory was built in Charlottenburg. To maintain production and to capitalize on the infrastructure at Pfalz (and to prevent it from going bankrupt) IdFlieg ordered 20 Roland D.I aircraft to be built by Pfalz. The aircraft would be built using the Roland Wicklerumpf semi-monocoque construction method, which Pfalz designers studied with intense interest. The Pfalz D.I or Roland D.I (Pfalz) was powered by the modern Mercedes D.III straight-six 160-hp engine and was capable of speeds up to 180 kph. The D.I had some drawbacks—same as the *Walfisch*: poor forward and downward visibility that made combat and landings difficult. These flaws were corrected in the Roland D.II, which featured a redesigned top wing attachment; it was reduced in thickness by 10 centimeters. The D.II also featured the Teves and Braun in-wing radiator and a lowered pilot's seat. Tests were successful in October 1916 and Pfalz received a license order of 100 Roland D.IIs (2830–2929/16). These were built as Pfalz D.IIs (Roland D.II [Pfalz]). During this production run, the engine was replaced by the 180-hp Argus AS.III engine, and termed the Pfalz D.IIa, giving rise to another 100 orders from IdFlieg (300–399/17). Initially they were termed Pfalz D.IIa but later changed to Roland D.IIa as that is really what they were. Pflaz also began producing the Roland D.III which was similar to the D.II except it had short, stocky cabane struts which greatly improved forward visibility and gun aiming. IdFlieg in turn ordered another 100 Roland D.IIIs (Pfalz), but only

The Pfalz E.V was a version of the E.IV except it had a Mercedes D.I inline engine. Its performance was better than the rotary-powered aircraft; however, it came too late as the new D types were rapidly phasing out the era of the *Eindeckers*. (Public domain)

30 fuselages were built before production was cancelled. During this period the Nieuport 17s began appearing over Verdun which were superior to everything the Central Powers had at the time.

Captured Nieuports were studied carefully by IdFlieg and aircraft manufacturers alike. Germany became fixated on the sesquiplane (literally meaning wing and one half) design, resulting in a strong Nieuport influence among new German aircraft—Euler and Siemens-Schuckert simply copied the French designs. However, the Nieuport's single lower wing spar was a drawback so manufacturers like Pfalz (and to a lesser extent Albatros) worked on new Nieuport-inspired desgins but retained characteristics of the aircraft they had been building.

At the beginning of 1917, Pfalz hired engineer Rudolf Gehringer who had been working under supervision of engineer Theodor Kober at the Friedrichshafen Flugzeugbau works. He became the chief constructor and remained in this position until the war ended. His closest co-workers were engineers Paulus and Goldmacher. A captured Nieuport was delivered to Speyr where it was tested and measured. Per IdFlieg's mandate, the team began working on a new design that utilized the best aspects of the Nieuports, which would result in the signature aircraft for this company: the Pfalz D.III.

Using the semi-monocoque fuselages that by this time they had mastered due their Roland work, which would feature the Mercedes D.III 160-hp inline engine, and two spar wings that had a moderate sesquiplane character. Armament was two LMG 08/15 machine guns installed below the turtle deck cowling to reduce drag. The monocoque fuselages demanded huge efforts which significantly extended the construction time.

The initial delay was most likely due to production of the necessary jigs and molds associated with the new aircraft, training new workers, and working out production snags as well as shortcuts that would make the new fighter profitable or at least cost-effective and competitive. The fuselage for the new fighter followed the construction method of the Roland D.II; each half was formed over a mold using "cold molding" technique. This was double diagonal planked using 1-mm ply that was 9 cm wide, while attachment points were strengthened with fabric strips.

From *Flight*, April 18, 1918:

> Each in the form of long narrow strips put on diagonally, the strips of the inner skin and those of the outer running at approximately right angles to one another. It would appear that this form of construction is of some advantage, inasmuch as difficulty is always experienced in getting three-ply

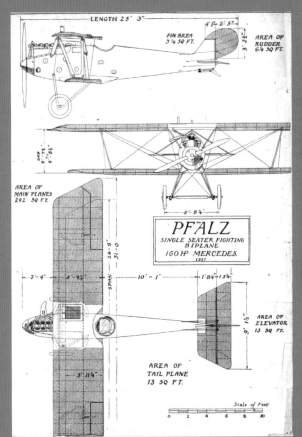

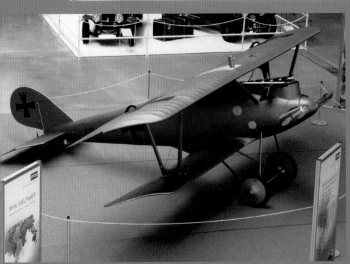

The Pfalz D.III was a breakthrough for the company that was cultivated by the construction of the Roland D.IIs by Pfalz, which had cold-molded double diagonally planked fuselages. The D.III incorporated Roland-style construction, Nieuport influence, as well as Pfalz designers' own sensibilities. Pfalz, unlike Albatros, did not repeat the Nieuport's fatal flaw: the single spar lower wing. Instead the D.III featured two spars that were linked by a U-shaped interplane strut that prevented wing flutter. (NARA and for the color image, public domain)

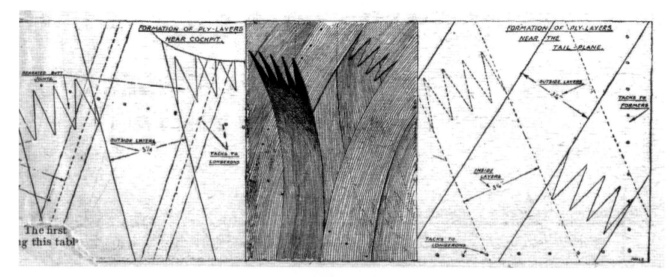

The first
g this tabl

wood to bend to a double curvature. A sheet of three-ply may be readily bent along one axis, but even a very thin sheet will protest if one tries to bend it in addition along an axis at right angles to the former. The fact is, therefore, almost certainly at the bottom of the Pfalz construction. However, this is a subject to which we hope to return later.

From *Flight* on July 25, 1918 a description of the Pfalz D.III fuselage:

> There are in all eight *longerons* … one at the top, one at the bottom, one half-way up on each side and four at what would be the corners in a rectangular section body. These *longerons* run the whole length of the body, with the exception of the top one, which is terminated just to the rear of the engine, and are attached to the formers as shown in the sketch. The *longerons* are stop-chamfered so as to leave them solid where they contact the formers, into which they are sunk and secured by a wood screw. The formers themselves are built up of smaller pieces of spruce, lap-jointed and covered each side with a facing of three-ply wood. Reference has already been made to the fact that wing roots are formed integrally with the body. These roots can be seen in the side view; and account for the peculiar shape of formers III and IV. Judging by these formers the cross-sectional area is unduly increased at this point, although this may be partly made up for by the shape of the-ply-wood covering, which merges the lines of the lower plane into the curves of the body.

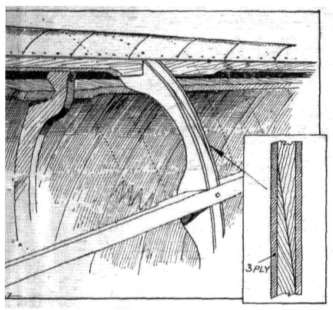

These two images illustrate the double diagonal strip planking of the Pfalz fuselages. The finger-jointed planking is also illustrated, although it was probably joined/glued off the fuselage before it was applied. Also illustrated is the former construction which featured solid stock sandwiched between two layers of plywood. (*Flight*)

One of the difficulties of monocoque (plywood) construction is that plywood does not conform readily to a compound curve. That is to say, thin sheet plywood will bend willingly to a cylinder (one direction), but as soon as this same cylinder tapers in either direction and thus forming a compound curve (second direction),

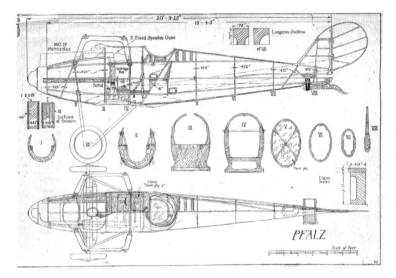

A construction drawing of the D.III from *Flight* magazine. Similar to the Albatros, the vertical fin was integrated into the last former. Also note that the stringers were coved or chamfered between joints to the formers to save weight. Another modern feature of the D.III was the integrated and faired wing root, which was beautiful and aerodynamic, albeit difficult to produce quickly.

plywood has difficulty conforming in two directions. In the Albatros aircraft this difficulty was overcome by using "gores" or tapered panels that would readily conform to a particular section of the fuselage form. Albatros calculated (and most likely experimented quite a bit) to figure out how best the fuselage could be covered, as explained in Chapter 7. Kolomon Mayrhofer of Craftlab stated that plywood of this period was more pliable than modern plywood, and that Albatros knew just exactly how far the plywood they used could bend and modified their designs accordingly.

As described with the Roland D.II and by extension the Pfalz, a different system was used than that of Albatros. The body covering consists of two layers of three-ply, each less than 1 mm thick. The plywood arrived at Pfalz in sheets, and was then ripped into strips of about 3 to 4 inches before it was applied to the molds. *Flight* mentioned that the width of the strips varied considerably throughout the body as dictated by the nature of a particular curve. The first layer of three-ply was then put on by bending it diagonally around the mold, and perhaps tapering the strips (like staves on a barrel) as they needed running toward the edges where they were tacked into a longeron at each edge of the half-fuselage. The second layer of strips was then laid on top of the first, but at a different angle, to which it was secured by gluing, and finally tacked to the longerons—which ran along the dorsal and ventral centerlines of the fuselage. *Flight* also mentioned that the inside of the fuselage was reinforced by gluing cloth tapes over the joints near the engine area.

Flight would not comment on the strength of these fuselages except to point out that they had heard "that the Pfalz machines have a habit of breaking their bodies just aft of the pilot's cockpit, but as for the accuracy of this statement we cannot verify. As a compromise between sheet three-ply covering and true monocoque construction the Pfalz method would appear to have certain advantages."

It is useful to try and reconstruct the production method of the Pfalz semi-monocoque system based on textual and photographic evidence. With regards to the fuselage, it can be readily observed that the D.III was built on its starboard side initially; that is to say, that the building jig seen at right (at the top of p.138) shows a rigid building deck to which vertical slotted struts were erected and braced at each station having a former.

The formers, after being cut out on a bandsaw and filed, rasped, or sanded smooth (including lightening holes) were then slid into their appropriate slots on the jig and clamped or temporarily secured by another means (perhaps a few screws). Pfalz designers thought about the exact placement of the formers such that the following observations were recorded:

> the former in the neighborhood of the pilot's seat slopes back so as to bring it approximately into line with the rear chassis struts, while rigidity is lent to the front portion of the body by sloping one of the formers carrying the engine bearers until its top meets the top of the next former. In this point also the formers are joined to the front struts carrying the top plane, while one of them serves, at the point of attachment of the bottom corner longeron, to transmit the load from the front chassis struts.

Similar to Albatros, Pfalz used a jig to secure the fuselage bulkheads for accurate installation of the longerons and stringers, which tied the whole structure together. A separate team crafted the cold-molded shell out of two layers of thin plywood running in opposing directions. This was then popped off the mold and fastened and glued to the endoskeleton of formers and stringers. The bulkheads seem to belong to a D.III whereas the fuselage "shell" being formed from thin veneers seems to be a D.XII due to absence of integrated vertical fin. (Greg VanWyngarden)

Next the spruce longerons and stringers were fitted into their appropriate slots in the formers and clamped temporarily to inspect fairness and fit. Any trimming would be done at this time. After all the stringers had been fitted to the port side (extending down to the centerline top and bottom), the formers could be beveled by means of a short, low-angle plane, sanding boards or a combination to achieve the rolling bevel as informed by the run of the stringers. Naturally any fittings that might get sandwiched between the endoskeleton and the monocoque shell (e.g. seat belt attachment clip) would need to be installed before the shell was mated to the internal skeleton. It is interesting to note that at least the bottoms of the formers along the longitudinal centerline were not notched, and we clearly see workers tacking the ends of the cold molded strips to a batten or stringer. Perhaps these stringers were then notched or "let in" to the formers during the sheathing process. The stringers on the sides of the fuselage are seen already installed on the formers.

A separate team (or multiple teams) would simultaneously or sequentially be building the shell of both the port and starboard sides of the monocoque shell over a form that exactly mirrored the form (but not the exact structure) of the stringers and framing previously described. The building jig was most likely a sturdy series of stations or molds to which robust battens were let in to each mold such that they were exactly flush with the mold's edge/contour and described the form of the fuselage perfectly with fair curves. Obviously having these "master molds" for port and starboard would occupy significant time to get right such that the shell produced

on them fitted the endoskeleton being built on the separate jig as described. After the shells had dried, they were removed from the molds and fitted, one at a time, to the framework, still held securely in the jig. After this was secured, by glue, nails, and screws, it was removed from the jig and anything that could be fitted before the other half was secured was done at this time.

Finally, the other half of the fuselage shell was attached to the framework and fastened. Next, the horizontal stabilizer could be finished and then skinned.

A Pfalz D.XII fuselage with one half of its shell attached to the framework. Note the other half-finished fuselages stacked upright in the background. (Greg VanWyngarden)

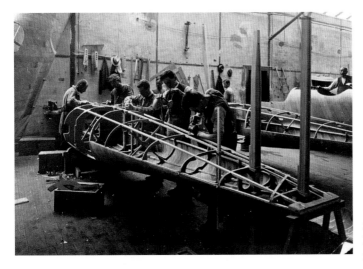

The fuselage of this D.XII has been rolled over to facilitate installation of the mating half-shell of the starboard side. Note the stabilizer struts protruding through the fuselage. (Greg VanWyngarden)

Unlike the Albatros, the vertical fin of the Pfalz D.XII (pictured) did not have the vertical fin built as part of the fuselage.

The horizontal stabilizer of early model D.IIIs was an inverted airfoil in section, making it easier to recover from a dive, *Flight* noted, and that the "the tail plane appears to be put on" the wrong way round. That is to say, it has a flat top surface and a convex bottom surface and was set at 0 angle of incidence.

The writers at *Flight* postulated "that during a steep dive the tail plane would exert a somewhat excessive righting force tending to 'flatten out' the machine rather abruptly. This is so unusual in a German machine, where frequently the tail plane is set at a positive angle of lift[incidence], as to give food for some speculation." *Flight* mentioned that a later model had a symmetrical airfoil stabilizer so obviously this was discontinued. Another interesting feature of the stabilizer was that it could be completely removed by removing five bolts and the elevator control cables from their attachments at the horns; thus, if damaged at the front, replacing this component could be done very quickly. The stabilizer was comprised of built-up spruce spars, poplar rib webs and ash flanges, and no internal rigging.

The leading edge was laminated (most likely steamed first) then hollowed out to keep weight down. The elevator was in one sturdy piece due to the characteristic and distinctive Pfalz rudder which was angled upward from its lower edge to allow upward deflection of the elevator.

The elevators and rudder were of welded steel, as most companies were doing at this point. The ailerons (unbalanced) were on the upper wing only, just as the Nieuports and Albatros. The wing structure was conventional, although it did have hollow spars of composite construction (solid stock and ply). The ailerons were actuated in a similar fashion as Albatros aircraft.

The aircraft was flown in the spring of 1917 and after minor tweaks brought before IdFlieg; its performance was similar to the Albatros D.III, but with the important difference that it did not develop lower wing flutter. In April, IdFlieg ordered 70 Pfalz D.IIIs and a further 300 in June; these orders saved Pfalz from almost certain ruin. By August, pilots who flew the new fighter complained of not being able to free jammed guns in their enclosures

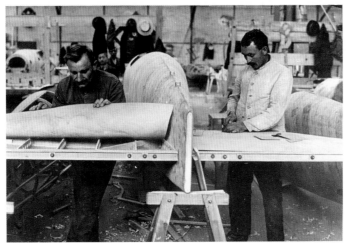

After the two shells are brought together over the framework (note bench dogs holding and drawing together the two halves), the sheathing and completion of the horizontal stabilizer is next. Note how thin and pliable the ply veneer is; the working is most likely gluing and tacking the skin to the framework as he rolls the veneer aft to complete the job. (Greg VanWyngarden)

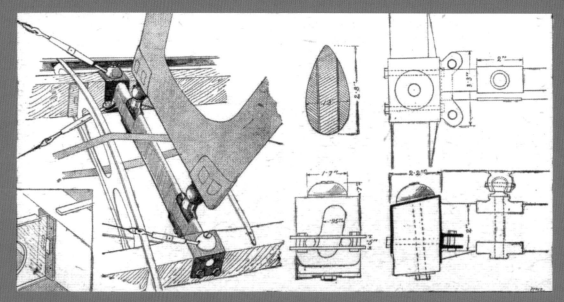

The drawing illustrates how sturdy the interplane attachment was to the spars; no need to worry about wing flutter here!

The wings for the D.III were a straightforward affair. The ribs were slid over the spars and then trued up and secured. Note the piles of fittings on the floor—presumably for the interplane and cabane attachment points, compression bar fixtures, and antidrag rigging. (Greg VanWyngarden)

Finally, Pfalz employed a variation of the system used by Albatros for aileron actuation; differing from Albatros, the Pfalz horn hooked over the spar on the topside of the wing.

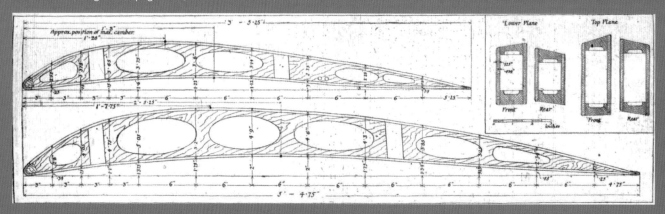

This drawing delineates the hollow spars of the D.III as well as the rib structure.

The Pfalz Dr.I was the company's response to the "triplane craze" that resulted from the appearance of the Sopwith Triplane over the front in late 1916. Of all the triplanes produced during this frenetic period, the Pfalz Dr.I is among the most attractive. It is interesting in that it had a very narrow chord middle wing, connected with a Y-shaped interplane strut.
(Greg VanWyngarden)

under the turtle deck. They also claimed the Pfalz was slower in level flight than the Alb. D.III and D.V; however, the Pfalz was superior in a dive. Overall visibility and rate of climb was good.

The construction and design team at Pfalz experimented constantly to improve the D.III, including more powerful engines such as a 195-hp V-8 Benz Bz.IIIb and 200-hp Adler Ad.IV, but they were difficult to source in sufficient quantity so this ended prospects of using them.

A D-type fighter called "wireless" was also designed, which could allude to experiments with cantilevered wings. The summer of 1917 was also the period in Germany known as the "triplane craze," spurred by the success of the Sopwith Triplane. Pfalz, along with every other major manufacturer, had to redirect its attention to pursuing this specious direction (when IdFlieg should have paid more attention to fast, stable gun platforms like the Spad VII).

The Pfalz triplane contribution was like the other Pfalz aircraft: semi-monocoque fuselage with standard (uncantilevered) wings. It was powered by the Siemens-Halske counter-rotating rotary engine. The Pfalz Dr.I was tested in August 1917. The Pfalz triplane had a fantastic rate of climb unmatched by any other: it reached 5,000 meters in 11 minutes 30 seconds; the Albatros D.V did the same in 35 minutes. IdFlieg ordered 10 of the Pfalz *dreideckers*, which were combat-tested by Jasta 73 at Mars sous Bourg in the spring of 1918.

Due to production problems with the Siemens-Halske Sh.III engine, Oberursel U.IIs were fitted to the new planes instead (Dr.II and Dr.IIa), subsequently reducing their performance and climb rate. Still they were superior in climb to the Dr.I, if not in maneuverability. Allied fighters such as the Camel, S.E.5a and Spad XIII outclassed the Pfalz Dr.IIs and they were not placed in production.

At the beginning of 1918, the D.III was modified according to input from pilots—including Richthofen—which resulted in the D.IIIa with the Mercedes D.IIIa engine, plus exposed machine-gun breeches so pilots could free jams more readily. In addition, the bottom wingtips were rounded as well as the leading edge of the horizontal stabilizer. Production of the preordered 300 D.IIIs was cancelled and replaced by the D.IIIa (beginning with number 4190/17), as the

The Pfalz Dr.I had a fantastic rate of climb—exceeding that of the Fokker Dr.1, although not as maneuverable. Manfred von Richthofen is pictured in the cockpit.
(Greg VanWyngarden)

The Pfalz D.VIII also had a high rate of climb—reaching 5,000 feet in 13 minutes 8 seconds. This aircraft had four sets of interplane struts and thin airfoil wings. (Public domain)

D.IIIa could reach 5,000 meters in 33 minutes. A total of about a thousand D.IIIs and D.IIIas were produced; they were however deemed inferior to both the Albatros DVa and the Fokker Dr.1; their advantage was near-perfect visibility and sturdiness owing to their monocoque construction and good craftsmanship.

Another experimental aircraft was the D.IIIa fighter with wings based on the Spad (very thin airfoils) with flanking radiators on the fuselage; the results of this experiment were later applied in the D.VIII and D.XII.

Ocurrring simultaneously to the development of the D.III using an inline engine, the company was also working on a sesquiplane with a rotary engine 110-hp Oberursel UR.II. The fuselage was standard monocoque, the cowling was open in front with three cooling holes in the bottom, and the propellor was covered with a spinner. In contrast to the V-strutters, it featured two attachment points on the bottom wings. The plane could get to 5,000 meters in 16 minutes, halving the time the D.III took to do the same.

The Pfalz D.VI, armed with twin machine guns, took part in the crucial fighter competition at Adlershof at the end of January 1918. The Pfalz D.VII beat the D.VI so it was withdrawn. The D.VII had a fuselage identical to the Pfalz Dr.I, and was powered by the same Siemens-Halske Sh.III engine (counter-rotating). It was built as a biplane and its wings were stiffened by struts and wire. Unbalanced ailerons on top wing only. The plane was built to utilize boom and zoom tactics (Spad). Another prototype was built using the same fuselage and engine but the wing cellule was based on the Spad VII (finally); wings were supported by two pairs of struts and robust rigging.

This aircraft was the D.VIII, which reached 180 kph at sea level and had a high rate of climb. These two planes climbed to 5,000 meters in 13 minutes 8 seconds and 11 minutes 1 second respectively, placing both these planes far ahead of the competition. Both machines were very maneuverable. Both designs were tested with two- and four-blade propellers and different engines: Oberursel UR.III (145 hp) and Goebel Goe Goe.III (200 hp). The four-blade propellers were made by Wotan. Obviously the scientific data from Gottingen about thicker airfoils having equal drag to thinner ones was lost on, or disregarded by, the design team at Pfalz.

The fuselages for the D.VIII were stubbier than the D.IIIs but were built the same way. (Greg VanWyngarden)

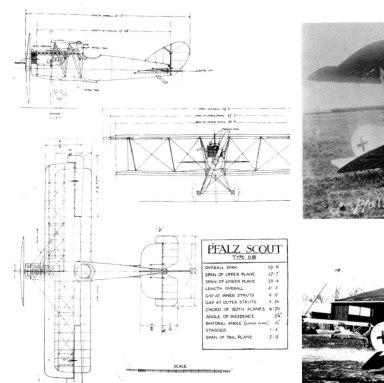

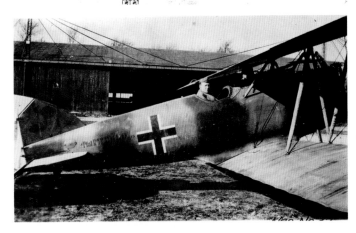

PFALZ SCOUT TYPE D.XII	
OVERALL SPAN	29·6
SPAN OF UPPER PLANE	27·7
SPAN OF LOWER PLANE	26·4
LENGTH OVERALL	21·5
GAP AT INNER STRUTS	4·6
GAP AT OUTER STRUTS	4·3½
CHORD OF BOTH PLANES	4·7¼
ANGLE OF INCIDENCE	3¾°
DIHEDRAL ANGLE (LOWER PLANE)	1½°
STAGGER	1·4
SPAN OF TAIL PLANE	7·3

The Pfalz D.XII was the most successful of a series of newer aircraft based on the Spad XIII. It featured an inline engine with the radiator up front, like the Fokker D.VII, and wings of longer span than the D.VIII but possessed the same thin airfoil. Its N struts were also influenced by the D.VII. (NARA)

The D.IX, X, and XI were transitional aircraft that resulted in the D.XII, that had thin airfoil wings like the D.VII and D.VIII but of longer span with balanced ailerons on the top wing only. The airfoil was based on Spad designs. It was powered by the 180-hp Mercedes D.IIIa engine. After witnessing the end of the fighting era as exemplified by the triplanes, Pfalz decided (a bit too late) to employ the boom and zoom tactics exemplified by the Spad and S.E.5a—and with the BMW engine the Fokker D.VIIF. The D.XII featured an auto-type rounded radiator in the front, as in the D.VII. Other engines were tried including a BMW 195-hp IIIa, and a 195-hp Benz Bz.IIIbou.

In terms of construction, its fuselage construction methodology was identical to the D.III, and its wings were of conventional construction and very similar to the Spad; many narrow ribs closely spaced. As such, two sets of interplane struts were fitted, resembling the Fokker D.VII in shape and construction, as was the radiator placed directly abaft the propeller.

The horseshoe-shaped lower cowling is about to be fitted over the nose of the D.XII to link the radiator's shape to the rest of the nose. (Greg VanWyngarden)

The Pfalz D.XIIa had the Benz Bz.IIIbou engine. The winner of the Second Aircraft Competition at Adlershof, May 27 to June 21, 1918, was the Fokker D.VII with a BMW IIIa engine (giving Fokker priority for these engines). Thus Pfalz was left with the Mercedes D.IIIa, Mercedes D.IIIau, and 84 BMW engines.

Pilots' opinions were that the Fokker D.VII and Pfalz D.XII were on par but that the Fokker was more maneuverable and easier to control. It was also easier to build due to the self-aligning wing structure discussed in Chapter 4. This was important as Germany was running out of experienced pilots, and skilled factory workers, and needed a fighter that was easy to fly, not necessararily easy to fly well. Pfalz tried to increase production from 10 to 30 planes a day—the war was not going to last much longer and more planes meant more money as well as more equipment to throw at the enemy. One way Pfalz saved time was by using metal on the vertical stabilizer that was attached later (not built as part of the monocoque structure). In October 1918, Pfalz built 180 D.XIIs.

Other Pfalz aircraft included the D.XIII, D.XIV, and finally the D.XV. This latter aircraft was very similar to the D.XII except the lower wing was detached from the fuselage and supported by a set of somewhat unwieldy struts; perhaps the construction time and cost of the wing root fairings had become too much. The D.XV also had only two sets of interplane struts.

This drawing from *Flight* depicts various wing and strut details, the hollow spars, and miscellaneous fittings. Figure 5 shows the robust attachment of the aileron spar to the aft main spar; given the speed of the D.XII in a dive, Pfalz wasn't taking any chances of having the ailerons come off!

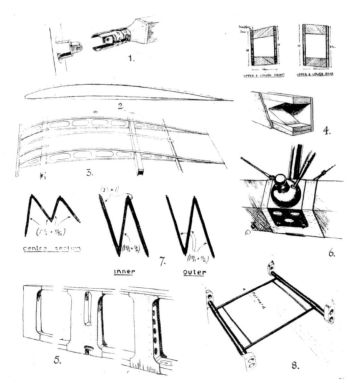

The Pfalz D.XV featured lower wings that were set off on the lower struts; obviously building the elegant but labor-intensive wing root fairings was becoming less economically viable, hence this awkward treatment. The XV also had only two sets of interplane struts. (NARA)

In Profile:
Pfalz D.III

Pfalz D.III (1370/17)
Lt Werner Voss, Jagdstaffel 10; Marckebeke, Belgium; September 1917.

RONNY
BAR
AIRCRAFT PROFILES
ronnybarprofiles@gmail.com

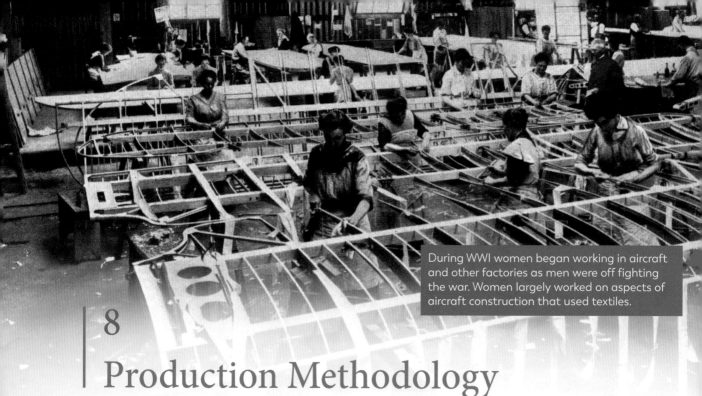

During WWI women began working in aircraft and other factories as men were off fighting the war. Women largely worked on aspects of aircraft construction that used textiles.

8
Production Methodology

Each aircraft manufacturer produced aircraft before the war: many cut their teeth on *Taubes* or licensed copies of proven designs. The challenge was a particular company's capacity for series production. It was challenging enough producing complex and exacting machines that were airworthy—as even the smallest overlooked detail could result in disaster—without the pressure of wartime production. However, this was the reality each company faced if they were going to succeed—let alone excel—during wartime Germany. The most successful (fighter) companies—Fokker, Albatros, Pfalz, and nominally Roland—each approached the problem of mass production differently, and, importantly, each company developed a system that worked for them and stuck with it. For Fokker it would be a combination of steel and plywood that would spell success, for Albatros and Pfalz semi-monocoque fuselages would be the method by which their companies flourished. Other companies like Siemens-Schuckert, Junkers, and Roland all experimented with different systems while striving to stay competitive. Of the larger companies, design teams thought of design and production as two interconnected facets of the same problem. It is certain that Albatros and Pfalz employed extensive jigs to assemble fuselages. With Albatros, the formers were set up much as one would set up molds in a wooden boat. With Pfalz, the port and starboard halves were cold molded over a form—insuring that each component was identical. In addition,

AGO Flugzeugwerke at Johannisthal, Berlin, and their hangar at the main flugplatz. (Fokker Team Schorndorf)

The wings and floats for the Ago floatplane are seen in the framing stage. Note the bracing on the interior of the floats, and the use of plywood bulkheads or possible removable molds. The wing structure seems very complex. Note the intermediary spar-like structures running parallel to the main spars. Companies that had mediocre designs that were difficult to build were weeded out quickly in the wartime context. (Fokker Team Schorndorf)

In this image the photographer must have felt like an intruder—such are the expressions of the workers seen here assembling an Ago floatplane. (Fokker Team Schorndorf)

Apparently the parts for the floats were first made in this shop, with its profusion of short benches and tool cabinets. In the distance a large curved form is being laminated, perhaps the main curved longerons for the floats. Note the two very small electric lights. (Fokker Team Schorndorf)

Seen here is a mixed-use shop for Ago: steelwork, wooden components, and subassemblies are strewn about seemingly in no apparent order. There also appear to be numerous people that are not really doing anything. Perhaps this seeming disorganization accelerated Ago's demise. (Fokker Team Schorndorf)

In this image an Ago wing is being covered while other workers perform miscellaneous tasks; again, there seems to be no systematic sequence for aircraft production. In the previous image, around 17 people are doing various tasks, but only one is actually working on the airplane. (Fokker Team Schorndorf)

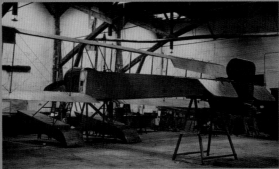

An Ago floatplane nearing completion. This aircraft seems crude when compared to some of the other designs of the time; however, it was a smaller company with insufficient political connections to break into the circles of Prussian military elites that would have been necessary for meaningful contracts. (Fokker Team Schorndorf)

The Ago pusher biplane featured a nacelle that projected well forward, and a rear structure reminiscent of British pushers like the Airco DH.2. (Fokker Team Schorndorf)

when one considers that many of the workers had to be trained in a short amount of time, training them to do relatively simple tasks like bending and tacking plywood strips over a form would have certainly been easier than setting up a box-girder fuselage with all attendant fittings and rigging. Fokker excelled at welded fuselages largely due to men like Reinhold Platz who, if nothing else, was an exceptional welder.

What follows is meant as an overview of some of the factories of the various aircraft manufacturers—some companies featured did not produce many noteworthy fighters (like LVG and AGO) but images exist of the interiors of their factories that speak volumes as to how production during this period was conducted (for better or for worse) so they are included. Although concerned primarily with the production of two-seaters and floatplanes, the factory images of the AGO company provide a fascinating insight into a mid-to-lower-level early German aircraft factory.

Gustav Otto founded AGO (Flugmaschinenwerke Gustav Otto) in Johannisthal in 1911 to handle repairs, pilot training and other services with the Prussian army—it was a subsidiary of Otto Werke in Munich. With much tension between the Bavarian and Prussian militaries, Otto hoped that AGO might be able to secure at least some business from the Prussian army. AGO built good floatplanes for the German navy; however, due to the animosity between the two nation-states, the Prussian army would not accept any AGO designs. The overall feel of the interior of the factory space is somewhat haphazard, bordering on disorganized. There is one gentleman with a hat, coat, and tie seen in many of the photographs, often going over plans, and most likely the company's chief designer. The lack of systematic production tenchniques at AGO most likely condemned it to obscurity.

At Schwerin Fokker D series biplanes fill this portion of the shop; contrast this to the haphazard layout at Ago in the previous images. (Fokker Team Schorndorf)

A Fokker E series in front of a factory building at Schwerin. (Fokker Team Schorndorf)

Fokker

Fokker's designs possess a utilitarianism that is appreciated by the modern eye for its simplicity and austere functionality. Anthony Fokker may have been many unflattering things—ruthless, opportunistic—but he did possess a curious mind, giving rise to the somewhat disparaging moniker of a "tinkerer." He was quick to adapt emerging technologies to a production framework like plywood and steel; he was also quick to

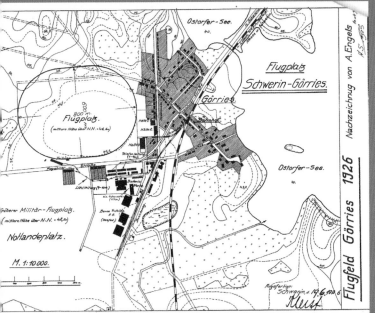

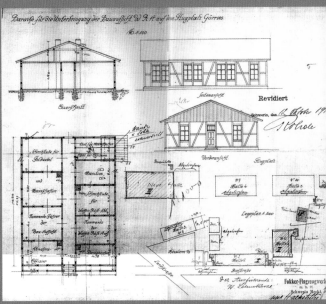

Drawings for the various factory buildings at Fokker's Schwerin plant. The main buildings were ideally situated between Lake Schwerin (for floatplanes), and the Flugplatz for his land aircraft. Test flights could be conducted over the lake in case of unexpected mishaps. (Fokker Team Schorndorf)

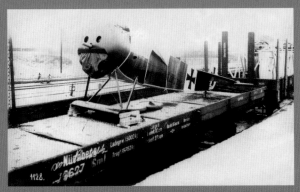

A Dr.1 has been loaded on a railway flatcar, the engine is tarped up as is the cockpit and machine guns. Similarly a D.VII is loaded on another flatcar. Having rail access was key to shipping aircraft to the front. (Fokker Team Schorndorf)

Schwerin factory buildings in the dead of winter. Obviously the roofs were not insulated, judging from the enormous icicles hanging from the eaves. (Fokker Team Schorndorf)

A rare aerial view of the Fokker factory complex and Lake Schwerin. (Fokker Team Schorndorf)

A Fokker Eindecker flies low over the factory complex at Schwerin. (Fokker Team Schorndorf)

A variety of different Fokker wings are being worked on in this room by primarily women. Fokker maximized on his space and crammed as much "work" in to it as possible. (Fokker Team Schorndorf)

In this shop solid stock milling appears to be the predominant activity: jointers, shapers, bandsaws, and tablesaws are all in operation here. The boy with the barrel waits patiently to clear away excess shaving and dust that could jam machinery and hold up production. (Fokker Team Schorndorf)

In this room Dr.1 box spars are being measured to accept rib webs. In the distance, a boy pulls another box spar from the rafters to begin another wing. (Fokker Team Schorndorf)

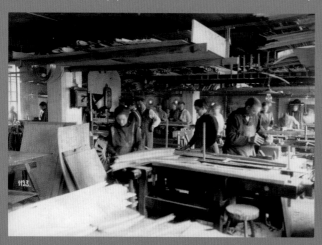

This room would appear to be for the production of wing rib webs. Templates, webs, and flange stock appear to be stored above, with assembly going on below. (Fokker Team Schorndorf)

Production of Dr.1 box spars is in full swing in this room. The man in the middle joins the two box spars with spacers. The women to the left are attaching the plywood webs, thus completing the box spar. Here again, materials are stored overhead, and there is very little wasted space. (Fokker Team Schorndorf)

The photographer has momentarily disturbed these men from working on Dr.1 wings. Note the very simple hand tools being used. (Fokker Team Schorndorf)

This shop was used to make the tapered box spars for the Dr.1 that were then joined together with ply webs and spacers. Note the stacks of finished tapered spars in the rafters. (Fokker Team Schorndorf)

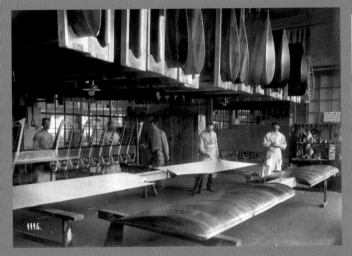

The framework of a Dr.1 wing is being varnished, then a pair is being doped (natural linen), and finally the one closest has been painted with the streaky olive paint scheme. Finished wings are in racks above. (Fokker Team Schorndorf)

In this image, some wings are being finished, while others are being ribstitched to comply with IdFlieg mandates after the series of accidents with early Dr.1s. (Fokker Team Schorndorf)

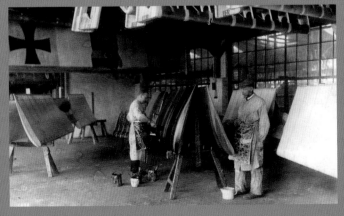

One worker applies the streaked camouflage scheme on the top of a wing, while another paints the German cross on the bottom of a Dr.1 wing. (Fokker Team Schorndorf)

Another image depicting a mixed-use operation: Dr.1 wings are being rib stitched (strengthened) while others are being finished. (Fokker Team Schorndorf)

An Albatros D series being framed on a jig that held the formers securely while stringers and longerons were installed. A fuselage that has been skinned with ply is behind the skeleton in the foreground. (Greg VanWyngarden)

capitalize on the breakthroughs of others (like Euler, Schneider, and Junkers) and quickly put those ideas into production, regardless of patent infringement. Fokker also relied on input from the ace pilots he wined and dined as he knew their opinions with regards to IdFlieg officials carried significant weight. IdFlieg set type and quantity mandates so it was in his best interest to keep the German aviator elites close. He was also willing to let those around him, like Reinhold Platz, influence the direction of aircraft construction, in this case the use of welded steel as a major structural component. There is evidence to support the assertion that Germany faced plywood shortages during the war, but nothing has been written about steel shortages, except that tubing was initially hard to obtain. Obviously Fokker overcame this problem as all his fuselages were of welded steel right up to the end of the war. Most likely, proven aircraft producers like Fokker and Albatros were given priority for materials.

It seems certain that Fokker must have used a building jig to set up his fuselages for welding. This way the lengths of tubing could simply be inserted into the building jig, welded, then erected on a mold to finish the fuselage. This would also have been a good way to keep the fuselage structure immobilized while the entire metal structure was carefully heated to eliminate any warps or internalized tensions in the metal from spot welding of the various supports and cross pieces.

Albatros

Albatros was quick to realize the potential of plywood as a structural component for aircraft. Their entire fuselages were built from plywood with the exception of the solid stock spruce longerons. This had a number of important advantages. Unlike solid wood which requires a specific moisture content to become dimensionally stable (and this was before kiln drying), plywood was dimensionally stable due to the thinness of the veneers and the multiple glue joints. It was also made in sheets which lent itself to planar shapes such as formers/

The leading edge of this Albatros wing is being worked on by the factory worker at right. Note the plywood sheathing of the leading edge and wingtip.

A worker uses a thin ply template of a German cross to paint the white outline around its perimeter, using his toe to keep the template firmly against the camber of the wing. (Greg VanWyngarden)

Pfalz fuselages were built on their side, to allow installation of one half of the laminated shell to be applied at a time. Once this side is finished, the fuselage can be removed from the jig. (Greg VanWyngarden)

bulkheads as well as sheathing. It was and is quite strong. Moreover, unlike the glues used in modern plywood, the casein glue used in World War I plywood was suppler, lending itself to compound curves with nominally greater facility. Albatros designs (and attendant curves used) were informed by the extent to which plywood sheets would bend, and no further. According to Kolomon Mahrhofer, who builds replica Albatros aircraft today, the plywood panels were either scarfed or butt-joined in the case of Oeffag, before they were bent on to the fuselage endoskeleton. They were not steamed in a mold (according to some), as this would have softened the glue—being thermoplastic, they were extremely sensitive to heat and moisture—of the plywood, resulting in delamination. In addition, since the fuselages were strong enough to require no internal bracing, this was a huge savings in expense and time as this step could be eliminated. In addition, rigging wires would never slacken or break in an Albatros fuselage: there simply were none. Finally, a monocoque fuselage did not require any stitched fabric work (except to reinforce scarfs on the Johannistal planes), so this too was a step that could be eliminated. Albatros aircraft relied on traditional methods of building wings however, which would cause problems in their D series, such as sesquiplane lower wing weakness, and D.V upper wing weakness outboard of interplanes.

Pfalz

When Pfalz received the Roland *Walfisch* to produce under license they were paying careful attention. Pfalz co-opted this construction method to produce all of their most successful fighters: the D.III, D.IIIa, D.VII, D.VIII, and D.XII. All of these were built identically: thin strips of 3-mm ply bent on the bias around a rigid form, much like cold-molded boats were and are built. Fabric strips reinforced the glue seam and were laid down first and tied together beneath the form to keep it out of the way. Next the first layer was laid and tacked to the edges. The subsequent layer was laid in the opposite direction to the first. This method allowed the strips to conform to compound curves readily, and since the strips were running almost perpendicular to one another, the dimensional stability was attained. Pfalz may have hired boatbuilders or coachbuilders for this process; it would be an easy transition from building cold-molded racing shells or coaches to fuselages at Pfalz—or Roland for that matter. Like Albatros, Pfalz did not have to worry about the time or expense to rig their fuselages with cable and turnbuckle bracing, and all attendant fittings.

Women apply glue to rib flanges, then apply fabric over the tops and down the sides as a method to secure the fabric covering. (Public domain)

A worker fits and secures an interplane attachment fitting before continuing to rig the antidrag cables.

The fabric shop at Pfalz. In the distance lozenge camouflage covering can be seen. In the foreground, natural, lozenge, and fabric tape are all present.

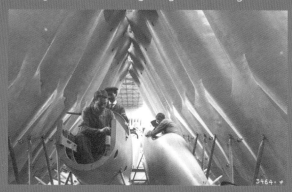

A cathedral of Pfalz fuselages create an interesting environment in which to work. Technicians prepare the engine compartment to receive the powerplant.

After the engine has been secured, the machine guns are next to be fitted.

Worker drill holes in the ball joints of Pfalz cabane struts. It appears as though the drill is fixed; a small piston jack is used to move the workpiece through the turning drillbit.

Workers use hand drills and other hand tools to fasten attachment points to Pfalz cabane strut assemblies. (Greg VanWyngarden)

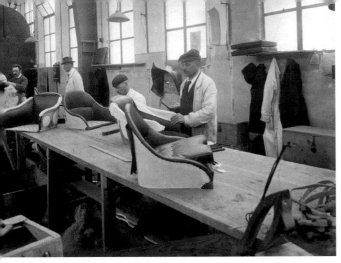

The upholstery shop for Pfalz. Note the rather comfortable-looking seats, especially when compared to the wicker seats of the Sopwith or the plywood seats of the Nieuport.

Technicians inspect the breeches of dozens of LMG 08/15 machine guns. In the background, a Pfalz D.XII waits for its engine and guns. (Greg VanWyngarden)

In addition to design and construction techniques that would facilitate rapid production, there was one other very important area that most aircraft producers tried their best to tackle: testing. During this period of rapid advances, experimentation, and practical trial and error, manufacturers could ill afford to produce a product that did not meet IdFlieg's performance specifications. We are fortunate that Fokker photographed so much of his testing—partly as proof that he was compliant with aircraft such as the Dr.1 with all its early production problems, but also partly as a desire to produce a superior product that would guarantee success if it could be produced in a cost-effective fashion.

This image of the LVG metal shop contains a wealth of informationL tubing benders, welding jigs, and finished components all are visible. Oxyacetylene tanks are in the background as is a partial fuselage. (Fokker Team Schorndorf)

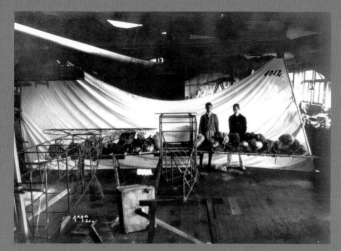

The middle wing of a Dr.1 is loaded with sandbags—and is showing the strain. At left is another welded fuselage, most likely a V.4 due to the curved leading edges of the stabilizer. In the background, the sheet obscures what appears to be another V.4, its top wings perched on its cabane struts.

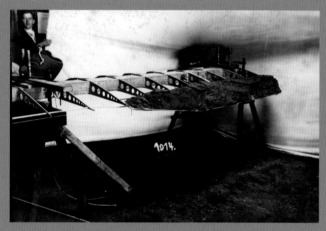

Sandbags been loaded onto the aileron and after portion of an early Dr.1 (it does not have the vertical stiffeners on the rib webs characteristic of post-crash models). Note that the rigging for the upper aileron horn is taut, while the lower is slack.

Load tests of a Fokker spar, though it is unclear which aircraft this is for.

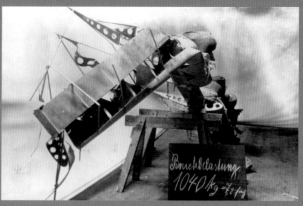

A load test of an early model Dr.1 wing. The breakage shows rib webs that appear paper-thin. Such trial and error tests were common at Fokker as well as other factories.

A load test of the modified rib web for the Dr.1 Note vertical stiffeners, and fabric-wrapped flanges. It appears to be holding up to the weight quite well; of course this is static and the weight is applied straight down. In the aerial context the loads would be constantly changing. It would seem that 200 kg was the breaking point of the rib.

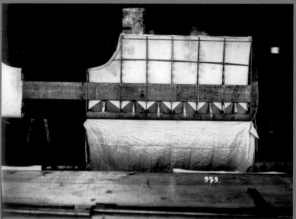

An early Dr.1 middle wing has its covering removed, presumably after a load test to see how the internal structure fared. Note the fabric strips that hold the ply-sheathed leading edge midpoint from puckering upward. This problem was solved on the D.VII by making both the top and bottom sawtoothed in shape and thus able to be secured to the box spars.
All images (Fokker Team Schorndorf)

A Siemens-Schuckert D. III is seen looking forward. The SS D. III borrowed from many other manufacturers; the tail feathers and semi-monocoque fuselage have an Albatros/Pfalz feel; the double ailerons borrow from British fighters,

9

Siemens-Schuckert Werke

This company began in 1847 as Siemens-Halske, a manufacturer of telegraphic equipment. In 1873 it merged with Nurnberg-Schuckert to form a large electrical combine: Siemens-Schuckert werke. In 1907 the company made its first foray into aviation with a non-rigid airship that had been requested by the General Staff. Between 1909 and 1911 it built three monoplanes which did not amount to much. At the outbreak of war in 1914 Germany requested that all manufacturers contribute to the war effort; thus Siemens-Schuckert revived its

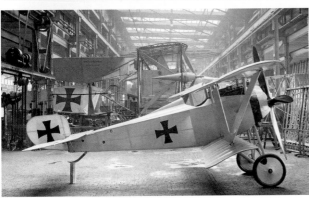

The Siemens-Schuckert D.I was based almost completely on the Nieuport 11, with the sole exception of the powerplant, which was a Siemens-Halske D.III engine. Shown is the massive four-blade propeller that was able to turn due to its counter-rotating spindle and cylinders. By the time the D.I was in production, the blush was already off the Nieuport such was the rapidity of aviation development during the war. (Greg VanWyngarden)

aviation department under the direction of Dr Walter Reichel. Others in the department were Dr Hugo Natalis, Forssman, Wolff, and Bruno and Franz Steffan.

The first fighter designed at the works was the Siemens-Schuckert E.I which appeared in mid-1915, and was the first aircraft to be powered by the Siemens-Halske Sh.I. This was a new type of rotary that had counter-rotating components: the cylinders and the propeller/crankshaft rotated in opposite directions. A small number of production machines were supplied to supplement supplies of the Fokker and Pfalz monoplane fighters, which at this time were used mainly for escort work. The prototype SSW E.II, powered by the inline Argus As.II, crashed in June 1916, killing Franz Steffen, one of the designers of the SSW R types. By early 1916 the first generation of German monoplane fighters was being outclassed by the Nieuport 11 and the Nieuport 17 which very quickly followed. Siemens-Schuckert was supplied with a captured Nieuport 17 to "study." Siemens-Schuckert responded by building an almost exact copy—except with a Siemens-Halske engine, spinner, and different tailskid—called the D.I. Production was held up due to problems with the Siemens-Halske engine. By the time the D.Is were ready, the efficacy of the Nieuport 17 had already past.

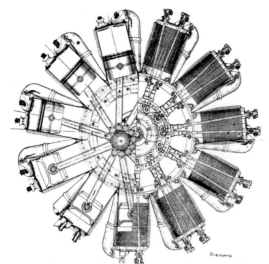

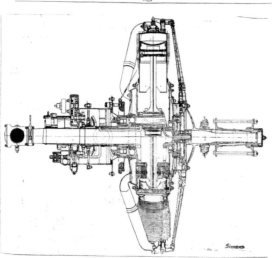

A drawing from *Flight* of the Siemens-Halske 11-cylinder 160-hp Sh.III engine. The cylinders in this engine rotated one way, and the crank shaft the other. This gave the engine high power with low torque (900 rpm) enabling it to swing a large propellor. (Public domain)

The Siemens-Halske division of the combine worked on a radical new 11-cylinder, geared, counter-rotating engine: one set of cylinders rotated in one direction at 900 rpm, the crankshaft in the opposite direction also at 900 rpm, which resulted in 1,800 combined rpm with a propeller speed of only 900 rpm. Thus the engine had tremendous torque and power at an efficient propeller speed. It was designated the 160-hp Sh.III engine. There were problems however due to the double-banked cylinders rotating slowly, and cooling was difficult as the aft set was blocked by the forward set. Overheating was exacerbated by the lack of genuine castor oil mentioned in Chapter 5. However, it did maintain its power at high altitudes, something other aircraft had trouble with, and its gyroscopic effect was mitigated by the counter-rotation of the cylinders and crankshaft, so refinement of the engine continued. Twin magnetos were fitted to the engine plus a proper throttle quadrant was installed, enabling the engine to idle down to 350 rpm.

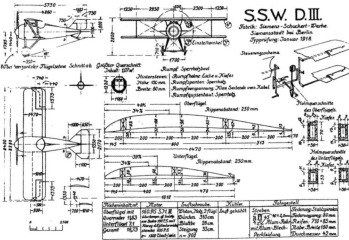

The SS D.III had an impressive rate of climb due to its powerful Sh.III engine, had a semi-monocoque fuselage, thin airfoil wings with interplane struts that supported two spars in the lower wings (like Pfalz), balanced control surfaces including ailerons on bottom and top wings, a nicely cowled engine, spinner, and a four-bladed propeller. (Public domain)

To capitalize on the new 160-hp engine, a new design was conceived by engineer Harald Wolff, who succeeded engineer Steffen after his death, assisted by engineer Glockner, and another junior engineer named Hauck. Three preproduction airframes were built—D.II (D 3501/16) D.IIa (D 3500/16), and D.IIb (D 3502/16)— as test beds for the new engine. Performance exceeded expectation with the D.IIb in August when 16,400 feet was reached in 15.5 minutes, resulting in an order for three additional prototypes. The problem remained that although they climbed very quickly, they were slow in level flight.

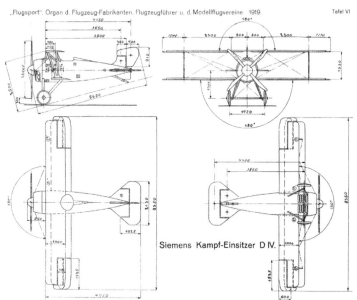

"Flugsport", Organ d. Flugzeug-Fabrikanten, Flugzeugführer u. d. Modellflugvereine 1919.   Tafel VI

Siemens Kampf-Einsitzer D IV.

The SS D.IV was similar to the D.III except it featured a reconfigured cowling shape to allow more cooling air over the engine which tended to overheat in the D.III due to the air blocked by the full cowling and spinner. Note the spinner on the D.IV is perforated as well to allow more airflow over the engine. The D.IV feature Fokker-style balanced ailerons. (Public domain)

After the additional prototypes were tested in October 1917, they were relabeled D.III and in weeks a preproduction order for 20 aircraft was placed.

In January 1918, the D.III was tested at Adlershof, which resulted in 30 more being ordered in February 1918. The D.III was used in home defense units as an interceptor, due to its outstanding rate of climb. In order to achieve the desired speed in level flight, some of its rate of climb was sacrificed, resulting in reconfiguring the size and shape of the wings, and leading to the D.IV. The Pfalz D.VIII was largely a copy of the D.IV, and it too used the Sh.III engine. Several offshoots of the design included triplanes and a parasol monoplane, but none saw production.

The SS series were all built in a very similar fashion: semi-monocoque fuselages similar to Pfalz's method of construction, with wings that were of conventional construction somewhat resembling the Pfalz D.XII or Spad type of wings. The engine was the revolutionary feature with the Siemens-Schuckert aircraft. And the airframe design was a good blend of many design challenges: the interplanes were similar to the Pfalz D.III in that the bottom of the V was connected by a short strut to connect the two lower spars, thus avoiding the wing flutter problem. The control surfaces were all balanced as well, making it light on the controls.

With the end of the war, production of the D.IV continued, mainly for sales to Switzerland, which flew them into the late 1920s. With the signing of the Treaty of Versailles the next year all aircraft production in Germany ceased.

Fokker D. VII reproduction built by Cole Palen at the Old Rhinebeck Aerodrome in New York. It has an original Mercedes straight six D.III 200 hp engine, a powerful engine for the time, and quite wonderful to hear! (Author)

10
Armaments and Engines

Firepower and speed were two elements in aircraft design that Germany (and the Allies) aspired to attain with increasing intensity. Early aircraft carried small arms strapped to the airplane or pilot and were almost an afterthought. The development of the aircraft as a point-and-shoot weapon was slow, but, once realized, there was no turning back. Initially a single machine gun was fitted to the aircraft, along with an interrupter or synchronizing gear—or this problem was eliminated by mounting the machine gun to fire over the arc of the propeller as with early Nieuports. The German machine gun was the same basic design as the ones used by the Allies—all of them stemmed from Hiram Maxim's "killing machine" of 1884.

The engine was the heart of the aircraft and many designs were developed exclusively around available engines—as discussed. The quest for engines of increased horsepower with low weight was the obvious design problem facing engine manufacturers and designers. As the war continued, engines that could perform well at high altitudes became another design challenge. Fortunately for

The Gnome monosoupape 9N, built under license at Oberursel as the U.I. These were installed on the Fokker E.II, E.III, D.II, D.V, the Pfalz A.II, E.II, E.III, E.VI, and the Siemens-Schuckert E.III. Oberursel also produced the Le Rhône 110-hp 9J under license that was relabeled the UR.II; this saw service on Fokker Dr.1s, the D.VI prototype, and the D.VIII. (Public domain)

The Le Rhône 9J 110 hp rotary engine—more powerful than the 80 hp engine and differentiated by intake manifolds placed on the aft side of the cylinders. The 110 was more powerful but less reliable as the 80 hp engine. It was produced in France, England, and Germany. It saw service on many aircraft including Nieuport 17s, Camels, Strutters, Pups, and Hanriots. (Public domain)

Germany, steel was available in quantity, but the same problem that faced the aircraft factories—namely tooling up for series production—plagued the engine manufacturers as well. Also, the extreme precision required to machine and tool engines on a compressed wartime timeline, compounded production problems. Many skilled machinists were already at the front; those who remained behind had to train new workers to do tasks that often required a long apprenticeship and much practice.

Rotary Engines

Early German aircraft featured rotary engines that were largely copies of the French Gnome and Le Rhône engines used by the Allies. These were made under license by Motorenfabrik Oberursel A.G. They were effective engines and posed no problems (except for their gyroscopic effect) until Germany began running low on high-quality castor oil upon which these lightweight powerful engines depended.

The Oberursel factory was located in its namesake town near Frankfurt. In 1913 the company produced Le Rhône 9C (UR series) and Gnome (U series) engines under license. The U.0, a copy of the Gnome Lambda 80-hp engine was used on early Fokker E.Is. By 1915, the 100-hp Oberursel U.I, a clone of the Gnome Monosoupape Type 9B 100-hp rotary, had the best power-to-weight ratio of any German engine. It was used on the Fokker and Pfalz E-series monoplanes. The 110-hp Oberursel UR.II, a clone of the Le Rhône 9J, was next and was popular. Fokker bought the company in 1916 in order to guarantee supplies of the UR.II, as supplies of the Mercedes D.III engine were limited. This acquisition obviously influenced the design path at Schwerin: the UR.II was used in the Fokker Dr.1 and Fokker D.VI. By 1917, the UR.II was obsolete due to its relatively low power compared to inlines, and poor performance at high altitudes. By 1918, IdFlieg preferred inline engines over rotaries as did the pilots. Moreover, the lack of high-quality castor oil and the inferior mineral oil substitute Voltol also conspired to bring an end to use of rotaries. Nevertheless, in the summer of 1918, the UR.II was installed in the Fokker D.VIII. The lightweight and aerodynamic cleanliness of the D.VIII allowed it to achieve excellent performance using the outmoded and underpowered UR.II. Oberursel also built a copy of Gnome's 14-cylinder Double Lambda double-banked rotary. This 160-hp engine, designated U.III in Germany, was difficult to build and tended to overheat quickly thus sealing its fate. It was used on the Fokker E.IV and D.III designs.

The Argus four-cylinder 100-hp inline engine. This was used by Aviatic, Rumpler, Otto, Goedecker, Harlan, and Jeanin. In 1914 this engine cost 7,500 marks. (Idflieg.com)

Inline Engines

With the emergence of the Halberstadt D series, the direction was clear to German designers: the inline engine became the preferred powerplant by all except Fokker who had a controlling share in Oberursel, and Siemens-Schuckert as discussed. Inline engines were efficient, powerful, and had no gyroscopic effect. The Argus four-cylinder inline was an early 100-hp liquid-cooled engine that was used on many of the *Taubes* and early aircraft at the outbreak of the war.

As the war progressed, Mercedes/Daimler led the way with their straight-six, liquid-cooled engines, but Benz and BMW also produced effective engines. The D.II was based on the Austro-Daimler (A.D.) engine, however had important differences such as the single overhead camshaft, half compression setting for the camshaft (for engine starting), dual carburettors on one side of the engine, and a unique cooling jacket design that enclosed two cylinders per jacket. It was like the Austro-Daimler engine in that it had six steel cylinders, and a cast aluminum crankcase that was built in two halves, being joined by bolts along its midline, a scavenger pump to circulate oil from the crankcase which was then pumped by a separate pump under high pressure to lubricate the engine. The Mercedes D.II was used on Aviatik B and C series reconnaissance planes, Albatros B.I and B.II, Halberstadt D.II, and Junkers J 1, to name a few.

The Mercedes D.II was a six-cylinder, single overhead, cam inline engine manufactured by Daimler, that produced around 100–120 hp. It was used on Aviatik and Albatros B series, Aviatik C.I, Fokker D.I, Halberstadt D.II, and Junkers J.I. It was replaced by the D.III and ended production by end of 1916. (Public domain)

The Daimler Mercedes D.III was the most widespread and reliable German inline of the war. It had many variations that focused on changing the shape of the piston heads to increase compression and, by extension, horsepower. It was originally rated at 160 hp but reached 200–217 hp by October 1918. It had a single overhead cam, cast aluminum crankcase, steel cylinders, double spark plugs and magnetos, and individual cooling jackets that covered two-thirds of each cylinder. (Idflieg.com)

The Mercedes D.III was perhaps the most widely used engine in German fighter aircraft. The Mercedes D.III was a straight-six, SOHC valve train, liquid-cooled inline engine built by Daimler. It differed from the D.II in that it had individual cooling jackets on each cylinder. The initial versions were introduced in 1914 at 160 hp, but a series of changes improved this to 170 hp (D.IIIa) in 1917 which was accomplished by using a flat-headed piston instead of the concave one used by the D.II and, as such, increased compression. It also featured a redesigned crankcase and carburetor.

By mid-1918 the piston head was changed to a domed or convex shape, thus increasing compression even more; this was termed the D.IIIau, and was rated at between 180 hp and 200 hp. These later D.III engines were used on almost all late-war German fighters, including the Albatros D series, Fokker D.VII, Pfalz D.III, Roland D.VI, and many others. The final iteration of this popular engine was the D.IIIav which increased compression yet again using longer aluminum pistons that saved on weight and allowed a higher rpm, but few of these saw active service.

The Austro-Daimler 6 was designed by Ferdinand Porsche. Originally it had copper cooling sleeves then was upgraded to welded steel. Like the Mercedes D.III, it saw gradually increasing compression due to exigencies of the war: it began in 1910 with 90 hp, and by 1918 had reached 225 hp. The BMW III rivaled the Mercedes D.III and A.D.6, but was difficult to source in quantity.

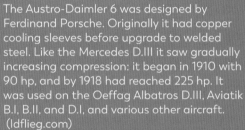

The Austro-Daimler 6 was designed by Ferdinand Porsche. Originally it had copper cooling sleeves before upgrade to welded steel. Like the Mercedes D.III it saw gradually increasing compression: it began in 1910 with 90 hp, and by 1918 had reached 225 hp. It was used on the Oeffag Albatros D.III, Aviatik B.I, B.II, and D.I, and various other aircraft. (Idflieg.com)

Believing that he had a solution to the crisis, Daimler-Benz designer Max Fritz proposed a new engine that used the same technology as the older Mercedes. But his ideas met with resistance, so he joined Bayerische Motoren Werke (BMW). There he designed BMW model IIIa—an engine that retained the six-cylinder inline configuration of the earlier Daimler-Benz engines, but was superior in that it had low fuel consumption and very good performance at high altitudes, which was the result of a "choked down" carburetor setting and a high compression ratio. It powered the Fokker D.VIIF. Pictured is the BMW IIIa in the Luftwaffenmuseum. (Arjun Sarup)

LMG 08/15

This was the nomenclature given to the machine gun used by the bulk of German fighters. It was a lightened air-cooled version of the original water-cooled rectangular pattern-receiver MG 08 machine gun used by ground forces, and was a variation on the basic gun developed by Hiram Maxim in the late 19th century. The lMG 08, was developed by the Spandau arsenal as a fixed, forward-facing aircraft machine gun and went into production in 1915, in single-gun mounts, for use on the E.I through the E.III production versions of the Fokker Eindecker. It was also fitted to the Halberstadt D.II and later in pairs by the time of the introduction of the Fokker D.III and Albatros D.I biplane fighters in 1916, as fixed and synchronized cowling guns firing through the propeller.

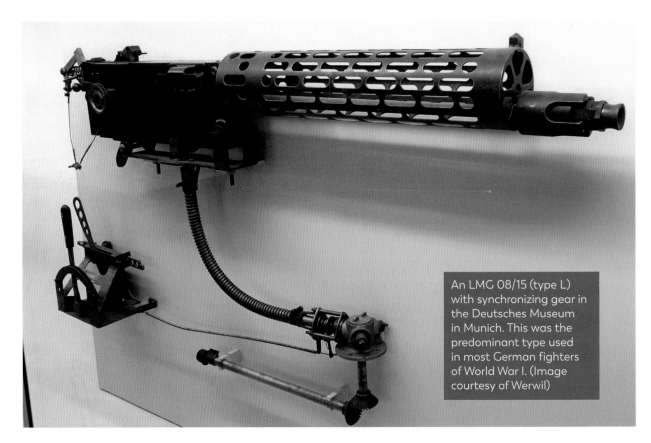

An LMG 08/15 (type L) with synchronizing gear in the Deutsches Museum in Munich. This was the predominant type used in most German fighters of World War I. (Image courtesy of Werwil)

The Parabellum MG14 made by Deutsche Waffen und Munitionsfabriken (DWM) was a lighter (22 lb) and quite different, air-cooled Maxim system gun with a very high rate of fire (600–700 rounds per minute). It was introduced in 1915, and was, but not without serious problems on occasion (as noted by Otto Parschau), prototyped on Parschau's own A.16/15 Fokker A.III "green machine" monoplane with the Fokker Stangensteuerung gun synchronizer, received back with the synchronized Parabellum by Parschau on May 30, 1915. It was first used in quantity as the synchronized, forward-firing armament on the five examples of the Fokker M.5K/MG Eindecker production prototype aircraft, and soon afterward served as a flexible aircraft observer's gun for rear defense.

| Conclusion

Before the war aircraft manufacturing was done in small batches by artisans coopted from boatbuilding, cabinet-making, coach-making, and even piano-making industries (Perzina factory used by Fokker). The training of workers initially varied from shop to shop, and series production was a term foreign to most of them.When war erupted in 1914, the rate of progress was sluggish before picking up rapidly in 1915. Effective aircraft that could fly over artillery-ravaged terrain were increasingly in demand for artillery and troop deployment reconnaissance, something that could not be by done on the ground. As reconnaissance aircraft were seen with increasing frequency in the skies over the Western and Eastern Fronts, the need for fighters to shoot them down arose on both sides. The German high command was fixated throughout the war on finding a "decisive weapon" as defined by Carl von Clausewitz, which translated to superior aircraft in overwhelming numbers—or series production of a good design. The production capacity for manufacturers evolved as the war continued: those who excelled in design and production and were lucky in their timing, received the biggest contracts. The methods by which these contracts were obtained were as varied, shrewd in their politics, and at times as perfidious as anything where potentially large sums of money are involved. Those who found a construction and production method that worked well for them, stuck with it, and were able to produce aircraft in quantity as well as quality. Fokker, Albatros, Pfalz, and to a lesser extent Roland, Siemens-Schuckert, and others were the leading producers of excellent aircraft. The path to this excellence was fraught with trial and error as testing and quality control were two areas that varied from factory to factory. Moreover, designers borrowed (or stole) ideas from each other, not only German designs but Allied as well as evidenced by the influence of Nieuport and Spad on German designers. Some were well ahead of their time—like Junkers—but cared less about winning the war, than advancing their own ideas and design sensibility.

As the war dragged on and Germany ran short of raw materials, skilled labor, and time to turn the tide, IdFlieg mandated that successful designs be produced under license by other factories (e.g. the Fokker D.VII built by Albatros). Patents, profits, and egos were swept aside in an effort to win the war. In the end it was too late for Germany, for with the United Sates now in the war with unlimited volumes of troops, supplies, and equipment, the air campaign could do little to stem the tide of events resulting in the Armistice on November 11, 1918.

| Appendix A

Zu der Patentschrift **26551**

Fig. 1.

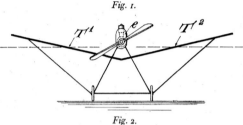

Fig. 2.

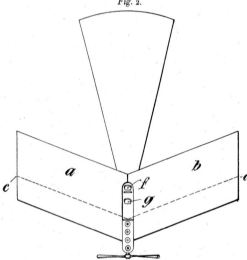

PHOTOGR. DRUCK DER REICHSDRUCKEREI.

ANTHONY HERMAN GERARD FOKKER
IN JOHANNISTHAL B. BERLIN.

Flugzeug.

Patentiert im Deutschen Reiche vom 26. Januar 1912 ab.

Um bei Flugzeugen die Längs- und Querstabilität zu erhalten oder wiederherzustellen, ist es allgemein notwendig, mechanische Vorrichtungen zu bedienen.

Mit Hilfe dieser Vorrichtungen ist es jedoch nicht immer möglich, allen äußeren, das Gleichgewicht störenden Einwirkungen in der gewünschten Weise zu begegnen, namentlich dann nicht, wenn Böen auftreten, denen gegenüber die mechanischen Vorrichtungen zu träge sind.

Zweck der Erfindung ist, ein Flugzeug zu schaffen, daß in sich, d. h. zufolge seiner Bauart, stabil ist, und zufolge dieser Eigenschaft das Bestreben hat, von selbst die Gleichgewichtslage aufrecht zu erhalten, oder sofort in sie zurückzukehren.

Nach den Erfahrungen und Versuchen des Erfinders (bei der noch bestehenden Unsicherheit der Gesetze über das Verhalten in der Luft bewegter Körper ist man auf solche hauptsächlich angewiesen) besitzt ein Flugzeug dann die erwähnte Eigenschaft, wenn es gleichzeitig drei Merkmale aufweist, 1. eine V-Stellung der Tragflächen nach oben, 2. eine V-Stellung der Tragflächen nach hinten und 3. Lage des Schwerpunktes über dem Auftriebsdruckmittelpunkt.

Der Beweis hierfür läßt sich indirekt führen. Es läßt sich nämlich mit einer Zuverlässigkeit nachweisen, daß ein Flugzeug beim Fehlen eines dieser Merkmale die Eigenschaft eigener Stabilität nicht besitzt.

Besitzt ein Apparat nur das erste der genannten Konstruktionsmerkmale, nämlich bei tiefliegendem Schwerpunkt V-Stellung der Tragflächen nach oben, so könnte diese höchstens insoweit günstig auf die Stabilität des Flugzeuges einwirken, als dieses sich senkrecht abwärts bewegt oder sinkt.

Die V-Stellung der Tragflächen nach hinten allein bei tiefliegendem Schwerpunkt sollte einen hohen Grad von Stabilität erwarten lassen, da bei einer Bö die getroffene Tragfläche eine Bremsung erfährt und dadurch das Flugzeug die zum Ausgleich der Bö erforderliche Kurve von selbst einschlägt. Damit indessen der Apparat aus dieser Kurve wieder von selbst in Gleichgewicht und Richtung komme, sind die beiden weiteren, oben angegebenen Konstruktionen erforderlich.

Der hochliegende Schwerpunkt für sich allein würde die Stabilität nur stören, weil er besonders in Kurven und im Gleitfluge beständig ein Kippmoment hervorbrächte.

Bei einem Flugzeug, welches bei tiefliegendem Schwerpunkt V-Stellung der Tragflächen nach oben und hinten besitzt, wird in der Kurve durch die Zentrifugalwirkung des mehr oder minder tiefliegenden Schwerpunktes die Stabilität vernichtet oder stark herabgesetzt. Beim Geradeausfliegen könnte ein derartiges Flugzeug immerhin einige Stabilität zeigen, soweit es nämlich aus der einer Bö entgegenwirkenden Kurve trotz des tiefliegenden Schwerpunktes wieder in Gleichgewicht und Richtung zu kommen vermag.

Ein Flugzeug, welches die V-Stellung der Tragflächen nach oben und hochliegenden Schwerpunkt aufweist, dem aber die V-Stellung nach rückwärts fehlt, würde nicht von selbst aus der von einer Bö verursachten Schrägstellung in die normale Lage zurückkehren, weil es sich nicht im Windstoße drehen und dadurch die gesenkte Tragfläche aufrichten könnte.

Gibt man endlich einem Flugzeug die V-Stellung der Tragflächen nach hinten und den hochliegenden Schwerpunkt, aber nicht auch V-Stellung der Tragflächen nach oben, so ist ein seitliches Abrutschen und ein Durchdrehen des Flugzeuges in der Kurve und mithin auch bei einer Bö unvermeidlich.

Dagegen haben Versuche einwandfrei ergeben, daß bei gleichzeitiger Anwendung der genannten drei Merkmale eine vollkommene Stabilität des Flugzeuges sowohl in der Kurve wie Böen gegenüber erzielt wird. Gerät ein gemäß der Erfindung gebautes Flugzeug durch einen Windstoß in eine Schräglage, so erfährt die getroffene gehobene Tragfläche eine Bremsung; dadurch kommt das Flugzeug ins seitliche Schieben und richtet sich infolge der V-Stellung der Tragflächen nach hinten wieder auf. Die V-Stellung der Tragflächen nach oben und der hochliegende Schwerpunkt spielen hier dieselbe Rolle wie bei einer Kurve, insofern auch hier ein seitliches Abrutschen verhütet wird, und die Zentrifugalbeschleunigung erst nach Vollendung der Kurve wieder eine richtende Kraft ausübt.

Die Zeichnung zeigt den Gegenstand der Erfindung in schematischer Weise an einem Ausführungsbeispiel, und zwar in Fig. 1 von vorn und in Fig. 2 von oben. Aus der Fig. 1 ergibt sich die V-Stellung der Tragflächen a und b nach oben. Die aus dieser Figur ersichtliche Verstrebung und Versteifung des Gestelles bildet keinen Teil der Erfindung. Das Merkmal der V-Stellung der Tragflächen nach hinten zeigt Fig. 2. Die auftreibenden Kräfte greifen mit ihrer Resultierenden in der V-förmig gebrochenen Linie c-d an. Denkt man sich die angreifenden Kräfte für jede Tragfläche in einem Punkt vereinigt, so ergeben sich die Auftriebsdruckmittelpunkte T^1 und T^2 deren Verbindungslinie in Fig. 1 eingetragen ist. Wie aus dieser Figur ersichtlich, liegt der Schwerpunkt (der Motor e) dem oben unter 3 genannten Merkmale entsprechend oberhalb dieser Linie. Flieger und Fahrgast befinden sich in gleicher Höhe auf den hinter dem Motor befindlichen Sitzen f und g.

Die Erfindung ist nicht auf eine bestimmte Gestalt der Tragfläche beschränkt. Notwendig ist nur, daß die Druckmittelpunktlinien selbst V-förmig verlaufen.

PATENT-ANSPRUCH:

Flugzeug, dadurch gekennzeichnet, daß die von der Längsachse ausgehenden Auftriebsdruckpunktlinien aufwärts und rückwärts verlaufen und der Schwerpunkt annähernd in dem bzw. über dem geometrischen Schwerpunkt der Flügel liegt.

Hierzu 1 Blatt Zeichnungen.

| Appendix B

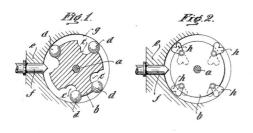

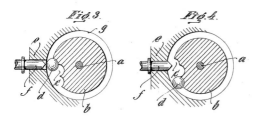

Fig. 1. Fig. 2.

Fig. 3. Fig. 4.

Inventor:
Anthony Herman Gerard Fokker.
By- B. Singer, Atty.

UNITED STATES PATENT OFFICE.

ANTHONY HERMAN GERARD FOKKER, OF AMSTERDAM, NETHERLANDS.

DEVICE FOR ACTUATING CONTROL GEARS FOR MACHINE GUNS.

1,426,849. Specification of Letters Patent. **Patented Aug. 22, 1922.**

Application filed September 1, 1920. Serial No. 407,537.

To all whom it may concern:

Be it known that I, ANTHONY HERMAN GERARD FOKKER, a subject of the Queen of the Netherlands, residing at Amsterdam,
5 Netherlands, have invented certain new and useful Improvements in Devices for Actuating Control Gears for Machines Guns (for which I have filed application in Germany, No. 307,649, filed June 21, 1917), of which
10 the following is a specification.

This invention is a new and useful improvement in the construction of devices commonly known as interrupter gears or firing gears on airplanes carrying machine
15 guns so mounted as to shoot through the plane of rotation of the propeller. These gears consist of a connection between the engine of the aeroplane and the machine gun, actuated by the engine in such a man-
20 ner that the gun is fired only at the time when the propeller blade is not in front of the muzzle of the gun, thus obviating damage to the propeller by bullets.

It is well known that in the construction
25 of such mechanisms great care must be taken to eliminate parts in which wear is likely to develop, which causes a lag between the actual actuation of the device by the engine and the firing of the gun, as this lag
30 would cause the gun to fire later than intended so that the bullets might hit one of the blades of the propeller.

The object of this invention is to provide a means to cause the gun to fire at the right
35 time, and on which the eventual wear has no detrimental effect, and which utilizes centrifugal force for keeping a rotating but loosely or pivotally mounted impact member in such a position as to stroke a suitably
40 placed projection on the firing pin, in order to actuate the mechanism of the gun, and cause the same to fire at the required times to avoid injury to the propeller.

In the accompanying drawings:—
45 Fig. 1 shows a transverse section.
Fig. 2 shows a second form of construction.
Figs. 3 and 4 show forms of construction similar to Fig. 1 in different positions.
50 A rotor disc *b* with peripheral recesses *c* in which balls *d* have been placed, is installed upon the shaft *a* and arranged to rotate in a circular chamber *g* of a suitable casing. The number of the balls *d* corresponds with the number of recesses *c*. The 55 firing pin *f* of the machine gun is adjustably installed in the casing *e* in such a manner, that its inner end protrudes into the wall *g* of the casing *e*.

In operation as the rotor disc *b* is made to 60 rotate, the balls are pressed against the edge of the wall *g* of the casing through the effect of centrifugal force, whereby they are made to push back, in passing, the firing pin *f* placed in the usual spring-bearings. (Fig. 65 3). The form of construction shown in Fig. 2 indicates, how the balls *d* have been replaced by rotatable blades *h*, whereby the dotted lines show the blades at rest. The balls *d* may be replaced by rollers or other 70 suitably shaped cam or impact members, which are flung into the uppermost aperture by centrifugal force, when the driving medium, in this case the plate *b*, is rapidly rotating and exercise in this position the oth- 75 erwise usual cam-pressure. (Fig. 3). When the rotor disc *b* is at rest, the centrifugal force ceases, so that the balls *d* are thrown out of their operative position. There is also no possibility of the device remaining 80 in such a position as to keep the firing pin *f* depressed when the rotation ceases, as is the case with devices using fixed cams or rollers.

Claims: 85
1. In combination with a controlling member of a machine gun firing mechanism, a rotor, and a centrifugally operated impact element, carried by the rotor and arranged to strike and actuate said controlling mem- 90 ber.

2. In combination with a machine gun firing pin, a casing having a chamber into which the inner end of said pin projects when said pin is at the inner limit of its 95 stroke, a rotor arranged in said chamber, and a centrifugally operated impact element, carried by the rotor and arranged to strike the inner end of said pin and hence actuate said pin. 100

In testimony whereof I affix my signature in presence of two witnesses.

ANTHONY HERMAN GERARD FOKKER.

Witnesses:
C. CJORTER,
H. Y. KUYPERS.

| Appendix C

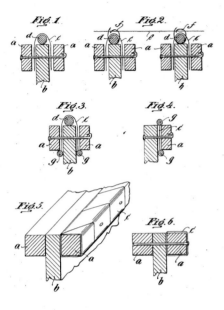

Fig. 1.　Fig. 2.

Fig. 3.　Fig. 4.

Fig. 5.

Fig. 6.

Inventor:
A. H. G. Fokker
By H. R. Kerslake.
Attorney

Patented Aug. 12, 1924.

1,504,817

UNITED STATES PATENT OFFICE.

ANTHONY HERMAN GERARD FOKKER, OF AMSTERDAM, NETHERLANDS.

FASTENING THE COVERING OF PLANES OF FLYING MACHINES TO RIBS OR SUCH LIKE.

Application filed December 9, 1920. Serial No. 429,557.

(GRANTED UNDER THE PROVISIONS OF THE ACT OF MARCH 3, 1921, 41 STAT. L., 1313.)

To all whom it may concern:

Be it known that I, ANTHONY HERMAN GERARD FOKKER, residing at 84 Rokin, Amsterdam, Netherlands, have invented certain new and useful Improvements in Fastening the Covering of Planes of Flying Machines to Ribs or Such Like (for which I have filed application in Germany, January 29, 1918), of which the following is a specification.

The object of the present invention is to provide an improved method of fastening the covering of supporting or steering planes of flying machines to the rib or such like.

By the means here described and which form the subject of my invention, the said covering, which may be of linen, cotton or any other suitable material can be fastened to a rib or other suitably constructed member over its entire length, by means of sewing, in the form of a continuous row of stitches, which may be as short as desired. Such a method has many advantages over the previously usual system of tying the covering to the rib at intervals by means of thread or string passing right around the rib; by the great number of stitches possible the covering is made to conform closely to the entire contour of the wing section, as determined by the shape of the rib, and the fastening is also greatly strengthened; a considerable amount of thread is saved, especially in the case of thick wings, and the whole process of fastening is much facilitated.

If it is desired for the sake of additional security, the well known system of tying the covering to the ribs at intervals, by means of thread or string passing around the rib, may be added to the method of stitching the fabric to the wrapping material on the frame members.

The attached drawing represents in Figs. 1-6 for instance, four different methods of execution of the invention, of which Figs. 1-4 and Fig. 6 are cross sections through the edge of a rib or other frame member.

Between the divided cap-strip or flange *a* and the web *b* a strip of cloth has been placed and glued and nailed together with the cap strip and the web. Underneath the strip of cloth *c* a cord *d* which may be of any suitable material and possessing any desired profile, has been placed. The covering *e* (Fig. 2) is sewn to the strip of cloth *c* and the cord *d* by means of yarn or such like *f* along the rib or frame member as shown in Fig. 2.

The method of execution in accordance with Fig. 3 shows the edges of the strips of cloth *c* provided with cords *g* which may already be woven into the strips *c* during the manufacture of the latter or separately let in or attached to them. Instead of the cords *g* the ends of the strips of cloth *c* may also be provided with re-inforced edges, or may be corded or bunched or such like.

By means of these reinforcing cords *g* the tearing out of the strips *c* has been prevented and a better means of fastening between the parts of the rib ensured, which, at the same time, improves the firmness of the fastening of the covering and is effected in a manner identical with the method as shown in Fig. 2.

The method of execution in accordance with Fig. 4 shows a single cap-strip, in which case the latter is glued and nailed to the rib *b*, after a strip of cloth *c* provided with reinforcing cords *g* has been placed between them.

The upper reinforcing cords *g* serve for being sewn on to the covering, while the reinforcing cords *g* of the lower edge offer a better security against being torn out or loosened.

The reinforcing cords *g* of the strip of cloth may be made during the process of weaving in the shape of a reinforced woven edge or separately put in at the upper and lower edge of the strip of cloth.

Figs. 5 and 6 show a somewhat different method of execution, in which one of the cap strips (*a*) is covered with cloth *c* or wound round with strips of cloth, before being glued and nailed to the other parts of the rib. Under this cloth a cord may be inserted, in a similar manner as shown in Figs. 1, 2 and 3, but this is not entirely necessary, as the wing covering material may be sewed directly to the covering of the cap-strip, as described. While in the above some preferred forms of construction have been described in which single or double cap-strips are used, I would have it understood that the methods described may be applied to frame members made up of any number of laminations, in which case a number of cloth strips may be used, as described, or any number of the laminations covered with cloth; furthermore I would have it understood that many more forms of construction may be devised without departing from the spirit of my invention and within the scope of the appended claims:

What I claim is:

1. In an arrangement of the character described, the combination of longitudinally divided frame members, of fabric insertions between the parts of said members, a covering, and means for securing the covering to the insertion.

2. In a plane structure of the character described, in combination, longitudinally divided frame members, fabric insertions arranged between the parts of said members, a covering, and stitches for securing the covering to the insertions.

3. In a plane structure of the character described, in combination, bracing ribs, strips secured longitudinally of the sides of the ribs adjacent the free edges thereof, a fabric insertion covering one of said strips, a covering and means for securing the covering to the fabric covered strip.

4. An arrangement as claimed in claim 3 wherein the fabric insertion is arranged in the form of a strip and wrapped about the longitudinal strip on the frame rib.

In testimony whereof I affix my signature in presence of two witnesses.

ANTHONY HERMAN GERARD FOKKER.

Witnesses:
W. HORTER,
H. NIEUWENHUIS.

Patent 1,504,817, registered with U.S. Patent Office, dated August 12, 1924.

| Appendix D

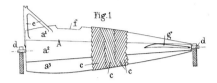

Fig. 1.

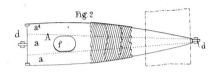

Fig. 2.

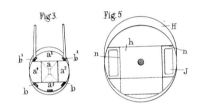

Fig. 3.   Fig. 5.

WITNESSES

INVENTOR
ARMAND JEAN AUGUSTE DEPERDUSSIN
BY
ATTORNEYS

Fig. 4.

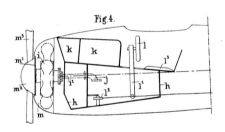

Fig. 6.

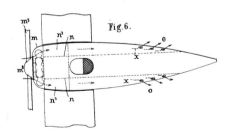

WITNESSES

INVENTOR
ARMAND JEAN AUGUSTE DEPERDUSSIN
BY
ATTORNEYS

ARMAND JEAN AUGUSTE DEPERDUSSIN, OF PARIS, FRANCE.

AEROPLANE-FUSELAGE.

1,106,193.   Specification of Letters Patent.   Patented Aug. 4, 1914.

Application filed April 22, 1913.   Serial No. 762,787.

To all whom it may concern:

Be it known that I, ARMAND JEAN AUGUSTE DEPERDUSSIN, a citizen of the Republic of France, and a resident of 19 Rue des Entrepreneurs, Paris, France, have invented a new and useful Aeroplane-Fuselage, of which the following is a specification.

This invention relates to an aeroplane fuselage constituted entirely by the juxtaposition and cohesion, at crossed directions, of very thin slats of small width of wood, cardboard, paper or the like. The fuselage obtained in this way, while being very light, is endowed with extraordinary rigidity and solidity.

A form of construction of the object of the invention is represented by way of example upon the annexed drawing which shows:

Figure 1 an elevation of a fuselage in course of construction; in this figure there is represented only a portion of the wooden slats which are broken away to show the crossed directions of the different layers. Fig. 2 is a plan view corresponding to Fig. 1. Fig. 3 is an end view from the left of Fig. 1. Fig. 4 represents on a larger scale a longitudinal axial section of the front part of the finished fuselage and in which there has been placed the frame which supports the different propelling and controlling devices. Fig. 5 shows the end view of the apparatus after fixing the frame and the engine being supposed removed. Fig. 6 is a plan view of the finished fuselage.

The construction of the fuselage is effected upon a mold or former A composed of several parts with a view to allowing removal when the fuselage is finished. In the example represented, this former is composed of a central part a of pyramidal shape upon which are fixed by any suitable means cheeks a^1 a^2 a^3 and a^4. These cheeks are provided with grooves b^1 to allow of accommodating the ribs b of the fuselage upon which are to be nailed the wooden slats c which form the fuselage body. The former is mounted preferably upon trunnions d which allow of revolving it around its axis during the construction of the fuselage. First therefore the different parts of the former are assembled, after which the ribs b upon which the uprights e for the shrouds may even be fixed in advance are placed in position in the grooves b^1 of the cheeks a^1 a^2 and a^4. Then the position of the openings to be formed in the fuselage is determined: the pilot's manhole

f, openings g for the accommodation of the rear empennage, etc. The wooden slats c are next affixed, which operation is effected in the following manner: These slats are nailed one beside another upon the ribs b, in this way forming a first layer upon which is applied and glued or affixed a second layer at a crossed direction and if necessary a third and a fourth. This work is greatly facilitated by the fact that the former can be revolved around its axis. Moreover it is advantageous to affix the wooden slats under tension; for this purpose when the slat is soaked or coated with glue and fixed to a rib b at one end, an energetic pull is exerted upon the other end by means of any suitable device, for example by fixing this end in a vise or tongs and exerting a pull upon the tongs by means of a tackle. It is evident that care be taken not to place the slats where openings have to be arranged. When the fastening of the slats is completed, the former is taken apart and removed; the fuselage can then be clothed externally and varnished. In this way there is obtained a monoblock or one-piece fuselage, which is very strong and very light and offers very little resistance to the air.

In a fuselage of this kind, it would be very difficult to proceed to fit the different propelling and controlling devices in the interior of the fuselage itself, as is done usually in other apparatus. There is available indeed only a space of very limited dimensions, so that fitting would be very long and troublesome to perform and moreover difficult to verify. The present invention has for object to avoid these disadvantages; it consists in mounting the whole or a part of the apparatus intended for the propulsion and the control of the apparatus upon an independent frame which is then introduced into the fuselage and secured upon the fuselage by means of any suitable device. In this way the fitting may be carried on upon an erecting table for example, which allows of avoiding any loss of time and lends itself readily to verifications. The frame upon which the different parts are mounted in this way, when secured in the interior of the fuselage, forms to some extent a partition or bulkhead in the fuselage and thereby increases rigidity. This partitioning may even be used to conduct toward the rear of the apparatus the burnt gases exhausted from the engine.

Fig. 4 is an axial section of the front part of the aeroplane showing the disposition of the frame h upon which are previously mounted the engine i and its shaft i^1, the carbureter j, the tanks k, as well as the controlling devices, viz. the wheel l and bridge l^1, foot-rail l^2, seat l^3, etc. After having received all these parts, the frame is introduced into the fuselage, in the interior of which it is fixed by any suitable means.

The fuselage when finished is provided at front with a bonnet m which incloses the engine. This bonnet has an opening m^1 in which is engaged the cap-shaped hub m^2 with which the propeller m^3 is provided. The opening m^1 is larger than the hub m^2 so as to leave an annular space through which the air serving for the cooling of the motor can penetrate.

Fig. 6 is a plan view of the finished fuselage showing the sub-division of the fuselage to allow the evacuation of the cooling air and the burnt gases. In this figure the frame A has been supposed to be provided upon its faces with tight-fitting walls n (see also Fig. 5) extending longitudinally so as to isolate completely the pilot's room from the space which contains the engine. There are formed in this way chambers or compartments n^1, which are bounded externally by the walls of the fuselage, in free communication with the space inclosing the engine and extending on either side of the apparatus. By forming in the shell at the rear of the planes suitable openings o there are constituted channels which allow the cooling air and the burnt gases to escape as indicated by the arrows x. The rear portion of the shell might even be used for the evacuation of these gases which would in this way take place at the rear of the apparatus.

What I claim and desire to secure by Letters Patent of the United States is:

1. A monoblock fuselage or body for aeroplanes, comprising a hollow frame formed of a plurality of superposed layers glued together, each layer consisting of thin plates, the plates of one layer crossing the plates of another layer.

2. A monoblock fuselage or body for aeroplanes comprising a hollow body formed of a plurality of superposed plates glued together each layer consisting of thin and narrow juxtaposed plates, the plates of one layer extending in a different direction to

the plates of another layer, the frame being provided with apertures in its sides.

3. A monoblock fuselage or body for an aeroplane, comprising a hollow frame formed of superposed layers, each layer consisting of thin and narrow juxtaposed plates, the plates of one layer crossing the plates of another layer, the frame being provided with an upright at one end, an opening adjacent its other end and a manhole intermediate of its ends.

4. A monoblock fuselage or body for aeroplanes comprising a hollow frame open at one end and formed of a plurality of superposed layers, each consisting of thin plates, the plates of one layer crossing the plates of another layer, and a frame-work carrying the engine and its appurtenances and extending into the hollow frame.

5. A monoblock fuselage or body for aeroplanes, comprising a hollow frame open at one end and formed of a plurality of superposed layers, each layer consisting of thin and narrow juxtaposed plates, a frame work carrying an engine and its appurtenances and arranged in the frame, with the engine outside thereof, and an apertured cover for the open end of the frame and inclosing the engine.

6. A monoblock fuselage or body for aeroplanes, comprising a hollow frame open at one end and formed of a plurality of superposed layers, each layer consisting of thin juxtaposed plates, a frame work carrying an engine and its appurtenances and arranged in the hollow frame with the engine outside thereof, an apertured cover for the open end of the frame and inclosing the engine, and a propeller on the engine shaft outside of the cover.

7. A monoblock fuselage or body for aeroplanes, comprising a hollow frame formed of a plurality of superposed layers, each layer consisting of thin juxtaposed plates, the frame being provided with apertures in its sides and interior walls forming longitudinal passages for circulation of air and burnt gases.

In testimony whereof I have signed my name to this specification, in the presence of two subscribing witnesses.

ARMAND JEAN AUGUSTE DEPERDUSSIN.

Witnesses:
   EDGAR MORGAN,
   JACQUES VANDER LINGO.

Appendix E

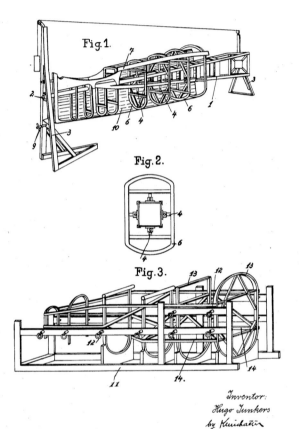

Fig. 1.

Fig. 2.

Fig. 3.

Inventor:
Hugo Junkers
by *Knichaein*
Atty.

HUGO JUNKERS, OF DESSAU, GERMANY.

ERECTION OF THE HULLS AND THE LIKE OF FLYING MACHINES.

Application filed July 22, 1925, Serial No. 45,380, and in Germany August 8, 1924.

My invention refers to the erection and assembling of the skeleton and covering of the hull or fuselage and similar hollow bodies forming part of an aeroplane or other flying machine. It is an object of my invention to provide means whereby such bodies can be erected and assembled in an easier and more effective manner than was hitherto possible.

According to the present invention the hollow body to be erected is built around a longitudinal support or girder supported at its ends and carrying the templets or the like. By thus supporting all the templets on a rigid inner support or girder the entire body is rendered freely accessible from without in all phases of erection and the cross frames can easily be mounted in place.

In the construction of fuselages for flying machines that part of the fuselage which connects the wings, rudders or elevators on the one hand and the part carrying the engine, crew and passengers on the other hand can be erected separately and are then only put together. This involves a great simplification inasmuch as in assembling the first mentioned part of the fuselage no consideration need be paid to the single frames required for supporting the engine in the front portion of the craft, these frames as a rule forming an obstacle to the erection of the other parts of the hull.

By aid of the present invention I am also enabled to easily and simply erect flying machines in which a wing structure extending right across the fuselage carries not only the fore part of the fuselage and the engine, but also the tail portion of the fuselage, each of these parts forming a structural unit.

I further provide an exterior fixture for the construction of the fore part of the hull designed to take up the engine, this fixture together with the templets required for the fixation in place of the several parts surrounding it from without.

In a preferred form of my invention the inner support has the form of a light lattice girder which carries the templets for the main parts to be mounted in place and which is mounted at its ends in bearings which are so arranged that the girder can easily be disengaged therefrom.

In the drawings affixed to this specification and forming part thereof a device embodying my invention is illustrated diagrammatically by way of example.

In the drawings:—

Fig. 1 is a perspective view of a longitudinal support or girder supported at its ends and carrying the templets and/or cross frames of the tail portion of a fuselage.

Fig. 2 is a cross section.

Fig. 3 is a perspective view of a fixture supporting the fore part of a fuselage.

Referring first to Fig. 1, 1 is a lattice girder rotatably and disengageably mounted with journals 2 in two supports 3. Templets 4 are mounted on the girder 1 for holding the single parts of the fuselage in correct position.

Fig. 2 shows the way in which the cross frames 6 are mounted on the templets 4. A pin 9 in the rear support 3, which can be inserted in the stern portion of the fuselage allows fixing the fuselage in position and prevents its rotation about the journals 2. By withdrawing the pin 9 the fuselage can easily be rotated about its longitudinal axis, thereby rendering all parts readily accessible. Fig. 1 further shows how, after the cross frames 6 have been mounted in place on the girder and templets, the longéron 7 and the outer skin 10 which also serves as a longitudinal bracing member can be mounted on the cross frames 6.

The fixture 11 illustrated in Fig. 3 and serving for the construction of the fore part of the fuselage has a number of adjustable pins or bolts 12 serving for fixing in place the main frame 13, and longérons 14, which have previously been constructed and are now connected with each other to form the skeleton. The covering is mounted in place after the skeleton has been removed from the fixture.

The two parts of the fuselage erected separately as shown in Figs. 1 and 3 are then connected by intermediate ties or struts or are mounted together on the central section of the wing.

I wish it to be understood that I do not desire to be limited to the exact details of construction shown and described for obvious modifications will occur to a person skilled in the art.

I claim:—

The method of building the fuselage of a flying machine comprising assembling the parts constituting the rear half of the fuselage around a rotary template support, the parts constituting the front half, which is designed to carry the engine, within a templet carrying jig, stripping the halves thus produced from their supports and uniting said halves.

In testimony whereof I affix my signature.

HUGO JUNKERS.

Patent 1,618,53X, registered with U.S. Patent Office, dated February 22, 1927.

Appendix F

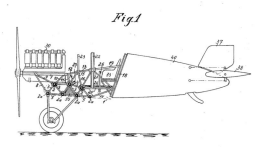

Fig.1

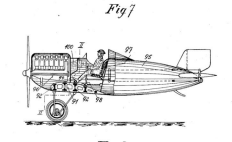

Fig.2

Inventor:
Hugo Junkers
by
Attorn

Fig.7

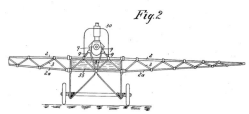

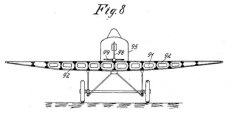

Fig.8

Inventor:
Hugo Junkers
by
Attorney.

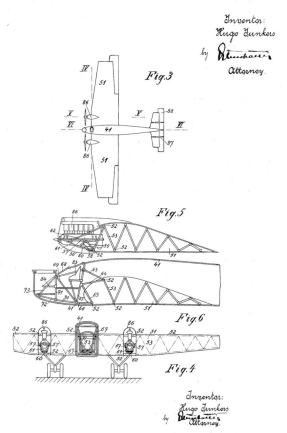

Fig.3

Fig.5

Fig.6

Fig.4

Inventor:
Hugo Junkers
by
Attorney.

HUGO JUNKERS, OF DESSAU, GERMANY.

FLYING MACHINE.

Application filed June 28, 1920. Serial No. 392,587.

(GRANTED UNDER THE PROVISIONS OF THE ACT OF MARCH 3, 1921, 41 STAT. L., 1313.)

To all whom it may concern:

Be it known that I, HUGO JUNKERS, a citizen of Germany, residing at Dessau, Germany, have invented certain new and useful Improvements in Flying Machines (for which I have filed application in Germany, March 12, 1918, and March 22, 1918; Netherlands, July 14, 1919; Sweden, December 6, 1919; Norway, December 31, 1919; Denmark, December 19, 1919), of which the following is a specification.

My invention relates to flying machines of the monoplane type with supporting-surfaces devoid of all external stay wires or the like. Although such self-supporting surfaces offer considerable aerodynamic advantages over supporting-surfaces braced by means of stay-wires or the like, they have been employed until now in monoplanes only to a small degree as their use involves great difficulties in the construction of the aeroplane and in the distribution of the loads. It is usual in monoplanes to attach the two halves of the supporting-surface laterally to the central body or shell, whose walls, considering their weight can however hardly be made strong enough to take up the strong flectional forces acting upon the supporting-surfaces.

It is an object of the present invention to fully utilize in monoplanes the aerodynamic advantages of self-supporting wings, viz, the absence of the resistance offered to the air by external stay-wires or the like. To this end the supporting-surface structure and more especially the longitudinal beams or runners are made to extend across the entire width of the flying machine, that is to say, also across the middle portion thereof which is usually formed by the body.

In the monoplanes constructed up till now and consisting as a rule of a body and the supporting-surfaces attached to both sides thereof, the supporting-surfaces are not directly connected with each other and are not constructively combined with the body to form a coherent structure, the more so as they are required to be easily detachable from said body for constructional and transporting reasons. In accordance with this peculiarity of construction the body generally represents to a certain extent the backbone of the whole flying-machine, which back-bone ultimately supports all other parts and in which all internal and external forces, which become effective in a flying machine, are collected and balanced. At the same time the body forms a kind of foundation for the loads, such as persons, motors, tanks or the like to be carried by the flying machine. The body accordingly does not only form an envelope for these parts, but also takes up directly their weight. This form of construction, which has been until now in general use in monoplanes, is fundamentally imperfect in so far as in the same the considerations playing a rôle in terrestrial vehicles are still too much emphasized, while the forces arising in flying are only given secondary consideration. Before all this construction involves the disadvantage, that during flight the transmission of power from the supporting-surfaces creating the buoyancy to the loads to be carried has to take place by means of a number of intermediate members. The same is true of the balance of the air resistance of the supporting-surfaces acting in the direction of travel by the tractive power of the propeller.

The monoplane according to the present invention offers the further advantage, that its construction can be substantially better accommodated to the sequence of forces corresponding to the real purpose of the flying machine thereby that the loads to be carried by the aeroplane are taken up as far as possible directly by the supporting-surfaces, the forces acting upon the aeroplane being also balanced as far as possible in the supporting surface itself. To this end the continuous supporting framework of the supporting-surface is made to take the place of the body as a kind of foundation for taking up directly the loads carried by the aeroplane. In thus using the supporting-surface as a foundation for the loads and as a kind of backbone for the whole flying machine advantage can be taken of the circumstance that the longitudinal beams of the supporting-surface according to this invention and which extend across the entire width of the flying machine, must be made very strong or be reinforced in the middle portion, where all loads are concentrated, such reinforcing of the middle portion of the supporting-surface beams being further necessitated by the circumstance that their bending movement assumes its maximum value in that portion.

In the case where the loads cannot be placed immediately upon the supporting surface framework, auxiliary frames for supporting such loads may be attached to the continuous beams or girders of the supporting surface.

In consequence thereof that part of the aeroplane body, which encloses these loads only serves as a resistance reducing envelope, not as a support for the loads and still less as a support for the wings. The rearwardly extending portion of the body, forming the connecting member between the main supporting-surface and the rear surface can now be attached, the same as the other loads, directly to the continuous supporting-surface beams or to an auxiliary frame connected therewith and can thus transmit the weight and steering forces acting upon said portion of the body to the main supporting-surface on the shortest way.

If in smaller monoplanes the supporting-surface provided with continuous cross-beams is attached in the usual position to the side walls of the body, there arises the disadvantage that the cross-beams extend through that part of the body, which is designed to take up passengers, motors, and loads, thus forming a great hindrance to the accommodation of such persons or loads. According to the present invention this disadvantage is obviated by placing the supporting-surface so low with respect to the body that its supporting framework such as the cross-beams or girders extends either below the body or through its lower part, so that in that part of the body, which is above the supporting-surface, there is left a sufficiently high space for the accommodation of persons, motors, loads, steering gear and the like, such space being entirely unobstructed by constructive parts of the supporting-surface. Passengers, motors and loads may thus be accommodated and distributed within the body as desired. It is true that in consequence of this arrangement the center of gravity of the flying machine is as a rule raised above the supporting-surface. However, experience has proved that this is of no avail whatever, the necessary stability of the aeroplane in the air being obtained by suitably dimensioning and adjusting the balancing surfaces.

In the drawings affixed to this specification and forming part thereof three different types of monoplanes embodying my invention are illustrated diagrammatically.

In the drawings—

Fig. 1 is a side elevation, and

Fig. 2 is the front elevation of the skeleton of a small single-seat monoplane.

Figs. 3 to 6 illustrate a large type of monoplane,

Fig. 3 being a plan view,

Fig. 4 a front elevation, partly in section on line IV—IV,

Fig. 5 a cross-section taken on line V—V and

Fig. 6 a like section taken on line VI—VI of Fig. 3.

Figs. 7 and 8 are illustrations of a small type of monoplane with a wooden framework surface,

Fig. 7 being a side elevation, partly in longitudinal section and

Fig. 8 a cross-secton on line 8—8 of Fig. 7.

Referring to Figs. 1 and 2 of the drawings, the supporting-surface, the sectional outlines of which are indicated in dotted lines at 1 (Fig. 1), encloses the supporting framework in the form of a lattice girder formed by upper and lower longitudinal beams 2, 2ª and diagonal rods 3 arranged between said beams. Further framework rods 4 and 5 form a connection between the top and bottom flanges, respectively, of the different girders. The beams 2, 2ª as well as the rods 3, 4, 5 arranged between them extend across the entire width of the machine.

The weight of the loads to be carried by the aeroplane are transmitted as far as possible directly upon this framework of the supporting-surface by means of auxiliary frames attached to the said framework and carrying the loads. The weight of the motor 30 is transmitted to the supporting-surface by an auxiliary frame substantially consisting of the motor supports proper 7 and the struts 8, 9, 10, 11; the weight of the pilot sitting in the chair 33, is transmitted by aid of the auxiliary frame 16—21 carrying also the steering gear 25, 26. The pedal 27 of the side steering gear is mounted directly within the supporting-surface frame. In order to brace the whole structure more rigidly the frames carrying the motor and the pilot are connected with each other by rods 12—15. Some of the elements of the frame such as 18 and 22 are preferably constructed to form frames adapted to carry the envelope of the body. The fuel tank 35 is mounted within the supporting-surface framework, its weight being thus taken up directly by the said surface. The body itself merely serves as an envelope for all these loads and mainly serves the purpose of diminishing the air resistance. In a like manner the tractive

effort of the propeller is transmitted directly upon the supporting-surface by the auxiliary frame carrying the motor. The rear portion 40 of the body carrying the rudders 37, 38 is attached directly to the auxiliary frame 18 secured to the supporting-surface, so that the weight of this portion of the body and of the rudders as well as the air forces acting upon the same are also transmitted to the supporting wing on the shortest possible way.

In the aeroplane shown in Figs. 3 to 6, the motors 30 arranged as far as possible in front are mounted with their supports on an auxiliary frame by the framework rods 58—62 and attached to the framework 52, 53 of the supporting-surface 51, said supporting structure extending across the entire width of the flying machine. Seats 83, 84 for the crew are provided in the front portion, said seats being mounted in a special auxiliary frame 63—73 directly combined with the main framework of the supporting-surface. The body envelope 41 mounted upon the frames 62—71, again serves merely for reducing the air resistance and not for taking up and transmitting the weight of the crew. The motors are enclosed in resistance reducing envelopes 86.

The monoplane illustrated in Figs. 7 and 8 has its supporting-surface 91 arranged in such low position relatively to the body 95, that above the framework of this surface a high space remains available within the body for the comfortable accommodation of the pilot as well as of the driving and steering gear, other accessories, loads, and so on. This arrangement warrants on the one hand a simple construction of the girder structure of the supporting-surface most perfectly adapted for the distribution of forces. On the other hand the arrangement and distribution of the loads to be accommodated in the body is not in any manner interfered with by the constructive members transmitting the bending stresses. As shown in Fig. 7 the motor 96, the pilot's seat 97, the steering gear 98 and 99, the fuel tank 100 and the like are arranged in the interior of the body above the supporting wings. Fig. 8 further shows that with the usual mode of arranging the supporting surfaces at about half the height of the body a transmission of the bending stresses from one side of the surface to the other by causing the transmission members to extend across the entire width of the aeroplane would meet with difficulties hardly to be overcome, unless the loads were distributed on an entirely different plan.

The body in order to offer the least possible resistance to the air extends downwardly so far that its bottom is flush with the bottom of the supporting-surface.

I claim:

1. In a flying machine of the monoplane type in combination, a substantially unbroken self-supporting bearing plane of streamline section extending substantially in a straight horizontal line across the entire width of the craft and a motor and pilot's seat mounted on and above said bearing plane.

2. In a flying machine of the monoplane type in combination, a substantially unbroken self-supporting bearing plane of streamline section extending substantially in a straight horizontal line across the entire width of the craft, a load carrying structure supported by said bearing plane and a motor on said structure.

3. In a flying machine of the monoplane type in combination, a substantially unbroken self-supporting bearing plane of streamline section extending substantially in a straight horizontal line across the entire width of the craft, a load carrying structure mounted forward of and supported by said bearing plane and a motor on said structure.

4. In a flying machine of the monoplane type in combination, a substantially unbroken self-supporting bearing plane of streamline section extending across the entire width of the craft, a load carrying structure supported by said bearing plane, a motor on said structure and a substantially non-load carrying tail piece fixed to said bearing plane.

5. In a flying machine of the monoplane type in combination, a substantially unbroken self-supporting bearing plane of streamline section extending across the entire width of the craft, a load carrying structure supported by said bearing plane, a motor on said structure and a substantially non-load carrying tail piece fixed to said load carrying support.

6. In a flying machine of the monoplane type in combination, a streamlined bearing plane comprising a plurality of straight girders forming the transverse spars and extending substantially in a straight horizontal line across the entire width of said plane and a motor and pilot's seat mounted on and above said bearing plane.

7. In a flying machine of the monoplane type in combination, a streamlined bearing plane comprising a plurality of straight girders forming the transverse spars and extending substantially in a straight horizontal line across the entire width of said plane and a motor and pilot's seat mounted on and forward of said bearing plane.

8. In a flying machine of the monoplane type in combination, a streamlined bearing plane comprising a plurality of straight girders forming the transverse spars and extending substantially in a straight horizontal line across the entire width of said plane, a load-carrying structure mounted on and above said bearing plane and a motor on and supported by said structure.

9. In a flying machine of the monoplane type in combination, a streamlined bearing plane comprising a plurality of straight girders forming the transverse spars and extending substantially in a straight horizontal line across the entire width of said plane, a load-carrying structure mounted on and above said bearing plane and a motor and pilot's seat on and supported by said structure.

10. In a flying machine of the monoplane type in combination, a streamlined bearing plane comprising a plurality of straight girders forming the transverse spars and extending across the entire width of said plane, a plurality of load-carrying structures mounted on and above said bearing plane and a motor and a pilot's seat mounted on and supported by separate load-carrying structures.

11. In a flying machine of the monoplane type in combination, a streamlined bearing plane comprising a plurality of straight girders forming the transverse spars and extending across the entire width of said plane, a load-carrying girder-shaped structure mounted on and above said bearing plane and a motor on and supported by said structure.

In testimony whereof I affix my signature.

HUGO JUNKERS.

Patent 1,576,977, dated March 16, 1926.

Appendix G

VILLEHAD HENRIK FORSSMAN, OF COLOGNE, GERMANY.

PROCESS FOR THE PRODUCTION OF HOMOGENEOUS WOOD MATERIAL AND THE
PRODUCT THEREOF.

No Drawing. Continuation of application Serial No. 593,650, filed October 10, 1922. This application
filed March 31, 1923. Serial No. 629,172.

To all whom it may concern:

Be it known that I, VILLEHAD HENRIK FORSSMAN, a subject of the King of Sweden, residing at Cologne, Germany, have invent-
5 ed certain new and useful Improvements in Processes for the Production of Homogeneous Wood Material and the Product Thereof, of which the following is a specification, the same being a continuation of my appli-
10 cation entitled "Process for the production of practically homogeneous wood material and wood bodies and the product thereof," filed October 10, 1922, Serial Number 593,650.

The objects of this invention are to pro-
15 vide a process for the production of homogeneous wood material, which may also be substantially free from tendencies towards deformation caused by variations in temperature or humidity, by reason of the treat-
20 ments described and claimed in my copending application entitled Process for the treatment of wood material and the product thereof, executed on even date herewith, and also to provide a wood material with new
25 and very valuable characteristics. The process hereinafter described for rendering wood material homogeneous is preferably employed after the treatment set forth in said application, although it may be independ-
30 ently utilized to advantage.

Wood material consists principally of fibres and superposed and interposed cells. The inner spaces of these cells enclose hygroscopic substances, whose changing de-
35 grees of humidity tend to cause inner tensions in the wood material and consequent deformations. There are also within the cells albumen or ferment substances which tend to putrefy, this affecting the form and
40 characteristics of the wood material.

The invention of my process consists broadly in treating a thin layer of wood with a cellulose solution, such as acetylcellulose in acetone, said layer having prefer-
45 ably a substantial number of its cells mechanically opened and preferably having had the contents of said cells rendered nonhygroscopic and non-fermentable.

The wood material to be treated is first
50 separated into one or more thin layers by suitable mechanical methods, such as by cutting, slicing, etc. If every cell is opened so that its contents can be treated, theoretical perfection will be attained, but it is un-

necessary as well as usually impracticable 55 to strive for such accuracy. In the case of woods of central Europe, I have obtained remarkable results with layers of about a tenth of a millimetre thickness, in which layers most of the cells were exposed, but it 60 is not necessary to employ such very thin layers in the use of my process, as thin layers of wood materials of two and a half millimetres thickness can be successfully treated by my process. 65

The reason therefore is that the cellulose solution which is applied to the thin layer penetrates it more thoroughly in proportion to the number of opened cells. The impregnation of one or more thin layers by a cellu- 70 lose solution has the extremely valuable effect of filling the interstices and opened cells with a solution having substantially the inherent properties and characteristics of the wood material itself, thus producing a sub- 75 stantially homogeneous material, which is peculiarly adapted for working and for the production of such wooden articles as boxes, trunks, canoes, automobile bodies, etc.

Preferably, I first subject the thin layer 80 to one or more of the treatments set forth in my said application, to which reference is here made, but which treatments may be briefly described as follows, namely, as consisting broadly in suitably treating the con- 85 tents of as large a number as practicable of these cells, the maximum results being obtained by mechanically opening as many as possible, either by washing out the hygroscopic and ferment substances therein or by 90 treating them with a suitable neutralizing solution, as for example, one containing chrome alum with or without formaldehyde, or by washing and then neutralizing the undesirable hygroscopic and ferment qualities of 95 the cell contents.

Thin wood layers when treated as above described become soft and pliable, so that superposed layers may be readily shaped by merely stretching over a core or placing in a 100 mould. The application of heat and pressure or either may be employed to facilitate the described treatment. During the treatment, the treated layers expand and swell considerably, there being a correspondingly 105 great contraction upon drying, which has the effect of causing to disappear during drying any folds occuring during the ex-

panding and swelling of the material. Wood material treated by my process possesses the very valuable characteristics of being substantially immune from deformations caused
5 by variations in temperature and humidity as encountered during usage. If desired, it can be subsequently treated with suitable solutions for the purpose of altering its shape.

The advantages of prior treatment by one
10 or both of the processes of my said application are that the homogeneous wood material will not warp, contract or otherwise change its form when exposed to usage conditions.
15 I claim:

1. The process of treating a thin layer of wood material, comprising impregnating it with a cellulose solution.

2. The process of treating a thin layer of
20 wood material, comprising impregnating it with a solution containing acetylcellulose acetone.

3. The process of treating a thin layer of wood material, a substantial number of
25 whose cells have been opened, comprising impregnating it with a solution containing acetylcellulose acetone.

4. The process of treating a thin layer of wood material comprising the subjection of the contents of a substantial number of its 30 cells to a solution adapted to neutralize the hygroscopic and ferment qualities of substances in said cells, and impregnating said layer with a cellulose solution.

5. The process of treating a thin layer of 35 wood material, comprising the washing out of hygroscopic and ferment substances from a substantial number of its cells and impregnating said layer with a cellulose solution. 40

6. Wood material and cellulose matter in a substantially homogeneous thin layer.

7. Wood material and cellulose matter in a substantially homogeneous thin layer, a substantial number of whose cells are sub- 45 stantially free from hygroscopic and ferment substances.

In testimony whereof I hereunto affix my signature in the presence of two witnesses.

VILLEHAD HENRIK FORSSMAN.

Witnesses:
GEO. ROSSWEG,
HENRY W. HEEDS.

| Appendix H

AUGUST 26, 1920

DURALUMIN

BY E. UNGER AND E. SCHMIDT

(Translated from *Technische Berichte*, Vol. III—Section 6, by STARR TRUSCOTT)

THE use of duralumin in the construction of aircraft makes an account of the properties of this material desirable, especially with reference to its working qualities as developed by experience.

Composition, Specific Gravity and Melting Point

Duralumin is made in various compositions, and has, with the exception of small quantities of impurities, the following composition :—

Aluminium	..	95·5 to 93·2 per cent.
Magnesium	..	0·5 ,,
Copper ..	..	3·5 to 5·5 ,,
Manganese ..	..	0·5 to 0·8 ,,

Lead, tin and zinc, which, as is well-known, have an unfavourable influence upon the permanence of aluminum alloys, are not found in duralumin.

The specific gravity of duralumin varies according to composition and hardness from 2.75 to 2.84. The melting point is about 650° C.

Duralumin is made under this name by the Dürener Metallwerke, Düren (Rhld.), and under the name of Berg-metall by Carl Berg, Eveking (Westf.).

Working of Duralumin

Like other metals, duralumin can be rolled into plates and shapes and behaves in a similar manner, in that the elongation decreases as the hardness of rolling increases. Tube blanks, however, can be made only by pressing, and not by the oblique rolling method.

Fig. 1 shows the increase in tensile strength and decrease in elongation of a duralumin plate as its thickness is reduced by cold rolling from 7 mm. to 2 mm. The strength increases from 41 kg. to about 54 kg. per sq. mm., while the elongation falls from 22.7 to 2.3 per cent. The curve shows that the elongation decreases very rapidly with the very first reduction in thickness.

However, duralumin can be worked hot at a temperature of about 400° C. very well.

Tempering

Duralumin can be tempered, like steel, by heating and sudden cooling. For this purpose plates, tubes, and shapes are heated to between 480° and 510° and quenched, then aged ; that is, the treated material is simply set aside. The original strength characteristics are very nearly restored after the quenching, but the tensile strength continues to grow with the time of ageing, from 35 to 50 kgs. per sq. mm. The elongation does not decrease, but remains at

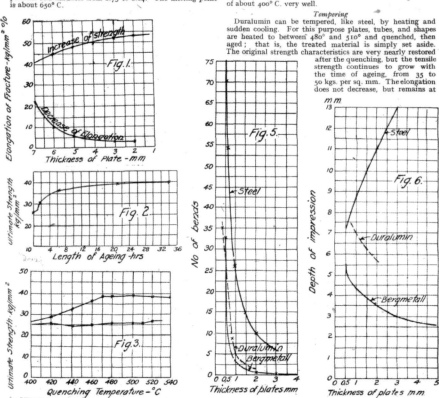

least the same, and usually increases slightly. In practice the greatest strength is reached after about five days of ageing.

When heated to over 530° C. duralumin becomes unusable. Consequently the treating is carried on in a bath of nitrates, whose temperature can be carefully regulated and watched. During the ageing of the metal, work cannot be done on it which would change the section, as in that case the strength will not increase any more. After the completion of ageing, the material can be re-rolled in order to obtain smooth

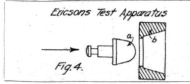

Fig. 4.

Appendix I

Dec. 8, 1925.

H. JUNKERS

ARMORED AEROPLANE

Filed June 28, 1920

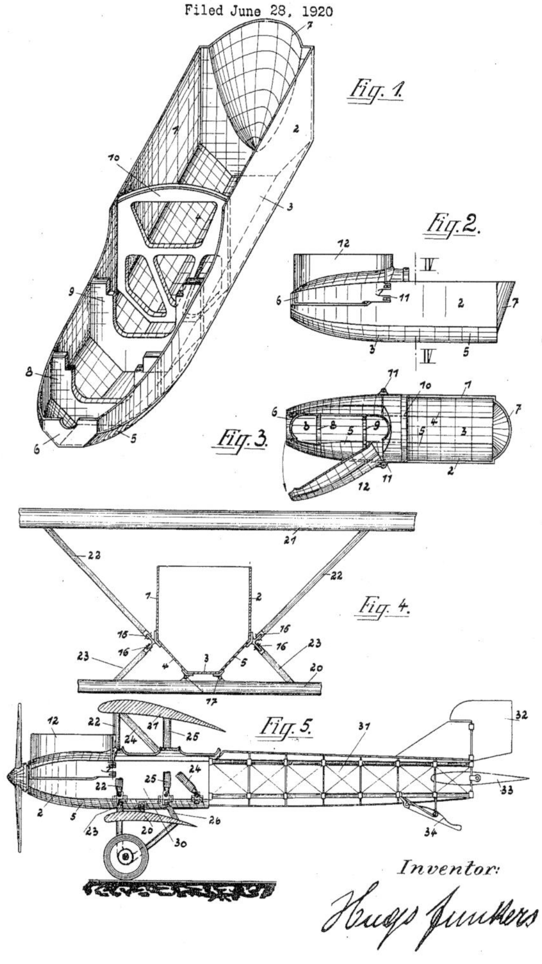

1,564,354

Fig. 1

Fig. 2

Fig. 3

Fig. 4

Fig. 5

Inventor:

Hugo Junkers

HUGO JUNKERS, OF DESSAU, GERMANY.

ARMORED AEROPLANE.

Application filed June 28, 1920. Serial No. 392,591.

To all whom it may concern:

Be it known that I, HUGO JUNKERS, a citizen of Germany, residing at Dessau, Germany, have invented certain new and useful Improvements in Armored Aeroplanes, of which the following is a specification.

This invention relates to flying machines and more especially to aeroplanes having their bodies protected by armor plate. Until now armored bodies were produced by covering the body structure with armor plates instead of the usual light covering. This construction offers the advantage that the armor plate can be attached to the body in a comparatively simple manner; however the drawback is connected therewith, that the considerable weight of the armor represents merely a dead load for the flying machine and that further the body frame has to be made especially strong in order to enable it to carry the heavy loads attached to it, whereby the weight of the flying machine is further considerably increased.

According to the present invention this drawback is obviated to a great extent by the armor plates themselves being utilized for transmitting forces arising within the body. To this end the individual armor plates are rigidly connected with each other so that the body formed by them represents a sort of plate girder. The body frame formerly used can now be dispensed with altogether, a substantial saving in weight being thus effected.

In the case where the body does not merely serve for sheltering persons, motors, loads, fuel tanks, artillery or the like, but also acts as a connection between the tail rudders and the supporting surface. I prefer providing with armor only the front portion of the body, where the persons and the objects to be protected are usually disposed, the rear portion of the body remaining unarmored. In such cases it suffices to construct this front portion after the manner of a plate girder composed of armor plates, the rear portion being formed as usual as a lattice girder covered with fabric or as a thin walled hollow girder covered with veneers.

By dispensing with the inner frame in the armored part of the body a substantial saving of space and weight is obtained inasmuch as the exterior dimensions of the body can be made correspondingly smaller, ing easy access to the motor, this portion of the armor is preferably imparted the form of a door 12 swinging about hinges 11.

Fig. 4 shows the armored body connected to the supporting surfaces 20 and 21 of a double deck aeroplane. The supporting surfaces 20, 21 as well as the struts 22 to 26 are preferably connected to the body in such places, where two armor plates contact with their edges, this being the points of highest rigidity.

In the aeroplane illustrated in Fig. 5 the armored front portion 30 of the body is constructed as described before. The rear portion 31, serving only for connecting the tail rudders 33, 33' and the spur 34 to the front portion, preferably forms a lattice girder, covered with fabric, as usual.

The curved faces of the body portion formed of armor plates are preferably constructed as so-called evolvable faces, so that the armor plates, cut out according to the evolution outlines of the individual faces, need be bent in one direction only. The construction is simplified thereby quite materially inasmuch as armor plates can be pressed or hammered only with difficulty; moreover an exact matching of the single plates at the curved edges is thus greatly facilitated, such exact matching being necessary inasmuch as the individual plates must be rigidly connected with each other along their edges in order to enable the body as a whole to act as a girder.

I claim:—

1. Fuselage for armored flying machines, consisting of two parts, a substantially stream lined front portion of polygonal shape and which is composed of armor plate, and an unarmored tail portion, the armor plates constituting the front portion being joined to each other at obtuse angles and being bent in a single direction to converge in forward direction.

2. In a fuselage for armored flying machines, in combination, a shell-proof front portion and an unarmored rear portion, although the space available within remains the same, the air resistance being diminished also.

Particular advantages are derived from this improved body construction with regard to the arrangement of the motor which may now rest with its longitudinal supports on a number of cross frames, transmitting its weight. as well as the thrust of the propeller immediately to the main supporting elements of the body, i. e. the walls formed of armor plates.

In the drawings accompanying this specification and forming part thereof two forms of an armored aeroplane embodying my invention are illustrated. In the drawings—

Fig. 1 is a perspective view of an armored body,

Fig. 2 is a side elevation and

Fig. 3 a plan.

Fig. 4 is a cross-section on line IV—IV in Fig. 2.

Fig. 5 is a side elevation of a modified form of aeroplane with the front portion only of the body protected by armor.

Referring to this drawings, the body shown in Figs. 1 to 4 consists mainly of the two side walls 1 and 2, the central bottom plate 3, the oblique bottom plates 4 and 5, the front wall 6 and the rear wall 7. For the purpose of reducing the air resistance the body is continuously tapered or contracted towards the front wall 6. The plates 1 to 5 transmit all forces acting in longitudinal direction, and quite especially the flectional forces resulting from the own weight of the body and the weight of the persons and objects accommodated therein, and further the forces, which arise in the constructive parts attached to the body.

The motor is arranged upon cross frames 8 and 9 immediately attached to the longitudinal walls 1 to 5 and thus transmitting thereto the weight of the motor and the thrust of the propeller. The supporting frames 8 and 9 serve at the same time for bracing the body transversely against lateral and torsional forces. Further cross frames may be provided for the same purpose, such as the frame 10, serving also as a support for the instrument panel.

As shown in Figs. 2 and 3 the armor may be supplemented so as to completely enclose the motor. For the purpose of providing said front portion comprising a substantially horizontal bottom, two substantially vertical side walls, and two inclined intermediate walls connecting said bottom and side walls and being joined thereto at obtuse angles, said front portion being formed of armor plate bent in a single direction so as to converge at the front end.

3. Fuselage for armored flying machines, consisting of two parts, a substantially stream lined front portion of polygonal shape and which is composed of armor plate, and an unarmored tail portion, the armor plates constituting the front portion being joined to each other at obtuse angles and being bent in a single direction to converge in forward direction and load carrying partitions extending transversely across said front portion.

4. In a fuselage for armored flying machines in combination, a shell-proof front portion and an unarmored rear portion, said front portion comprising a substantially horizontal bottom, two substantially vertical side walls and two inclined intermediate walls connecting said bottom and side walls and being joined thereto at obtuse angles, said front portion being formed of armor plate bent in a single direction so as to converge at the front end and load carrying partitions extending transversely across said front portion.

5. Fuselage for armored flying machines comprising a polygonal front portion consisting of armor plate and an unarmored tail portion, the armor plates constituting the front portion being joined to each other at obtuse angles and being bent in a single direction to converge in forward direction, load carrying partitions extending transversely across said front portion and a hood for said front portion comprising a pair of armor plate leaves hinged to said front portion.

In testimony whereof I affix my signature.

HUGO JUNKERS.

| Appendix J

Dec. 2, 1924.

H. JUNKERS

CORRUGATED SHEET METAL

1,517,633

Filed June 28. 1920

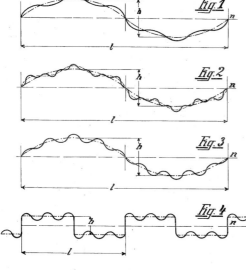

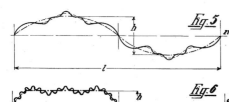

Inventor:

Hugo Junkers

HUGO JUNKERS, OF DESSAU, GERMANY.

CORRUGATED SHEET METAL.

Application filed June 28, 1920. Serial No. 392,592.

To all whom it may concern:

Be it known that I, HUGO JUNKERS, a citizen of the German Empire, residing at Dessau, Germany, have invented certain new and useful Improvements in Corrugated Sheet Metal, of which the following is a specification.

My invention relates to corrugated sheet metal and more especially to a novel profile or cross-sectional configuration of such corrugated sheet metal. In various cases of application of corrugated sheet metal, for instance in using same in the construction of walls in flying machines, the problem arises of supporting heavy loads per unit of surface, at the same time keeping the weight of the corrugated sheet metal as low as possible, although the distance between the supporting members is relatively great.

In order to comply with the requirement of small weight sheet metal of very slight thickness has to be employed. However, such sheet metal involves the disadvantage of the point of maximum load at which permanent deformation or destruction of the sheet metal will take place, being as a rule much lower than would be assumed from the customary rules of strength or resistance. As has been ascertained by experiments, this is caused thereby, that in those parts of a corrugated sheet metal, whose thickness is very slight in proportion to the corrugation, on their being subjected to pressure or breaking stress, a local formation of folds will occur already before the maximum load is reached, such formation of folds continuously spreading farther and ultimately causing a premature crushing or crumpling of the whole sheet.

According to the present invention the rigidity of corrugated sheet metal is increased by superposing to the main or primary corrugation secondary corrugations of smaller radii. For I have ascertained that the crumpling of sheet metal of a given thickness and load is the more retarded, the more the sheet is curved at the point in question, in other words, the smaller the average radius of curvature at that point. If now the secondary corrugation superposed to the main corrugation is curved too slightly in proportion to the thickness of the sheet, so that the danger of the sheet

crumpling locally is still present, a tertiary corrugation of a still greater curvature may be superposed to the secondary corrugation, and so on.

According to the present invention the superposing of corrugations of a higher order to corrugations of a lower order is effected primarily at those points which are most exposed to crumpling, that is those points, which are subjected to strong pressure and more especially those portions of the main corrugation, which are remote from the neutral plane of the corrugated metal, and of these portions again those points which are comparatively slightly curved. As the direction in which the corrugated sheet metal is subjected to strains, changes, according to the manner in which it is used, the corrugations of the higher order will in general be arranged relatively to corrugations of the lower order in symmetry with the neutral plane. With corrugated sheet metal, which is always subjected to strains in a predetermined direction only, the corrugations of the higher order need only be arranged on that side of the neutral plane which is subjected to pressure.

In the drawings affixed to this specification and forming part thereof several embodiments of the present invention are illustrated in a diagrammatical manner, the full lines indicating sections of the novel profile, while the primary profile (main corrugation) is shown in dotted lines, the neutral plane being indicated by n, the length of the main corrugation by l and its height by h.

Figure 1 shows a sinus-shaped main corrugation in dot and dash line with a superposed sinus-shaped secondary corrugation extending uniformly throughout the main corrugation, in full line.

Figure 2 shows a secondary corrugation in dash dash line superposed upon a sinus-shaped main corrugation delineated by a dot and dash line, and a tertiary corrugation in full line superposed upon the secondary corrugation, the corrugations of the higher order extending uniformly throughout those of a lower order.

Figure 3 shows a sinus-shaped main corrugation with a superposed secondary corrugation increasing in height and average

curvature from the neutral plane toward those points of the main corrugation which are most heavily subjected to flexion.

Figure 4 shows a main corrugation of rectangular configuration, in which a secondary corrugation is arranged only at the external planes while the vertically extending walls of the main corrugation have no secondary corrugations.

Figure 5 shows a sinus-shaped corrugation having tertiary corrugations superposed only upon those portions of the secondary corrugations extending over the entire main corrugations which are subjected to the most heavy strains.

Figure 6 shows a main corrugation of trapezoidal profile depicted by a dash and dot line, those parts of said corrugations which are remote from the neutral plane being provided with sinus-shaped secondary corrugations, and tertiary corrugations depicted in full lines extending throughout the main corrugation.

Apart from the illustrated forms of corrugations various further combinations of the different kinds of corrugations are possible. Thus for instance the corrugations of the higher order may have other than sinus shapes, such as for instance rectangular, triangular or trapezoidal shapes.

I claim:—

1. Corrugated sheet metal having main corrugations, secondary corrugations superposed on the main corrugations, and tertiary corrugations on the secondary ones.

2. Corrugated sheet metal having corrugations of a higher order superposed to the main corrugations, the average curvature of the corrugations of a higher order increasing towards the points of higher stress.

3. Corrugated sheet metal having corrugations of higher orders superposed to the main corrugations, the corrugations of higher order extending partly over an entire

main corrugation and partly only over those portions of a main corrugation which are designed to take up high strains.

4. Corrugated sheet metal comprising in combination, flat primary corrugations and corrugations of a higher order uniformly distributed over the said primary corrugations.

5. Corrugated sheet metal composed of primary corrugations and superposed secondary and tertiary corrugations extending continuously throughout the primary corrugations.

6. Corrugated sheet metal for aeroplane construction having main corrugations, each main corrugation being composed of a plurality of secondary corrugations, said secondary corrugations varying in degree of curvature from the neutral plane.

7. Corrugated sheet metal having main corrugations each main corrugation being composed of a plurality of secondary corrugations, the degree of curvature of said secondary corrugations increasing toward the points of application of greatest stress to the surface of the metal.

8. Corrugated sheet metal for aeroplane construction having main corrugations, secondary corrugations extending continuously throughout the plane of the main corrugations, the secondary corrugations having tertiary corrugations at and throughout the point of application of greatest stresses to the sheet metal.

9. Corrugated sheet metal for aeroplane construction comprising main corrugations and superposed secondary corrugations increasing in height and average curvature from the neutral plane toward those points of the main corrugations most subjected to flexion.

In testimony whereof I affix my signature.

HUGO JUNKERS.

Appendix K

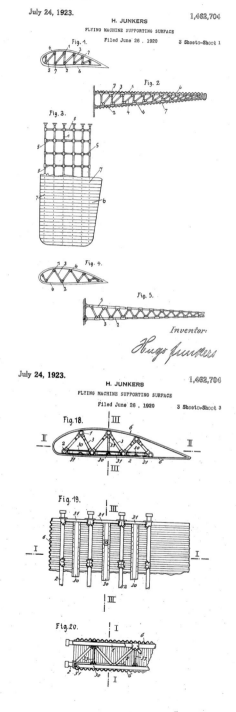

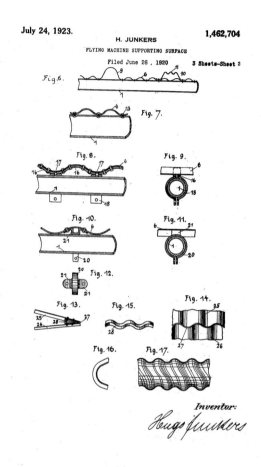

HUGO JUNKERS, OF AACHEN-FRANKENBURG, GERMANY.

FLYING-MACHINE SUPPORTING SURFACE.

Application filed June 26, 1920. Serial No. 392,161.

(GRANTED UNDER THE PROVISIONS OF THE ACT OF MARCH 3, 1921, 41 STAT. L., 1313.)

To all whom it may concern:

Be it known that I, HUGO JUNKERS, a citizen of the German Empire, residing at Aachen-Frankenburg, Germany, have invented certain new and useful Improvements in Flying-Machine Supporting Surfaces (for which I have filed application in Germany, December 22, 1916; Germany, June 26, 1919; Austria, February 11, 1918; Holland, July 29, 1919; Sweden, December 18, 1919; Switzerland, December 23, 1919; Denmark, December 31, 1919; Norway, January 17, 1920; Czechoslovakia, January 17, 1920), of which the following is a specification.

My invention refers to supporting surfaces for flying machines and more especially to all-metal surfaces of the self-supporting type, i. e. such as are not externally stayed or stiffened.

Now the customary manner of constructing the supporting surfaces of flying machines consists in covering a frame composed as a rule of two longitudinal beams and a plurality of cross beams (frames or ribs) with a covering of cloth, or the like.

The essential drawbacks appertaining to this form of construction reside in the use of elastic material for the covering, which at best is suitable for the transmission of tensile forces. Thus the fact of the covering being elastic renders it necessary, for example for the purpose of securing and maintaining the proper shape of the supporting surfaces, as also for taking up twisting strains to arrange a great number of cross beams or transverse girders, as a consequence of which the construction of the surface is rendered more difficult, and its weight increased. Moreover, for the purpose of transmitting the forces of air resistance acting on the surface it is as a rule necessary to interpose a special connection resistive against air pressure between the longitudinal beams and the cross frames.

According to my present invention, now, the supporting surface has the form of a hollow body comprising a number of beams disposed in the longitudinal direction of the supporting surface and preferably constructed after the manner of lattice girders, and a sheet metal covering, entirely enveloping said girders, and provided with protruding portions such as corrugations, or the like, extending in the direction of flight, and serving to reinforce the covering, which latter is rigidly connected with the various parts of the frame at various points distributed all over the wing surface.

This novel form of wing construction involves a number of highly important advantages, as will be explained in full hereinafter.

Owing to the peculiar profile given to the sheet metal covering, the possibility is afforded of providing a cover, even with sheet metal of slight thickness, such as is required to avoid too large an increase in weight which possesses a sufficient rigidity of its own to enable it to transmit both the forces coming to act on it perpendicularly and tending to deform the cross sectional shape of the supporting surface (such as air pressure, local loads, as when, for instance, the wing is being trod on), as also the forces acting in the direction of the profile given to the sheet metal, and all this without any excessive alteration of shape and for relatively big distances. The fact that the improved cover constitutes in and for itself a rigid body, renders it possible to transfer to it either partially or even entirely the functions which it was hitherto necessary to provide special members in the wing frame for.

For this reason, the transverse beams or girders (cross-frames, ribs) which were otherwise required for the purpose of securing the true cross sectional shape of the wing, for the mutual connection of the longitudinal beams, and for taking up the twisting strains, may now be dispensed with either in part or entirely. Besides, the covering may itself constitute the air pressure resisting connection between the single longitudinal beams. By these means, the construction of the wing is simplified to a very considerable extent.

In the event of a member or section of the frame being damaged, the forces, which would otherwise be taken up by this particular member or section, may be transmitted through the cover across the section damaged, or else transferred to adjoining portions of the frame, so that thereby the safety of the novel supporting surface, even in the event of any section thereof being injured, is increased.

The main beams disposed in the longitudinal direction of the wing, are preferably constructed after the manner of panel works composed of tubes. Now, in accordance with the fact that the load diminishes towards the free ends of the supporting surfaces, the top and bottom flanges of said girders are suitably composed of members or sections of different diameter or different wall thickness.

It will also be found expedient to so dispose the cover that the raised portions thereof, facing the inner side of the wing, will come to repose directly upon the top and bottom flanges of the main girders. If the cover be then rigidly connected at every point of contact with the frame girders, say by rivets, then there will be created a very large number of fastening points uniformly distributed all over the wing, as a result of which arrangement the carrying out of the aforementioned functions on the part of the covering is essentially facilitated.

Instead of forming a simple rivet connection at the points of contact between cover and frame members, it is obvious that also any other manner of connection may be selected, say for example by clamping.

In the case of supporting surfaces of the kind hereinbefore described, the twisting (torsional) forces arising in the wing are also for the main part transmitted by the cover, which in this case is subjected to shearing stresses. In particular in the case of large sized supporting surfaces, i. e. such wherein the distance between the longitudinal beams or girders is relatively large, it has been found that the sections of the wing covering located between two such beams or girders on being subjected to great strains will more and more tend to lose their original shape, which will in one course lead to the wing cover bulging out and crumpling up. This drawback may be successfully overcome by arranging between the longitudinal beams or girders on the corrugated sheet metal and firmly fastening to this latter, special stays in such wise that the said stays will cross the corrugations formed in the wing cover either obliquely or vertically. The action of these stays is such that both in the case of locally confined strains as also in that of more extended strains exerted on the wing cover, the normally corrugated shape, and therewith the power of resistance proper to the wing cover, cannot be prematurely impaired or lost.

By the provision of stays or stiffening members of the said kind, the wing covering is enabled to withstand increased shearing stresses. To utilize this fact to the utmost extent possible, and accordingly to be able to safely transmit even increased shearing forces from the cover to the point where the wings are secured (wing base or girder junction points), respectively, at the points of division between one wing section and another, the cover is suitably reinforced at the said points of connection or division by additional members serving for the transmission of forces, disposed in the plane of division of the wings or in the plane of the girder junction from girder to girder, that is to say, about vertically to the girders.

The front face of the wing, the so-called wing head is not as a rule provided with a sharp edge, but is rounded off. As this rounded off portion possesses a rather small radius relatively to the profile formation of the remaining wing section, it is somewhat difficult to bend the corrugated or otherwise shaped sheet iron into this particular form. It will therefore be found expedient to construct the wing head as a distinct part, duly connected with the upper and lower portions of the cover which are likewise constructed separately for themselves. In this connection, it is again possible to carry this out in manifold ways. Thus, for example, the head may be primarily constructed after the manner of a channel or groove, the internal extremely bent portion of which is level, while the two lateral portions, which are less curved, are provided with corrugations, or the like, gradually increasing in depth toward the outside, and corresponding in shape to the profile formation of the wing covering. However, the head of the wing may also be fitted out with through going corrugations or the like, formed by means of special dies, or else by forging, or a similar operation. Finally, the profile formation of the wing cover may also be made to gradually run down to a level surface in the direction toward the junction point for the head which, for its part, is in the main also level.

In the drawings affixed to this specification and forming part thereof several modifications of the subject matter of my invention are illustrated diagrammatically. In the drawings—

Fig. 1 is a cross section of a supporting surface,

Fig. 2 a longitudinal section,

Fig. 3 a plan with part of the cover removed.

Fig. 4 is the cross section of another modification.

Fig. 5 is a side elevation of a longitudinal beam or girder;

Fig. 6 is a cross section of a particular profile formation;

Figs. 7 to 12 are details showing the manner of attaching the corrugated or otherwise shaped sheet metal to the frame girders;

Figs. 13 to 15 illustrate one modification of the terminal edge of the wing, while

Figs. 16 and 17 show a form of execution of the head,

the purpose of increasing the resisting capacity of the sheet metal cover against torsional or shearing stresses. These reinforcing stays are disposed in a line with the longitudinal beams, and similar to these, they are rigidly connected to the corrugated sheet metal, say by riveting. In the example illustrated, the cross sectional shape of these stays is that of a corrugation, however, also other cross sectional forms may be made use of. In the case of large sized supporting surfaces there may be arranged between each pair of longitudinal girders a plurality of stays of this kind, and these latter may in addition be provided with special props supporting them relatively to the girders. Thus, for instance, the reinforcing stay of the central field is propped up by means of the rods 33 relatively to the oppositely disposed top flange common to the adjoining longitudinal girders.

According to requirement either all, or else only some of the corrugated sheet metal sections disposed between the longitudinal girders may be provided with such reinforcing stays.

The reinforcing members 31 disposed in a line with the corrugations are connected at the junction point of the wing with the edge of the corrugated sheet metal, the ends of said members being connected to the bottom flanges 2, which thus effectively assist the wing cover in transferring the shearing forces on to the points of junction with the longitudinal beams. The aforesaid reinforcing members may, moreover, be arranged, as shown in the drawing, either only between always two longitudinal girders within the fields or wing sections subjected to the greatest amount of strain, or else around the entire cross sectional area of the wing.

In a like manner, other hollow bodies appertaining to air craft, and subjected to stress in the same way as the supporting surfaces, such as rigid rudder surfaces (so-called fins) and the like, may be constructed in a similar manner, in accordance with this invention.

I claim:

1. In a flying machine surface in combination, a plurality of longitudinal girders and a sheet metal covering surrounding the said girder structure and connected therewith in a plurality of places, said sheet metal covering being provided with narrow corrugations substantially uniformly extending in the direction of flight over the entire length of said covering.

2. In a flying machine surface in combination, a plurality of longitudinal girders converging towards each other and having each one flange in common with the adjacent girder and a sheet metal covering surrounding the said girder structure and connected therewith in a plurality of places.

3. In a flying machine surface in combination, a plurality of longitudinal girders converging towards each other and having each one flange in common with the adjacent girder and a sheet metal covering surrounding the said girder structure and connected with the top and bottom flanges, respectively, of said girders.

4. In a flying machine surface in combination, a plurality of longitudinal girders, a corrugated sheet metal covering surrounding the said girder structure, a corrugated reinforcing member closely applied to the inner side of said covering and clamping means adapted to connect said covering with said girders.

5. In a flying machine surface in combination, a plurality of longitudinal girders and a sheet metal covering surrounding the said girder structure and connected therewith in a plurality of places, said sheet metal covering being provided with corrugations substantially extending in the direction of flight, the corrugations on the upper and lower portions of the covering being stagged in such a way as to form a keen edge at the rear end of the said surface.

6. In a flying machine surface in combination, a plurality of longitudinal girders and a sheet metal covering surrounding the said girder structure and connected therewith in a plurality of places, said covering being provided with corrugations substantially extending in the direction of flight, the corrugations on the upper and lower portions of the covering being staggered in such a way as to form a keen edge at the rear end of said surface, and the rounded head portion being formed of a separate piece of plain sheet metal.

7. In a flying machine surface in combination, a plurality of longitudinal girders and a sheet metal covering surrounding the said girder structure and connected therewith in a plurality of places, said covering being composed of a plurality of separate parts, the rounded head portion formed of plain sheet metal and the top and bottom portions formed of corrugated sheet metal, said portions being fixed to each other in any suitable manner.

8. In a flying machine surface in combination, a plurality of longitudinal girders and a sheet metal covering surrounding the said girder structure and connected therewith in a plurality of places, said covering being composed of a plurality of separate parts, the rounded head portion and the top and bottom portions fixed to each other in any suitable manner, said top and bottom portions being provided with corrugations

Figs. 18 to 20 illustrate a supporting surface construction, the corrugated sheet iron cover of which is provided with special stays in order to render the cover more capable of resistance against torsional (shearing) stress.

Fig. 18 being a cross section of the supporting surface taken in the direction of flight on line I—I in Figs. 19 and 20;

Fig. 19 a plan taken on line II—II in Fig. 18, and

Fig. 20 a sectional view on line III—III in Fig. 18, taken in the longitudinal direction of the supporting surface.

Referring to the drawings, the frame arranged within the interior of the hollow supporting surface according to Figs. 1 to 3 consists of a relatively large number of longitudinal lattice girders, comprising a top flange 1, a bottom flange 2, perpendicular stays 3, and diagonal stays 4. A cover 6 consisting of corrugated sheet metal is fitted across the frame, being rigidly jointed to the flanges 1 and 2 at the sunken portions 7 of the corrugations. The said cover thus constitutes a substitute for the resisting connection otherwise required to be arranged between the single main girders of the frame for the purpose of taking up the forces that come to act upon the supporting surface in a horizontal direction. Diagonal rods 5 are arranged to run from the bottom flange of the one longitudinal girder to the top flange of the adjacent girder, said rods, conjointly with cover 6, enabling the wing to take up torsional stresses.

Fig. 4 is a cross sectional view of a wing similar to that shown in Fig. 1, the difference being that in this case the top and bottom flanges of the main girders are staggered so that the frame cross section will be composed of approximately equilateral triangles. The top and bottom flanges 1 and 2, (Fig. 5) are composed of tubular members, the diameter of which gradually lessens in the direction toward the wing end.

In the modification illustrated in Fig. 6, the profile formation is reinforced at certain points, distributed over the full length of the wing, for the purpose of rendering the cover still more capable of resistance against deformations, in other words to render the entire supporting surface still more rigid, without, however, essentially increasing the weight thereof. The cover 6, possessing a profile formation of any kind whatsoever, and fixed to the frame section 1, is provided at certain intervals with projections 9, 10 either disposed along the outside over the entire width of the wing, or else arranged within the wing between always two longitudinal girders; said projections, while having a greater depth, preferably resembling in shape the general profile formation, and they may either be integral with the sheet metal cover (as at 9), or else they may be superposed separately, as shown at 10. These projections may further be reinforced by providing them with corrugations in the manner shown at 11.

Fig. 7 illustrates a simple way of attaching the corrugated sheet metal cover 6 to a tubular frame member 1 by means of rivets 13 traversing the tube walls.

Figs. 8 and 9 show a different form of connection. In this case, a flat reinforcing strip 16 extending in the direction of the frame girder 1 is riveted from below to the sheet metal cover 6, this latter being also corrugated. In the sunken portions 7 of the corrugations, the strip 16 is rigidly joined to the clip 18, said clip being clamped to the frame member 1. By these means any weakening of sections of the frame owing to the presence of rivet holes is avoided, while moreover the number of fastening points between the frame section and the cover is further increased, in consequence of which arrangement the distribution of force over the sheet metal cover is enhanced to a still greater degree, and any danger of said cover being wrenched off is obviated.

A similar form of joint is shown in Figs. 10 to 12. In this case, a clip 20 serves to connect the sheet metal cover 6 to the frame member 1, the upwardly bent laps 21 of said clip being attached to the corrugated or otherwise shaped sheet metal in the vicinity of its neutral layer.

Figs. 13 to 15 illustrate one form of construction of the rear edge of the supporting surface. The corrugations formed in the upper section 25 and in the lower section 26 of the wing, respectively, are staggered for the distance of half a pitch relatively to each other, so that the corrugations at the rear edge of the wing will converge to a sharp edge 27 running in a line with the corrugations of the wing cover. For the purpose of connecting the upper and the lower wing sections 25, 26 at the rear edge of the wing, both sheet metal sections are fixed to a wedge 28 of wood, or the like, in the faces of which corrugations are formed corresponding to those of the wing cover.

Figs. 16 and 17 are, respectively, a cross section and a front view of a specially constructed head for a supporting surface, the front edge of which is rounded off, and corrugated or otherwise shaped for the extent of its entire length. These corrugations, as seen from the front (Fig. 17), are disposed at an incline for the purpose of suitably staggering the profile formation of the upper and lower wing faces relatively to each other in order to secure their converging smoothly at the rear edge of the wing.

In the wing structure shown in Figs. 18 to 20, stays 30 are arranged along the lower wing face between the bottom flanges for

staggered in such a way as to form a keen edge at the rear end of said surface, while the said head portion has corrugations formed thereon which extend in an oblique direction so as to connect the staggered corrugations of the said top and bottom portions.

9. In a flying machine surface in combination, a plurality of longitudinal girders, longitudinal stiffening members extending substantially in parallel with and between said girders and a sheet metal covering surrounding the said girder structure and said stiffening members and connected to both said girders and said stiffening members in a plurality of places.

10. In a flying machine surface in combination, a plurality of longitudinal girders, longitudinal stiffening members extending substantially in parallel with and between said girders, a sheet metal covering with corrugations substantially extending transversely to said girders surrounding said girder structure, and stiffening members extending substantially in parallel with and between said girders, said covering being fixed to said girders and said stiffening members.

11. In a flying machine surface in combination, a plurality of longitudinal girders, longitudinal stiffening members extending substantially in parallel with and between said girders, a sheet metal covering surrounding the said girder structure and said stiffening members and connected therewith in a plurality of places and stays between said stiffening members and the opposite flanges of said girders.

In testimony whereof I affix my signature.

HUGO JUNKERS.

Appendix L

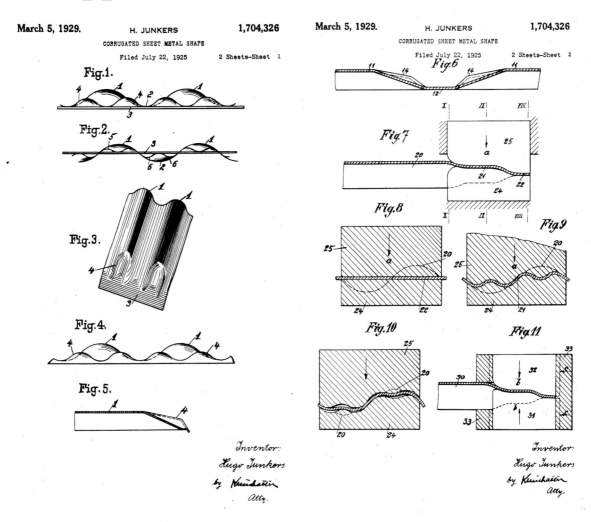

March 5, 1929. H. JUNKERS 1,704,326
CORRUGATED SHEET METAL SHAPE
Filed July 22, 1925 2 Sheets—Sheet 1

Fig.1.

Fig.2.

Fig.3.

Fig.4.

Fig.5.

Inventor:
Hugo Junkers
by Knudsen
Atty.

March 5, 1929. H. JUNKERS 1,704,326
CORRUGATED SHEET METAL SHAPE
Filed July 22, 1925 2 Sheets—Sheet 2

Fig.6

Fig.7

Fig.8

Fig.9

Fig.10

Fig.11

Inventor:
Hugo Junkers
by Knudsen
Atty.

HUGO JUNKERS, OF DESSAU, GERMANY.

CORRUGATED SHEET-METAL SHAPE.

Application filed July 22, 1925, Serial No. 45,382, and in Germany August 9, 1924.

My invention refers to corrugated sheet metal and more especially to the connection between corrugated sheet metal and other corrugated or non-corrugated parts of a structure, more particularly a flying machine, boat or the like.

It is a particular object of my invention to provide means whereby such connection can be effected in an easier and more efficient manner than was hitherto possible.

In effecting the connection between corrugated sheet metal shapes, such as form part for instance of flying machines or boats, it is necessary in order to obtain a satisfactory connection, which will also keep tight, that either the abutting ends of the two corrugated sheet metal parts to be connected register exactly both regarding the configuration and the position of the corrugations or, in the case of non-corrugated parts, such as transverse bulkheads, that the abutting end of such part be adapted exactly to the corrugations of the sheet metal, or else the abutting edge of the sheet metal must be made plane in order to enable it to be easily connected to the other part by riveting, welding or the like. Such conversion is however accompanied by a considerable upsetting of the sheet metal, which presents great difficulties more especially if high grade light metal sheets of great hardness such as duraluminium are used.

According to the present invention a simple and efficient connection is effected between the parts by shaping the abutting portion of the corrugated sheet metal in such manner that the corrugations are first subdivided into a great number of smaller substantially coaxial corrugations and the adjoining edge portion is then upset so as to form a plane surface. For instance, in sheet metal having comparatively large corrugations each of these corrugations is first converted into two smaller corrugations without any considerable upsetting being required, and these smaller corrugations can if necessary be subdivided so as to form still smaller corrugations and so on, until the width of the final corrugations has been reduced to such an extent that they offer only very little resistance to the upsetting and smoothing. By thus subdividing the corrugations I obtain a uniform distribution of the upsetting effect all over the respective parts of the corrugated sheet and I thereby enable it to be smoothed down without any folds being formed. In many cases the smallest corrugations obtained by the subdivision of larger ones need merely be upset in such manner that a plane edge is formed, riveting or the like being then effected intermediate the corrugations at some distance from the plane edge.

The subdivision of the corrugations and the upsetting is preferably effected by means of a top and a bottom die, each of which is formed with larger and smaller corrugations and with a plane portion, and I prefer employing dies extending over a plurality of large corrugations and if possible all over the width of the piece of sheet metal being treated.

In the drawings affixed to this specification and forming part thereof several corrugated sheet metal shapes embodying my invention are illustrated diagrammatically by way of example. In the drawings

Fig. 1 is an end view of a sheet metal shape having large corrugations, the ends of which are subdivided into two smaller corrugations each.

Fig. 2 is a similar view showing each half of the large corrugation subdivided into two smaller corrugations.

In both cases the smaller corrugations gradually merge into a plane edge portion.

Fig. 3 is a structural view, drawn to a smaller scale, of the shape illustrated in Fig. 1,

Figs. 4 and 5 are an end view and axial cross-section of a further form.

Referring first to Figs. 1 and 3, 1, 1 are a large or main corrugation, 2 is the depression between two such corrugations, and 3 is the plain edge portion. The ends of the large corrugations adjoining these large portions are subdivided each into two smaller corrugations 4, so as to represent the aspect of forks, the plane edge portion being formed by simply smoothing down by pressure the outer ends of the small corrugations 4. In order to obtain this shape, the ends of the large or main corrugations can be transformed into smaller corrugations extending to the edge of the sheet, whereupon the edge portion of the smaller corrugations is smoothed down by pressure exerted upon it by a further pair of dies.

In the majority of cases, however, the large or main corrugations can be converted into a plane edge portion with smaller corrugations adjoining it, by shaping the edge portion by means of a single pair of dies, either in a single operation or in several subsequent operations, the extreme edge portion of the sheet being first inserted between the dies and the sheet being then gradually introduced further between the dies, so that the edge portion of the sheet is shaped in several consecutive operations.

As shown in Fig. 2 the smooth edge portion 3 is formed in the central layer intermediate the ridges 1 and the depressions 2 of the main corrugations, each ridge 1 being subdivided into a pair of smaller corrugations 5 and in a similar manner each depression 2 being subdivided into two smaller corrugations 6. These smaller corrugations 5 and 6 have only one half of the width of the smaller corrugation 4 illustrated in Fig. 1, and in consequence thereof can be upset or smoothed down in an easier way. Obviously therefore, this latter modification is more suitable for thin sheets and it further offers the advantage of the smooth edge portion being arranged in the neutral intermediate part of the corrugated sheet, which is desirable in order to keep the sheet as strong as possible. In those cases where the corrugations abut against an edge in oblique direction, the ends of the smaller corrugations can extend in a corresponding oblique direction, inasmuch as the alternately unequal shapes of these ends of the smaller corrugations do not form any obstacles to the transformation of large corrugations into smaller ones nor to the pressing down of the ends of the smaller corrugations.

The sheet illustrated in Figs. 4 and 5, while corresponding in all other respects to the form illustrated in Figs. 1 and 3, shows an end formation of the smaller corrugations 4 by which a plane connecting edge is obtained. In this case riveting is effected in the single depressions between the corrugations, and the smaller corrugations 4 are preferably upset in such manner that before the riveting operation has started the connecting edge is formed somewhat below the deepest depression, so that it is applied with particular force against the other part when riveting is started. In the same manner as shown in the drawings with reference to an outer edge of a corrugated sheet, plane transverse webs can also be formed intermediate the ends of an endless web of corrugated sheet metal, these plane webs extending either at right angles or at an acute angle or in a curve with reference to the corrugations. I may further form the corrugated sheet with plane portions having any desired configuration, and in all these cases these plane portions merge into the large or main corrugations by way of smaller corrugations. On the other hand a corrugated sheet metal cover can be formed in a similar manner with a plane circumferential edge.

While in Figs. 1–5 the invention is shown as applied to the marginal portion of a piece of sheet metal, Fig. 6 illustrates in longitudinal section the planing down of an intermediate part.

11 is one of the main corrugations and 12 is the part planed down by pressure. 14, 14 are the smaller corrugations.

In Figs. 7–10 several forms of a pair of dies for acting on corrugated sheet metal in accordance with the present invention are illustrated, Fig. 7 being a lateral end view, while Figs. 8, 9 and 10 are cross-sections on the lines VIII—VIII, IX—IX, X—X of Fig. 7, respectively.

The dies shown in Fig. 7 allow transforming in a single operation the main corrugations of a piece of sheet metal 20 into smaller corrugations 21 and also to transform the end portion of these smaller corrugations into a plane edge portion 22. The device consists of a matrix or bottom die 24 and a patrix or top die 25, this latter acting in the direction of the arrow, *a*.

Fig. 11 illustrates a device adapted for being first applied to the marginal portion of the piece of sheet metal such as 30, and by means of which the main corrugations are transformed into smaller corrugations and part of these latter into a plane edge portion by gradually displacing the dies relatively to the sheet metal or vice versa in the longitudinal direction of the corrugations. The device here comprises a matrix 31 and patrix 32, both being guided in guides 33. The arrows *b*, *b* indicate the direction of movements for the transformation, while arrows *c*, *c* indicate the direction of relative movement of the dies and the metal. The parts are shown in Fig. 11 in the position which they assume after the last portion has been carried through.

I wish it to be understood that I do not desire to be limited to any details of construction or operation shown and described for obvious modifications will occur to a person skilled in the art.

I claim:—

1. As a new article of manufacture, a piece of corrugated sheet metal having part only of a corrugation subdivided into a plurality of smaller corrugations parallel thereto and merging into a plane metal portion.

2. As a new article of manufacture, a piece of corrugated sheet metal comprising a comparatively large corrugation, a plurality of smaller corrugations parallel thereto and extending over part of said large corrugation and a plane metal portion adjoining said small corrugations.

3. As a new article of manufacture, a piece of corrugated sheet metal comprising a plurality of comparatively large corrugations, smaller corrugations formed in the end of every large corrugation adjoining the edge of the piece and a plane metal portion adjoining said ends.

4. As a new article of manufacture, a piece of corrugated sheet metal comprising a plurality of comparatively large corrugations, smaller corrugations formed in the end of every large corrugation adjoining the edge of the piece and a plane metal portion adjoining said ends, said plane portion extending in the middle between the crests and the depressions of the corrugations.

5. The process of treating corrugated sheet metal for the purpose of connection, comprising forming by pressure a plurality of smaller corrugations in part only of one of the regular corrugations so as to subdivide part of this latter.

6. The process of treating corrugated sheet metal for the purpose of connection, comprising forming by pressure a plurality of smaller corrugations in part of one of the regular corrugations so as to subdivide part of this latter and transforming by pressure part of the metal adjoining said smaller corrugations into substantially plane metal.

7. The process of treating corrugated sheet metal for the purpose of connection, comprising forming by pressure a plurality of smaller corrugations in the ends of the regular corrugations adjoining an edge and transforming by pressure the edge portion adjoining said smaller corrugations into plane metal.

8. The process of treating corrugated sheet metal for the purpose of connection, comprising transforming the regular corrugation in several consecutive pressing operations, beginning at the ends and progressing in the longitudinal direction of said regular corrugations into a plurality of smaller corrugations and thereafter transforming by pressure the edge portion into plane metal.

9. The process of treating corrugated sheet metal for the purpose of connection, comprising transforming the regular corrugations in several consecutive pressing operations, beginning at the ends and progressing in the longitudinal direction of said regular corrugations into a plurality of smaller corrugations, treating in a similar manner the said smaller corrugations so as to subdivide each of them into a plurality of still smaller corrugations and thereafter transforming by pressure these still smaller corrugations into plane metal.

In testimony whereof I affix my signature.

HUGO JUNKERS.

Notes

Introduction

1 Many German designs included quick-release lugs on the lower wings, making changing these panels straightforward.

2 www.bbc.com/bitesize/guides/z36wycw/revision/2

3 Franz Kollmann, E. W. Kuenzi and A. J. Stamm, *Principles of Wood Science and Technology: II Wood Basic Materials*, p. 155.

1 The *Taube*

1 Ernst H. Hirshel, Horst Prem and Gero Madelung, *Aeronautical Research in Germany: From Lilienthal Until Today*, p. 29.

2 Ibid.

3 Ibid.

4 During an earlier flight in an earlier *Taube*, Etrich wrecked the plane and nearly broke his back; as a result, Illner would make all subsequent initial test flights for Etrich.

5 60/70-hp engine designed by Ferdinand Porsche, who worked for Daimler at this time. *Aeronautical Research in Germany*, p. 30.

6 Ibid.

7 Ibid.

8 Lohner originally was a high-end coachbuilding company (see fig.) and was affiliated with Daimler, and employed Porsche until 1905.

9 Hirshel, Prem and Madelung, *Aeronautical Research in Germany*, p. 30.

10 *Flight* magazine, August 21, 1914, p. 880.

11 Ibid, October 9, 1914, p. 1019.

12 *Flight*, September 11, 1914, p. 939.

13 Ibid.

14 *Flight*, August 28, 1914, p. 897.

15 *Flight*, September 4, 1914, pp. 923–4.

16 Ibid, p. 924.

17 *Flight*, September 18, 1914, p. 958.

18 Ibid.

19 *Flight*, July 9, 1915, pp. 490–2.

2 Aviatic

1 *WWI Aero*, No. 76, Nov. 1979, p. 27.

2 Terry Treadwell, *German and Austro-Hungarian Aircraft Manufacturers 1908–1919*, p. 48.

3 Ibid.

4 *WWI Aero*, p. 27.

5 Ibid.

6 *Flight*, February 15, 1917, p. 152.

7 Ibid, pp. 152–3.

8 Ibid, p. 55.

9 Peter Grosz, *Aviatik D.I*, p. 3.

10 George Haddow, *The O Aviatik (Berg) D.I*, p. 3.

11 Ibid, p. 4.

3 Halberstadt Flugzeugzelte

1 Marian Krzyzan and Holger Steinle, *Die Halberstadt CI. IV D-LBAO*, p. 29.

2 Ibid, p. 31.

3 Combination of stabilizer and elevator hence the term.

4 Krzyzan and Steinle, *Die Halberstadt CI.IV D-LBAO*, p. 29.

5 Peter Grosz, *Halberstadt Fighters*, p. 2.

6 Ibid, p. 3.

7 Ibid.

8 Ibid, p. 2.

9 Ibid, p. 3.

10 Ibid, p. 2

11 Ibid, pp. 2–3.

12 Ibid, p. 3.

13 Ibid.

14 It has been successfully argued that the skill of just a few pilots with the Fokker E series was transmuted to mean that it was a great fighter aircraft, when in fact, it was unstable and somewhat difficult to fly, and challenging to fly well.

15 Grosz, *Halberstadt Fighters*, p. 13.

16 *Flight*, April 5, 1917, p. 318.

17 Ibid.

18 Grosz, *Halberstadt Fighters*, p. 5.

19 Ibid, p. 5.

20 Ibid.

21 Ibid.

22 Ibid, pp. 13–14.

23 Some later models were included such as the D.III and the D.V

24 Grosz, *Halberstadt Fighters*, p. 6.

4 Fokker Flugzeugwerke

1. It was called the "spider" due to all the rigging wires which made it look like a spider.
2. Ernst H. Hirshel, Horst Prem and Gero Madelung, *Aeronautical Research in Germany: From Lilienthal Until Today*, p. 39. Goedecker worked for Hugo Junkers in the mechanics laboratory at Aachen, and had developed a cantilever wing based on a seagull wing.
3. Alex Imrie, *Fokker Triplane*, p. 9.
4. Marc Dierikx, *Anthony Fokker: The Flying Dutchman Who Shaped American Aviation*, p. 51.
5. Ibid, p. 53.
6. Imrie, *Fokker Triplane*, p. 9.
7. Dierikx, *Anthony Fokker*, p. 53.
8. Ibid, p. 55.
9. Ibid, p. 75.
10. Fokker was guaranteed 30 army customers per year which would generate 240,000 marks per annum. Dierikx, p. 77.
11. Alex Imrie, *The Fokker Dr. 1*, p. 9.
12. Dierikx, *Anthony Fokker*, p. 74.
13. Ibid.
14. Ibid, pp. 76–7.
15. Ibid, p. 79.
16. A. R. Weyl, *Fokker the Creative Years*, p. 58.
17. Dierikx, *Anthony Fokker*, p. 82.
18. Ibid.
19. Ibid.
20. Sixteen-year-old cousin of Germany's "Iron Chancellor" (Bismarck) and pupil at Fokker's flight school in October of 1913, Dierikx, p. 82.
21. Dierikx, *Anthony Fokker*, p. 82.
22. Ibid.
23. Ibid, p. 82.
24. Ibid, p. 85.
25. Capitalized at 300,000 marks.
26. Ibid.
27. Ibid, p. 96.
28. Designed by Martin Kreutzer.
29. Ibid.
30. Dierikx, *Anthony Fokker*, p. 97.
31. *Flight*, November 16, 1956, p. 796. Assertion was by Mr. Weyl.
32. Abstract of the patent: 16,726. Schneider, F. July 21. Safety appliances applicable generally. Consists in controlling the firing-mechanism of guns mounted on aerial machines and discharging through the propeller, by a device coupled to the propeller in such a way that the gun can only be fired when no propeller blade is in front of the muzzle of the gun. In the form shown, the trigger is locked and unlocked by a lever e pivoted at f and worked by a cam d geared to the propeller shaft a.
33. *Flight*, November 16, 1956, p. 796.
34. J. M. Bruce, *The Fokker Monoplanes*, p. 5.
35. Imrie, *Fokker Triplane*, p. 11
36. Dierikx, *Anthony Fokker*, p. 99.
37. The Fokker team worked from late December 1914 until around end May/early June on the interrupter gear. Dierikx, p. 100.
38. Bruce, *The Fokker Monoplanes*, p. 5.
39. Dierikx, *Anthony Fokker*, p. 100.
40. Ibid.
41. Bruce, *The Fokker Monoplanes*, p. 5.
42. Ibid.
43. Ibid, p. 6.
44. Ibid.
45. Ibid.
46. Ibid.
47. Ibid, p. 7.
48. Ibid.
49. Ibid, p. 8
50. Ibid, p. 17.
51. Imrie, *Fokker Triplane*, p. 15. J. Bruening & Sohn produced all manner of products from plywood, including cigar boxes and plywood wallpaper! They received several patents for their plywood products, and Forssman received patents in the early 1920s for a plywood manufacturing process he had developed using formaldehyde; this would become the industry standard henceforward.
52. Alex Imrie wrote that Bruening's plywood was "extremely thin, diagonally bonded, weatherproof veneer plywood" although it seems dubious that the glues available were weatherproof; and certainly were not waterproof. Imrie, p. 15.
53. Imrie, *Fokker Triplane*, p. 15.
54. Ibid.
55. Ibid, p. 17
56. Dierikx, *Anthony Fokker*, p. 117.
57. Imrie, *Fokker Triplane*, p. 119.
58. Ibid, p. 103. Fokker eventually won the lawsuit.
59. Imrie, *Fokker Triplane*, p. 104.
60. Ibid, p. 119.
61. Ibid, p. 21.
62. Incidence was changed by using a crank worm-gear.
63. Imrie, *Fokker Triplane*, p. 23. It was calculated that this spreader could provide enough lift to offset the weight of the landing gear.

64   Imrie, *Fokker Triplane*, p. 25.

65   Ibid.

66   The drag of its three wings acted as a brake in a steep dive; biplanes would generate greater speeds leading to wing shearing or disintegration.

67   Imrie, *Fokker Triplane*, p. 25.

68   Ibid, p. 27.

69   Dierikx, *Anthony Fokker*, p. 120.

70   Peter Gray, *The Fokker D.VII*, p. 3.

71   Dierikx, *Anthony Fokker*, pp. 120, 134–5.

72   Ibid, p. 121. Albatross would build them under license; by the time of the Armistice, 800 were at the front with only 300 built at Schwerin.

73   Dierikx, *Anthony Fokker*, p. 135.

74   *Flight*, October 3, 1918. p. 1114.

75   Ibid, p. 1115.

76   Ibid, p. 1161.

77   Fokker patent filed in Germany in 1918, in the U.S. in 1920 (see appendix).

78   The bottom edge of the ply leading edge was straight, running spanwise, and as such, the midpoint between ribs had to be pulled slightly downward with a glued piece of fabric tape to keep the ply from bowing upward, and thus deforming the fabric covering.

79   J. M. Bruce, *The Fokker D.VIII*, p. 3.

80   Ibid.

81   Ibid, p. 4.

82   Ibid, p. 5.

83   Ibid.

84   Ibid, p. 6.

85   Ibid.

86   Weyl, *Fokker the Creative Years*, pp. 330–1.

87   Bruce, The *Fokker D.VIII*, p. 7

88   Ibid, p. 8

89   Ibid, p. 9.

5 Junkers Flugzeugwerke

1   Hugh Cowan, *Junkers Monoplanes*, p. 3.

2   Peter Grosz and Gerard Terry, "The Way to the World's First All-Metal Fighter" in *Air Enthusiast, Twenty-Five*, p. 60.

3   Eric Reissner, *Profiles in Engineering Science*, p. 5.

4   Grosz and Terry, *Air Enthusiast, Twenty-Five*, p. 60.

5   Cowan, *Junkers Monoplanes*, p. 3.

6   Ibid. Other engineers that contributed to the J 1 at Forschungsanstalt were Franze Brandenburg, Becker, Viktor Entler, Kurt Erfurth, Grisson, Matthias Lurke, Friedrich Schmidt, Sonnenleiter, Wagenseil, and Emil Wergien. Hans Steudel headed the Materials and Structures testing laboratory—key to developing the lightweight airframes Junkers wanted. Grosz and Terry, p. 61.

7   Eric Byers, "An Unhappy Marriage: The Junkers-Fokker Merger" in Journal of Historical Biography 3, p. 7.

8   Sheet steel came in large sheets in thicknesses of .1 to .2 mm and was able to be joined via arc-welding.

9   Cowan, *Junkers Monoplanes*, p.4

10   Byers, *Journal of Historical Biography 3*, p. 7.

11   Ibid, p. 8.

12   Cylindrical metal public urinals were at this time being built in Berlin.

13   Byers, *Journal of Historical Biography 3*, p. 8.

14   Cowan, *Junkers Monoplanes*, p. 5.

15   Grosz and Terry, *Air Enthusiast, Twenty-Five*, p. 64.

16   Ibid, p. 6.

17   Grosz and Terry, *Air Enthusiast, Twenty-Five*, p. 6.

18   Marc Dierikx, *Anthony Fokker: The Flying Dutchman Who Shaped American Aviation*, p. 117.

19   Ibid.

20   Dierikx claimed it was 15 percent in *Anthony Fokker Flying Dutchman*, p. 117.

21   Dierikx, *Anthony Fokker*, p. 117.

22   Can there be any doubt as to the origins of this design?

23   Cowan, *Junkers Monoplanes*, p. 7.

24   Ibid.

25   Ibid, p. 13.

26   Ibid.

27   Ibid.

28   Marc Dierikx, *Anthony Fokker*, pp. 118–19

29   Ibid, p. 119.

30   Cowan, *Junkers Monoplanes*, p. 8.

31   Ibid.

6 Albatros Flugzeugwerke

1   James F. Miller, *Albatros D.I–D.II*, p. 226. Huth eventually earned his PhD in 1912.

2   Terry Treadwell, *German and Austro-Hungarian Aircraft Manufacturers 1908–1919*, p. 34.

3   Ibid.

4   So named for one of his favorite specimens from his years of study as a biologist; moreover, his love of birds would inspire the very designs of Albatros aircraft from the D.I right up through the D.Va.

5   Miller, *Albatros D.I–D.II*, p. 231.

6   Tomasz Kowalski, *Albatros D.I–D.Va Legendary Fighter*, p. 3. Schneidemuhl was originally Polish (Pita), but became part of the Kingdom of Prussia—becoming a Prussian military garrison town during the late 19th

century. During the Great War it was home to OAW and a POW camp.

7   Treadwell, *German and Austro-Hungarian Aircraft Manufacturers 1908–1919*, p. 34.

8   Ibid.

9   Miller, *Albatros D.I–D.II*, p. 243.

10 Jack Herris, *Albatros Aircraft of WWI*, Vols 1–4.

11 *Flight*, October 4, 1914, p. 1019.

12 Kolomon Mayrhofer heads up Craftlab in Germany, a firm that produces exact replicas of Albatros aircraft.

13 Production shortcuts that achieve a uniform result without sacrifices to quality.

14 Miller, *Albatros D.I–D.II*, p. 243. Heinkel claimed he designed the B.I although this has not been verified. Some sources say Grohmann designed the B.I.

15 Miller, *Albatros D.I–D.II*, p. 249.

16 *Flight*, April 4, 1914, p. 360.

17 Ibid, p. 361.

18 Historical film #1106, U.S. Army Signal Corps, Berlin, Germany, 1917.

19 *Flight*, April 4, 1914, p. 362.

20 Ibid.

21 Herris, *Albatros Aircraft of WWI*.

22 Miller, *Albatros D.I–D.II*, 147.

23 Ibid, p. 214.

24 Kowalski, *Albatros D.I–D.Va*, p. 5.

25 Craftlab's website at www.craftlab.at/

26 NASM's Stropp DVa was restored in the 1970s and this was thus discovered during the restoration. Robert Mikesh, *Albatros D.Va German Fighter of World War I*, p. 33.

27 The same method is used when coppering the hull of a ship: working from stern to bow such that the water flow does not lift the edges of the copper plates, or even simpler, roofing shingles of a house such that the water runs downhill and not up under the shingles.

28 This is a quantitative description of the washout integrated into the framing of the wings and ailerons.

29 *Flight*, June 28, 1917, p. 641

30 Ibid.

31 Ibid, p. 642

32 Ibid, p. 643.

33 Ibid, p. 644.

34 Kowalski, *Albatros D.I–D.Va*, p. 7.

35 Ibid.

36 Ibid, p. 8

37 Ibid.

38 Ibid, p. 9.

39 Ibid, p. 10.

40 Ibid, p. 11.

41 Ibid.

42 Ibid, p. 12.

43 Ibid.

44 Treadwell, *German and Austro-Hungarian Aircraft Manufacturers 1908–1919*, p. 236.

45 Ibid.

46 Ibid.

47 Ibid.

7 LFG Roland and Pfalz Flugzeugwerke

1   Paul Leaman, "The Luft-Fahrzeug-Gesellschaft (LFG) Seaplanes," 45.05845.058

2   www.rapidttp.co.za/milhist/vol122jm.html

3   Peter Grosz, *The Roland C.II*, p. 3.

4   Ibid.

5   See Deperdussin patent in appendices.

6   Grosz, *The Roland C.II*, p. 4.

7   Ibid.

8   Ibid, p. 3.

9   Terry Treadwell, *German and Austro-Hungarian Aircraft Manufacturers 1908–1919*, p. 182.

10 Grosz, *The Roland C.II*, p. 4.

11 Treadwell, *German and Austro-Hungarian Aircraft Manufacturers 1908–1919*, p. 182.

12 *Flight*, July 11, 1918, p. 765.

13 Treadwell, *German and Austro-Hungarian Aircraft Manufacturers 1908–1919*, p. 183.

14 The "fingers" of this joint serve to increase the glue surface of two mating pieces over a specific distance; e.g. if a standard scarf was 8:1 a finger-jointed joint might be 16 or 20:1 depending on the length and quantity of the "fingers."

15 Tests conducted after the war at McCook Field, Dayton, Ohio by the U.S. Army Air Service.

16 Treadwell, *German and Austro-Hungarian Aircraft Manufacturers 1908–1919*, p. 227.

17 Peter Gray, *The Pfalz D.III*, p. 4.

18 Treadwell, *German and Austro-Hungarian Aircraft Manufacturers 1908–1919*, p. 227.

19 www.pfw.aero/en/history#1445499493184–71496f20–50c1

20 Tomasz Kowalski, *Pfalz Fighter Aircraft from Rheinland the Wine Country*, p. 3.

21 www.pfw.aero/en/

22 Kowalski, *Pfalz Fighter Aircraft*, p. 3.

23 Powered by 100-hp Rapp engine.

24 Kowalski, *Pfalz Fighter Aircraft*, p. 3

25 Ibid.

26   Ibid, p. 4.

27   Ibid.

28   Ibid.

29   Ibid. p. 5.

30   Ibid.

31   Ibid. p. 6.

32   Ibid.

33   Ibid.

34   Ibid.

35   Ibid, p. 9.

36   Ibid, p. 11.

37   Cold-molding meaning use of laminations and glue joints to establish a curve rather than steam-bending which could be called "hot molding."

38   Kowalski, *Pfalz Fighter Aircraft*, p. 12.

39   *Flight*, April 18, 1918, p. 418.

40   Ibid, p. 822.

41   Ibid, p. 826.

42   Ibid, p. 827. It is important to view statements by *Flight* with some circumspection regarding enemy planes in a wartime context; the bias is evident and complements are begrudging at best.

43   Ibid, p. 826.

44   Ibid, p. 418.

45   Kowalski, *Pfalz Fighter Aircraft*, p. 12.

46   Ibid.

47   Ibid, p. 14.

48   Ibid, p. 15.

49   Ibid, p. 16.

50   Ibid, p. 17.

51   Ibid.

52   Ibid, p. 18.

53   Except there was no integrated vertical fin; this was installed after the fuselage was completed.

54   Kowalski, *Pfalz Fighter Aircraft*, p. 20.

55   Ibid, p. 21.

8 Production Methodology

1   Terry Treadwell, *German and Austro-Hungarian Aircraft Manufacturers 1908–1919*, p. 207. Otto had also acquired stock in Pfalz.

2   Ibid, p. 205.

3   Ibid, p. 207.

4   The Forssman plywood patent in the appendices suggests that much of this wartime/early plywood was susceptible to hygroscopic and fungal issues, leading to rot; his patented use of formaldehyde largely solved this problem. This may have been a factor that contributed to some of Fokker's problems with his wings in the Dr.1 and D.VIII.

5   Achim Engels stated that it takes him 20 minutes to make a spliced eye in steel cable. There are dozens of these eyes in a fully rigged box-girder–contructed fuselage.

9 Siemens-Schuckert Werke

1   Peter Gray, *The Siemens Schuckert D.III & IV*, p. 3.

2   The SSW R (Riesenflugzeug) types were huge multi-engine bombers made by the company, that had three 150-hp Benz Bz.III engines in the cabin driving two propellers connected to a common gearbox through a combination leather-cone and centrifugal-key clutch in SSW R.I to SSW R.VII models (the SSW R.VIII utilized four engines). In the case of engine failure, which was extremely common at the time, the bomber could continue flying on two engines while the third was repaired by the inflight mechanic. These aircraft were so costly that the military eventually abandoned them in favor of more cost-effective aircraft. A few served on the Eastern Front.

3   Gray, *The Siemens Schuckert D.III & IV*, p. 4.

4   Ibid.

5   Ibid. p. 5

6   Ibid.

7   *Flight*, March 13, 1919, p. 332.

8   Ibid.

10 Armaments and Engines

1   Postwar statistics formulated by the British rated this engine at 180 hp

2   The "u" was an unofficial label that denoted "uber" or super compression.

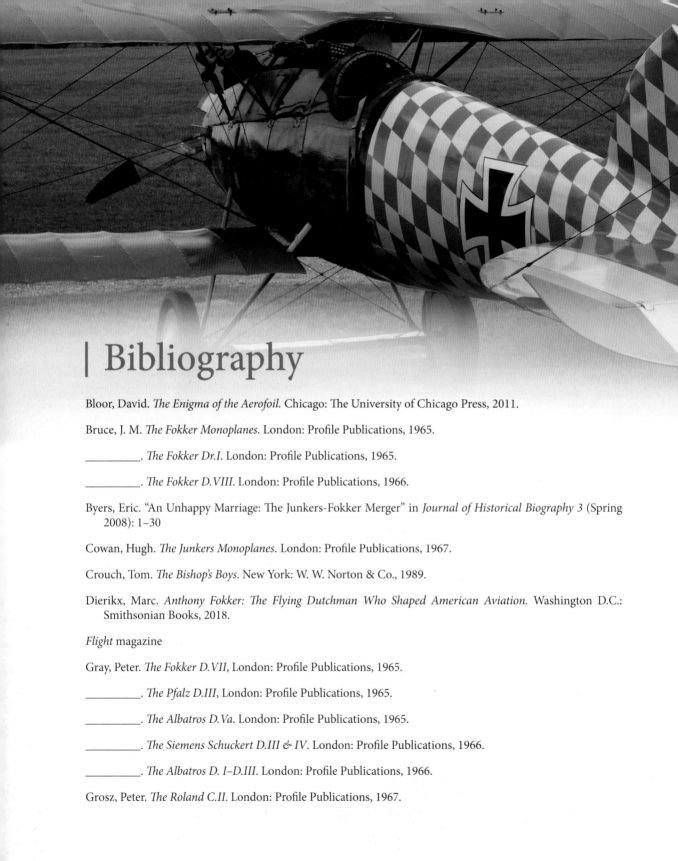

| Bibliography

Bloor, David. *The Enigma of the Aerofoil*. Chicago: The University of Chicago Press, 2011.

Bruce, J. M. *The Fokker Monoplanes*. London: Profile Publications, 1965.

_____. *The Fokker Dr.I*. London: Profile Publications, 1965.

_____. *The Fokker D.VIII*. London: Profile Publications, 1966.

Byers, Eric. "An Unhappy Marriage: The Junkers-Fokker Merger" in *Journal of Historical Biography 3* (Spring 2008): 1–30

Cowan, Hugh. *The Junkers Monoplanes*. London: Profile Publications, 1967.

Crouch, Tom. *The Bishop's Boys*. New York: W. W. Norton & Co., 1989.

Dierikx, Marc. *Anthony Fokker: The Flying Dutchman Who Shaped American Aviation*. Washington D.C.: Smithsonian Books, 2018.

Flight magazine

Gray, Peter. *The Fokker D.VII*, London: Profile Publications, 1965.

_____. *The Pfalz D.III*, London: Profile Publications, 1965.

_____. *The Albatros D.Va*. London: Profile Publications, 1965.

_____. *The Siemens Schuckert D.III & IV*. London: Profile Publications, 1966.

_____. *The Albatros D. I–D.III*. London: Profile Publications, 1966.

Grosz, Peter. *The Roland C.II*. London: Profile Publications, 1967.

_____. *The Pfalz D.XII*. London: Profile Publications, 1967.

Grosz, Peter and Terry Gerard. "The Way to the World's First All-Metal Fighter" in *Air Enthusiast, Twenty-Five*, 1984, Pilot Press.

Haddow, George. *The O Aviatik (Berg) D.I*. London: Profile Publications, 1967.

Hirshel, Ernst H., Horst Prem and Gero Madelung. *Aeronautical Research in Germany from Lilienthal to Today*, Volume 147. New York: Spring-Verlag, 2004.

Imrie, Alex. *The Fokker Triplane*. London: Arms and Armour Press, 1992.

Kollmann, Franz, E. W. Kuenzi and A. J. Stamm. *Principles of Wood Science and Technology: II Wood Based Materials*. New York: Springer Publishing, 1975.

Kowalski, Tomasz. *Albatros D.I–D.Va Legendary Fighter*. Lublin: Kagero Publishing, 2010.

_____. *Pfalz Fighter Aircraft from Rheinland the Wine Country*. Lublin: Kagero Publishing, 2013.

Krzyzan, Marian and Holger Steine. *Die Halberstadt CI.IV D-LBAO*. Herford: Verlag E. S. Mittler & Sohn GmbH, 1992.

Leaman, Paul. "The Luft-Fahrzeug-Gesellschaft (LFG) Seaplanes." 45.058, Cross & Cockade International, Spring 2014.

Mikesh, Robert. *Albatros D.Va German Fighter of World War I*. Washington D.C.: Smithsonian Institution Press, 1980.

Miller, James F. *Albatros D.I–D.II*. Oxford: Osprey Publishing, 2013.

Reissner, Eric. "Profiles in Engineering Science" in The Engineering Science Perspective, Vol. 2, No. 4, December, 1977.

Treadwell, Terry. *German and Austro-Hungarian Aircraft Manufacturers 1908–1919*. Gloucestershire: Amberley Publishing, 2010.

Weyl, A. R. *Fokker the Creative Years*. New York: Funk & Wagnalls, 1965.

WW1 Aero, No. 76, November 1979.

Index